The Communitarian Moment

ALSO BY CHRISTOPHER CLARK

The Roots of Rural Capitalism:
Western Massachusetts, 1780–1860

CHRISTOPHER CLARK

THE

COMMUNITARIAN

MOMENT

The Radical Challenge of the
Northampton Association

Cornell University Press

ITHACA AND LONDON

First published 1995 by Cornell University Press.

Printed in the United States of America

⊗ The paper in this book meets the minimum requirements of the
American National Standard for Information Sciences—
Permanence of Paper for Printed Library Materials, ANSI Z39.48–1984.

Library of Congress Cataloging-in-Publication Data

Clark, Christopher, 1953–
   The communitarian moment : the radical challenge of the Northampton Association /
Christopher Clark.
      p. cm.
   Includes bibliographical references and index.
   ISBN 0-8014-2730-4 (alk. paper).—ISBN 0-8014-8012-4 (pbk. : alk. paper)
   1. Northampton Association of Education and Industry.   2. Collective settlements—
United States—History—19th century.   3. Utopian socialism—United States—History—
19th century.   4. Abolitionists—United States—History—19th century.   5. Capitalism—
United States—History—19th century.   I. Title.
HX656.N75C53 1995
335'.974423—dc20   94-46310

AJN4290

to Margaret

CONTENTS

Illustrations ix

Preface xi

1 "One Common Enterprise" 1

2 Founders, Origins, and Contexts 15

3 "They Will Soon Convince the World":
Shelter, Base, and Mission 56

4 "To Live in the Common Cause":
Life in Community 98

5 The Business of Utopia:
Output, Silk, and Debt 135

6 "Too Despotic Power":
Members and Leaders 163

7 From Community to Factory Village 183

8 The Communitarian Moment 220

Abbreviations Used in the Notes 225

Notes 226

Index 263

ILLUSTRATIONS

Map of Broughton's Meadow, Northampton, Mass., 1831.   16

George W. Benson, about 1845.   19

Samuel L. Hill, about 1850.   21

Sojourner Truth, 1850.   75

Roxana Maria Gaylord Hill, about 1845–46.   79

Former Northampton community silk mill and boarding house.   110

Stages in the growth of the silkworm.   150

Map of Florence, Mass., 1860.   206

Stockholders of the Nonotuck Silk Company in the late 1860s.   209

Cosmian Hall, Florence, Mass.   214

Florence Kindergarten.   216

PREFACE

In 1843 the popular Hutchinson family of singers visited the Brook Farm community in West Roxbury, Massachusetts. In April of the following year they stayed and performed at another "utopian" community, the Northampton Association of Education and Industry, in the western part of the state. They found much in common with the members at Northampton, many of whom were committed abolitionists like themselves. But their visit also crystallized an idea that had been developing among them since their visit to Brook Farm, that living in "community" was a step toward a better way of organizing society as a whole. When they returned that summer of 1844 to their farm in Milford, New Hampshire, they discussed forming a community themselves. At the particular urging of John Hutchinson, they resolved to run their farm collectively for a year, putting their concert earnings into a "community treasury" and sharing responsibility for it equally. In doing so they joined thousands of Americans who, in the 1840s, set up, entered, or debated schemes for community reform that they hoped might transform their nation's way of life.[1]

The optimism of many of the men and women who joined communities soon faded, and although some remained committed to the search for an ideal community most turned their attention to other reforms from the late 1840s onward. (The Hutchinsons' experiment itself came to an end when they left for a singing tour of Britain in 1845.) As a scholar concerned with the history both of capitalist societies and of utopian visions, I am interested in tracing how such moments of optimism come and go. That is one of the purposes of this book.

It used to be virtually axiomatic that history belonged to the successful. Individuals and movements deemed "failures" were usually disregarded or entirely forgotten. Now the work of an entire generation of social and cultural historians has taught us that attention to failures is essential to understanding the past: that "success," "failure," power, and the lack of it serve as filters to distort our retrospective view, and that a rounded analysis depends on our ability to recover perspectives that have been lost in the processes of historical change. Communitarians of the 1840s set forth a variety of radical critiques of contemporary American society, based both on their own experiences and on their visions of a better world. Their attempts to realize these visions met with strong opposition and practical obstacles. Even as they began to retreat, they were cast by their opponents as insignificant or as fanatics, and those views have influenced most subsequent historical accounts of them. This book joins other recent studies that have sought to reevaluate the efforts of communitarians on their own terms, to locate them in their social and political contexts, and to understand the dilemmas that they faced.

The Northampton Association provides an ideal opportunity for a study of this kind. It is easily the most obscure of the main New England utopian communities of the 1840s—a victim of its own aftermath, the loss of crucial documentary evidence, and of the forgetfulness of later generations—so its story is unfamiliar even to many specialist scholars. It existed during a period in which moral critiques of social institutions were both radical and effective, and its members sought to build an American society in which the inequalities of class, race, and gender would be destroyed.

Since their vision has never been realized, and other efforts to the same end have still to prove successful, it seemed important to reexamine their attempts at social transformation and to cast off the condescension with which we so readily tend to regard such groups. This book aims not to celebrate the men and women of the Northampton community, but to understand them better, to trace how their vision was formed, and how it came to fade again into something less radical, less ambitious, and more forgettable.

Recovering the story of the Northampton community has involved extensive work in manuscript and printed sources throughout New England

and elsewhere. It is a great pleasure to thank the many friends and institutions whose kindness and generosity made this possible. Special thanks are due to Carol MacColl and Don Michak, who so many times have let us make our home with them, and to Annie S. Lamb, Alan and Alicia Lamb, Louis Wilson, Stanley and Dorothy Elkins, David Blight and Karin Beckett, and Nancy Grey Osterud for their hospitality.

I gratefully acknowledge the financial support that enabled me to conduct research in the United States: a Kate I. and Hall B. Peterson Fellowship of the American Antiquarian Society; a Small Personal Research Grant from the British Academy; a Research Grant from the American Philosophical Society; a visiting fellowship at the Essex Institute, Salem, Massachusetts; research travel grants from the Twenty-Seven Foundation and the Scouloudi Foundation; and a Benjamin F. Stevens Fellowship of the Massachusetts Historical Society.

I was especially dependent on the dedication and enthusiasm of archivists, librarians, and others who helped me track down source material, much of it obscure. Thanks are due to the staff at the following institutions for their unfailing courtesy and helpfulness: the American Antiquarian Society; Baker Library, Harvard Business School; the Barnstaple County (Massachusetts) Registers of Deeds and of Probate; the Beinecke Rare Book and Manuscript Library, Yale University; the Belmont Memorial Library, Belmont, Massachusetts; the Boston Public Library; the British Library; the British Library Oriental and India Office Collections; the British Newspaper Library; the Brooklyn (Connecticut) Town Clerk's Office; the Connecticut Historical Society; the Connecticut State Library; the Essex County (Massachusetts) Register of Probate; the Essex County Superior Court; the Essex Institute; the Florence Civic and Business Association, Northampton, Massachusetts; the Forbes Library, Northampton; the Hampshire County (Massachusetts) Register of Deeds and of Probate; Harvard University Archives; Historic Northampton; the Historical Society of Pennsylvania; Houghton Library, Harvard University; the Lynn Historical Society; the Mansfield (Connecticut) Historical Society; the Manuscript and Archives Department, University of Massachusetts Library, Amherst; the Massachusetts Historical Society; the Massachusetts State Library; the New England Historic Genealogical Society; the Rhode Island Historical Society; the Sophia Smith Collection, Smith College; and the Unitarian Society of Northampton and Florence. I am also grateful to staff at Duke University Library, the Illinois Historical Collections, the Kansas Historical Society, the Kansas State

Library, the University of Rochester Library, Swarthmore College Library, Syracuse University Library, the Western Reserve Historical Society, and the Worcester Historical Museum for answering questions and sending me materials.

Many individuals have taken an interest in this project and provided information or advice; I am grateful to them all: David Blight, Richard D. Brown, Mario De Pillis, Elise Feeley, Paul Gaffney, William Gilmore-Lehne, Robert A. Gross, the late Sidney Kaplan, John R. McKivigan, Mrs. Earl W. McSweeney, Ruth V. Munsell, Nell I. Painter, James Parsons, Jane Rendall, Daniel Scott Smith, James Walvin, and participants in seminars and lectures in Boston, Cambridge, Chicago, Milan, Salem, Worcester, and York. Edward James and the students who have taken our "Utopias" seminar at York have been a special inspiration.

I am particularly indebted to Carl J. Guarneri, Stephen Nissenbaum, Nancy Grey Osterud, and Edward Royle, who each took the time to read a draft version of the book and gave me thoughtful comments and criticisms that were a great help.

My editor, Peter Agree, has enthusiastically supported this project from its early days; to him, and to the staff at Cornell University Press who have brought it to fruition, many thanks as well.

Margaret Lamb has shared this project and much more; I dedicate this book to her with love.

CHRISTOPHER CLARK

York, England

The Communitarian Moment

"One Common Enterprise"

T his is a book about people who stepped outside society in an effort to change it by constructing a way of life that could serve as a model for the future. The men and women who came together in western Massachusetts in 1842 to form the Northampton Association of Education and Industry were among dozens of groups in North America and Europe who at that period saw forming communities as the best opportunity for social progress. Like most such groups, the Northampton community failed to realize its founders' hopes, and the members disbanded after four-and-a-half hard years. But they were part of a crucial moment in American history, a moment in which ideas about society, culture and religion were tested and reshaped. That they sought to alter society, and in doing so explored its boundaries and ideological limits, makes their story a revealing one that we can use to help understand the broader patterns of cultural and ideological change for which the 1840s were so important.

To identify communitarianism particularly with the 1840s has long been conventional among American historians, and like many conventions this one has been reexamined. Recent scholars of utopian movements have pointed out that communities were being founded throughout the nineteenth century and were not much less common at other times than they were in the 1840s. Otohiko Okugawa found 119 communal societies established in the United States between 1800 and 1859, and Robert S. Fogarty lists 141 more that were set up between 1860 and 1914, rightly noting that such movements continued to flourish even as many of those founded in the 1840s declined and disappeared. In a purely numerical sense, therefore, communities never faded from the American scene.[1]

Nonetheless, there is merit in the view that the 1840s were an especially significant period for communitarianism. At least fifty-nine new communities were founded between 1840 and 1849, more than in any other decade; some existing groups—especially the Shakers—also experienced revival and spiritual renewal. More important, though, at no other time in the nineteenth century were communal groups so closely connected with wider strands of reform, or apparently such feasible models for social, political, and economic change. In the context of the 1840s, when most institutions were still small in scale, communities were comparatively large organizations; by the end of the century, when there was another upsurge of interest in communitarian solutions, they appeared puny, dwarfed by huge corporations and powerful state institutions. We can therefore speak of the 1840s as a "communitarian moment" in American history, when the possibilities for and potential impact of communal groups were at their greatest. As an American Fourierist noted, this was a time when radical reformers could do more than sit by and imagine the perfect world: by joining communities, "we are permitted to be actors in the drama."[2]

The fifty-nine or so communities founded between 1840 and 1849 lasted, on average, two years or less. The Northampton community endured longer than forty-three of them. Over its four-and-a-half years at least 240 men, women, and children lived at the community as members, probationary members, boarders, scholars, or employees, though the maximum resident at any one time never exceeded 120. Estimates of the size of such communities are notoriously unreliable, so comparison among them is virtually guesswork, but even this modest membership made Northampton larger than average among contemporary groups.[3] Members lived on a substantial property purchased from the bankrupt Northampton Silk Company, on the Mill River in the western part of the town of Northampton. Some lived in one- and two-family houses, most in the upper floors of the silk mill, which were turned into a community boardinghouse, with a common dining room. More prosperous members subscribed for stock in the association and, under its original constitution, retained some control over affairs through a board of stockholders; among them were several silk manufacturers from Connecticut, led by a man called Joseph Conant, who had already been involved in the silk company.

Subscriptions, however, fell far short of the capital the association required, and so from the outset many thousands of dollars were owed on mortgages to wealthy abolitionists and to the merchant who had been the silk company's chief investor. Shortage of capital and heavy debts, which grew worse when Conant's group withdrew in October 1842, played a major role in the association's failure. Silk manufacture was the principal aim, and repeated efforts were also made to raise silkworms and produce raw silk for the factory. The community ran its own farm; shoemakers and bakers kept members supplied, and other goods were obtained by trading lumber and carpentry work. Workshops made knives, tools and machinery; a tannery was planned. From 1843 to 1845 the community's education department, which schooled the children of member families, attempted to raise further cash by taking in fee-paying pupils.[4]

New England, especially Massachusetts, pioneered the brief upsurge in community experiments that captured reformers' imaginations in the early 1840s. Though broader movements such as Fourierism, and to a lesser extent Owenism, embraced most American communities founded in this period, early in the decade Massachusetts produced distinctive communities that Fourierists in particular then sought to influence.[5] Of the four most significant Massachusetts communities founded between 1841 and 1843, Brook Farm at West Roxbury near Boston and Bronson Alcott's short-lived, anarchic Fruitlands community on ninety acres of farmland in the town of Harvard have long been prominent in memory and imagination because of their strong connections to transcendentalism and the New England literary renaissance.[6] The other two groups have not been so well remembered, perhaps because their pursuits were more industrial and their literary and intellectual traditions less durable. Adin Ballou's "Practical Christian" community at Hopedale is well documented in surviving records and in Ballou's own voluminous publications, but except to determined scholars his brand of religious and reformist writing has long ceased to resonate.[7] The Northampton Association, the fourth of these Massachusetts communities, has suffered from the relative obscurity of its members, its weak literary connections, and the loss of its records for almost ninety years.

Any study reveals as much about the purposes of its author as it does about the subject in hand; even the slender historiography of the Northampton community is no exception. John Humphrey Noyes's short chapter on it in his *History of American Socialisms* (1870) was occupied largely by the (misidentified) memoirs of a former member, but also contained

Noyes's criticisms, designed to fit the wider purpose of showing that his own Oneida Community was the best expression of the American communitarian tradition. The longest nineteenth-century account, in Charles A. Sheffeld's *History of Florence* (1895), was a respectful, though not uncritical work of remembrance by the grandson of one of the community's leaders, including memoirs by men and women who had lived there or grown up among its former members. A perceptive magazine article published the same year by Olive Rumsey stressed the community's economic arrangements and hinted at the relevance of its example for contemporaries concerned with solving the antagonism between capital and labor. Both Sheffeld and Rumsey made use of the community's records, but these subsequently disappeared, and the handful of studies that have appeared since have either been antiquarian, misleading and derivative, or acceptable but hampered by the lack of essential primary sources. Arthur E. Bestor's fine article of 1940 was aimed at correcting the misapprehension of another scholar that the Northampton community was Fourierist. Alice Eaton McBee's study of 1947—the fullest of all—recovered excellent local evidence, but portrayed the community, vaguely, as an expression of "middle class" reform, and in paying relatively slight attention to its ideological context rather misleadingly labeled it "transcendentalist." McBee's approach foreshadowed the consensus interpretations of the 1950s and 1960s that emphasized the "extremism" of a few radical reformers who pushed their crusade outside the bounds of mainstream American society. John L. Thomas in 1965 saw the Northampton community as part of a perfectionist movement whose excessive radicalism helped push the South toward rebellion; but by portraying it as an institutional failure from its outset he both undercut his own argument and overlooked the resilience of members who kept the community going for almost half a decade. In 1954, the Northampton writer Hope Hale Davis confronted the local historian's dilemma: how to deal with people in the past who would definitely not "fit in" today? She unconvincingly portrayed the members of the community as "discontented souls," "dreamers," and "drones" and, simultaneously, as "the same intelligent, normal citizens who today make a good living from the industrial community."[8]

A fuller treatment of the Northampton community is now possible. In 1983 several volumes of the lost records were found at an auction in central Massachusetts. They were acquired for the American Antiquarian Society, which then obtained another volume offered by a dealer. The collection includes some account books, a membership register, minutes of proceedings, and copies of outgoing correspondence from 1843 to 1846. It is not complete: incoming correspondence and internal reports referred to in the records as well as some account books are still missing.[9] Still, these records, in conjunction with a host of other manuscript and printed sources, provide the best opportunity in a century to explore the Northampton community and its activities. A generation of scholarly work in social history, reform movements, and utopian studies has also made it easier to tackle broader questions about the meaning and implications of the experiences, even of the relatively obscure people who joined communities. It is now feasible, in other words, not only to uncover the Northampton community's story more fully than before, but to interpret its significance.

The very identification of a community as "utopian" entails possibilities and also problems. It asks scholars and readers to assign a significance to the group under study far greater than they might accord to a similar-sized group of people who had not claimed to be creating a new form of society. The genre also commits us to a set of questions and assumptions that tend to follow from that claim; it is a discourse that tends to write its own story. "Utopian" communities never "succeed," but always "fail." Were that not so they would have rejoined with a dominant social pattern and become indistinguishable again. They create and seek, unsuccessfully, to propagate "alternative" visions of a future society. We tend to see them either as repositories of an "alternative tradition" that continues to challenge our social structures and assumptions, or—with hindsight—as indications of potential "paths not taken" in the evolution of capitalist societies. But there are reasons to break out of this discourse and to ask different sorts of questions.

To talk of communities only as impracticable and short-lived is to close discussion about them before it can begin. That communities "fail" is much less relevant than how they work as testing grounds for issues significant to contemporaries, and how the process of trying out new social forms and conventions can tell us a great deal about wider processes of change. The convention that dwells on the "failure" of utopian communities rests on a perception of them as distinct institutions, set apart from a "dominant" or "mainstream" society. This, of course, often correctly reflects the intentions of their founders, who saw withdrawal from the "world" as a necessary precondition for reforming it. But it has consequences that it might prove useful to avoid. Though the self-image of community founders must be taken seriously and incorporated into our analysis, we do not have to accept uncritically their tendency to assume that their own institutions and those of the "mainstream" society were static, monolithic, and permanently opposed. Most often, utopian communities challenged the cultural assumptions behind a whole range of contemporary debates. Community members both continued these debates among themselves, and conducted a dialogue (however hostile) with the "world" outside. The fluidity of these connections with a wider society, and the susceptibility of parts of society to influence by communitarian movements, gave them potential significance as radical challenges to the social order. This, in turn, meant that "utopia" had influence not only as the upholder of potential "alternatives" or "lost paths," it also fed ideas and arrangements into the wider society around it.

Surveys of utopian and communal history have long sought to categorize groups by ideological affiliation, form of organization, or type of leadership. That the Northampton Association is hard to fit into a single framework was evident to contemporary sympathizers. The New Hampshire abolitionist Nathaniel P. Rogers remarked that "it is a peculiar body, and of peculiar individual character."[10] Robert S. Fogarty, in his recent study of later nineteenth-century communities, distinguishes between "cooperative," "perfectionist," and "socialist" groups, but the Northampton community could be said to have been all of these. Other scholars distinguish between religious and secular communities, and some associate religious groups particularly with sectarian organization or individual charismatic leadership. The Northampton community was religious in purpose, but secular in organization, nonsectarian, not dependent on a single leader and lacking prophets, seers, or mystics who wanted to make it a vehicle for their beliefs. It defied categorization in other respects too. Founded just as interest in Fourierism was growing, it had some superficial similarities to Fourierist communities and members who watched the larger movement keenly, but it was not Fourierist itself.[11]

This inability to fit the Northampton community into a category would make it easy to dismiss it as an oddity, of no wider significance. But its varied characteristics are precisely what make it interesting, because it touched on and helps reveal so many aspects of antebellum culture and society. It was located in a rural area, but largely dependent on manufacturing for its income; it reflected, therefore, crucial tensions in the transition of New England society from agrarianism to industrialism. It was a joint-stock community that initially conformed to the patterns of industrial capitalism, but soon adopted a more radical economic system.

Started by abolitionists dedicated not only to ending slavery but to promoting women's rights and religious toleration, the Northampton community plunged into issues that seemed to many New Englanders to call the very foundations of their society into question. Abolitionism and a professed commitment to equality also led the mainly white membership to accept black men and women among them as equals—one of the few places anywhere in the United States to do so in this period.

The history of utopian communities did not begin and end with the institutions themselves, but with the lives of their members, who to varying degrees sought to share the vision of a better world that they were gathered to realize. We need to ask what brought people to participate in groups like the Northampton community, what influenced them to stay long or leave quickly, and what difference it later made to them that they had once shared in community life. Studies of utopian communities have, until recently, tended to focus most heavily on the ideas and actions of utopian theorists and community leaders. Clearly, these are important. But the evidence that can be recovered about the Northampton community and its members gives us an opportunity to look as well at the ordinary members and the networks of family, kinship, neighborhood, and religious and reforming commitment that led them to join and influenced their experience of community life.

To most who joined them, "utopian" communities were only one phase in a lifetime of work and of campaigning for reforms. Accordingly, in this book I am much concerned with antislavery, especially the radical abolitionist and connected movements, from which the Northampton community recruited many members and took its distinctive character. Recent historians in the field have considered not just the social status of abolitionists and their influence on the course of events in the United States, but the groupings and interconnections between abolitionists that shaped their lives, their reform outlook, and their campaigns. Such studies of the abolitionist "community" are essential to understanding reformers who self-consciously went about creating communities of their own. Connections of family, locality, and ideological loyalty between them became a crucial aspect of their campaigns. In a study of popular support for abolitionism in New York State, Judith Wellman emphasizes its roots in particular types of local community, and that "community institutions were one of the main avenues by which abolitionist activity was sustained." Support for a venture such as the Northampton Association was also based on particular social networks. Nancy Hewitt and others have, however, suggested that commitment to radical change also entailed a break with existing neighborhoods and communities, in order to gather like-minded individuals together for the sake of the cause, and that such gatherings could occur where people had "deeper commitment to a cause than to a [local] community." The historian Lawrence J. Friedman has noted that "small groups lay at the heart of the immediatist crusade"; abolitionists were themselves conscious that they were, as Charles Follen put it, "a world in ourselves and in each other." This combination of separateness and cohesiveness gave radical abolitionists a distinct culture, one which, as two recent scholars have suggested, was particularly prone to internecine quarrels and bitter divisions.[12]

"Utopian" communities resulted from this kind of breaking away of individuals and families from contexts in which their ideals had already been formed. The early 1840s provided a series of circumstances conducive to this. And yet it is important not to overemphasize the inward-looking nature of abolitionist groups. We also need to grasp the character of the commitment abolitionists had to their fellows and the cause of reform. As they joined or left communities like that at Northampton, these people altered their relationships with the society around them. As they took part in an effort to change society, they claimed universal, not just personal, significance for what they were doing. As they debated and struggled with the issues that confronted community members, they reflected on matters that resonated throughout society.

In this book I also address the history of capitalism. Ever since Marx and Engels's stringent criticisms of utopian socialism, utopian movements and abolitionism have appeared to possess well marked-out roles in the evolution of capitalist societies. As efforts to avoid the class struggle, or as naive blueprints of a perfect society ("duodecimo editions of the New Jerusalem"), utopian communities have been seen as distractions from the main path of working-class movements. That some communitarians and abolitionist leaders were professionals or proprietors, some quite rich, seemed to suggest that they could be labeled chiefly as "bourgeois" reformers unconcerned with addressing the true evils of the capitalist society they were dependent on.[13] But it is worth recalling that these interpretations of capitalism and the class struggle were themselves in part products of the changes of the 1840s to which the utopian movement had contributed. The American utopian communities of the early 1840s were not already lined up as supporters of further capitalist development. On the contrary, many members tried to resist and divert capitalism. The internal debates of groups like the Northampton Association would rehearse some of the wider points of conflict between capital and labor that were already emerging with the spread of factory and merchant-controlled production in the 1830s and after. Only as they dissolved did these communities contribute to the further evolution of capitalist ideologies.

In the early 1840s communities appeared to many radical reformers particularly promising vehicles for social change. As historians have long realized, antebellum reform movements were notable for the interconnections between seemingly different campaign issues. Communities concentrated these disparate themes in an effort to build entirely new ways of life. Yet they were created in response to reformers' difficulties, as well as their sense of opportunity. They reflected a wish to carve new paths out of the problems and evils that American culture, politics, and society seemed to present. Not only was American society itself riven with conflicts, but these were conflicts within a political, religious, and cultural world whose character and boundaries were still new and relatively fluid.[14] Portrayals of American radicalism perhaps too often underestimate this.

The tendency to interpret "utopian" visions as "alternatives" to a dominant "mainstream" culture directs attention away from the extent to which dominant social and cultural patterns were themselves shifting, contested, and open to influence. In religion, the twin challenges of Unitarianism and the evangelical revivals were still stirring the consciousness and activities of the New England churches, creating a rich field for theological innovation and debate. In politics, the notion of popular democracy based on universal white manhood suffrage had only quite recently evolved (and in Rhode Island, as the Dorr War of 1843 was to show, it was yet to emerge), and two-party politics was a novelty. To radical abolitionists, the Whig campaign of 1840, with its public sacrifice of principle to expediency, strengthened an abhorrence of the political processes that seemed to captivate the minds of voters: "I feel sorry," wrote the Quaker abolitionist Gertrude K. Burleigh, "that so many men can see *no further* than the ballot-box."[15] The capitalist transformation of the northern economy was also at a relatively early stage. Markets, communications networks and systems of production were all novel. The factory system, the most expressive symbol of a new manufacturing order, was little more than a generation old; only in the 1820s and 1830s had it begun to generate the social and political debate that would put it at the heart of social consciousness about the capitalist system in general. Much production, especially in commercial towns and in rural areas of New England where utopian communities were set up, still took place at the level of farms, families and small workshops. Business ventures were uncertain and prone to failure.[16] And many institutions and systems that would ultimately become established parts of American life were themselves new, experimental and of questionable practicality at this point: penal systems, school reforms, science and technology, railroads, suburbs, large publishing firms, paper money, and a host of other institutions, schemes, and proposals were as "utopian" in their inception as these communities. Precisely because this world was so new and so fluid, communities could appear to have reasonable chances of influencing the pattern of change. They were a radical challenge, but not to a fixed social and cultural hegemony, and the early 1840s was the moment when there was room for them to make a difference.

Evangelicalism, the new politics, and economic expansion had sown the seeds of the radical abolitionists' challenge to southern slavery in the 1830s. The fierce, often violent, responses—North and South—to their campaign revealed to abolitionists the glaring injustices of American society. Accordingly, during the late 1830s, abolitionism itself had begun to spawn a variety of interconnected movements to correct these wrongs and to pursue what William Lloyd Garrison would call "equal rights and radical reform." These movements—nonresistance, the challenge to the churches, the rejection of politics as an instrument of change, and the campaign for the right of women to participate in reform movements— would split the abolitionist campaign at the end of the decade and make a major contribution to New England communitarianism. They raised questions of class, race, and gender that utopian communities, both by circumstance and design, were obliged to confront.

Both from contemporaries and from historians, abolitionists have faced severe criticism for their "misguided" tactics. Critics often tried to have things both ways. On one hand, abolitionists who focused on the evils of southern slavery were accused of ignoring the problems of northern society. On the other, abolitionists who raised questions about race, women's rights, politics, and the state of the churches were accused of "diversionary" tactics and of distracting attention from the central issue of slavery. The interest in community ventures in the early 1840s was an attempt by some radical abolitionists to unite their criticisms of society under the single banner of "moral suasion" and to find a means of condemning the injustices of slavery, capitalism, and all the institutions that tolerated or supported them. Communities were a means of putting into practice a principle set forth by the New England Non-Resistance Society, that "every truth strengthens and forms part of every other truth."[17]

Though abolitionists challenged American social and political institutions, they were unable to agree on how to achieve their objectives. Three overlapping, but conceptually distinct patterns of reform were available to them. One, proposed as prudent and pragmatic, saw political institutions as the channel for change, and debated only whether to work within existing political parties or to create new third-party institutions to promote the abolitionist cause. Another, identified most readily with Owenite and other radical reformers of the 1820s and 1830s, saw the root of social evils in material circumstances, and proposed that change could come about only through the reformation of social institutions themselves. Many labor reformers, advocates of land reform, and Owenite and Fourierist communitarians of the 1840s shared this view to some degree. A third position, held in different forms by evangelical abolitionists and their radical opponents, put no faith in political or social change alone. The fierce and entrenched resistance to abolitionism in the 1830s proved that the political system would not free slaves. The emphasis that Owenites and Fourierists placed on material circumstances implied a lack of faith in God. Instead, Garrison and others argued, social reform would come about only through the moral regeneration of individuals and their commitment to renouncing sin. Years later the former Hopedale community member D. S. Whitney would recall abolitionist Oliver Johnson's reply to the taunt that no slaves had been freed: "If we had not freed the slaves we had freed ourselves."[18]

Historians tend to emphasize the conflict between the "social" and "moral" approaches. But participants in the Massachusetts communities of the early 1840s took the distinctive step of combining them. They sought to create social institutions in which moral reformation would be possible. The founders of Hopedale, Brook Farm, Northampton, and Fruitlands hoped to build models for the spiritual and moral, as well as social, regeneration of America. Like other radical reform movements, such as the contemporary Washington Total-Abstinence Societies with which they had some connections, they rejected the common view that economic behavior could be treated separately from moral concerns. In a literal sense, communities tried to establish "moral economies." Uniting social, economic, and moral perspectives, they set out to provide a terrain in which morality could escape the "slavery" of existing social institutions and so create a new world.[19]

Radical abolitionists took note of these community experiments as promising efforts to remove the "shackles" of inequality and oppression that they saw as enslaving northern society. All immediatist abolitionists influenced by the evangelical tradition perceived southern slavery as a sin to be removed, and some saw "freedom" as an absolute value whose achievement would unproblematically solve America's ills. But by the late 1830s a number of radical abolitionists were also inspired by a dawning realization that the North was not only implicated in the sin of slavery but was itself sinful for its economic, political, and religious competitiveness and for its denial of rights to black people and women. Even if it could be achieved, releasing slaves into such a sinful world would not be good enough. It would be necessary to prepare a better way of living for all free Americans. Communities were a means of overthrowing the North's own constraints on freedom. As an Ohio abolitionist wrote to a member of the Northampton community in 1843, "Men have the same natural wants . . . , they have equal rights to the soil and all other gifts of nature." But society "seems inevitably to circumscribe our efforts to obtain the right. We must therefore take such measures as can be carried out. . . . [M]uch may be gained from a properly regulated community system."[20] Community was a path to emancipation.

An important, though not essential, element in the impulse to form communities was the belief evolved in both liberal and biblical-literalist Christian theology, and accepted by freethinkers, that human perfectibility was possible on earth, not merely in heaven. This idea set perfectionists firmly apart from the more widespread, conservative doctrine that mankind was inherently depraved and dependent either on divine grace (Calvinism) or on faith (Arminianism) to achieve redemption. Perfectionism took many forms—including communitarian efforts by its leading proponent, John Humphrey Noyes, quite distinct from the ones we are considering here—but among its consequences was optimism that the creation of better institutions was a feasible, necessary step toward the achievement of a perfected human society. Since, presumably, all aspects of life needed reform and since perfection could not evidently coexist with the imperfect institutions and customs of contemporary society, the withdrawal of seekers into communities was a logical first step toward the wider goal.[21]

Perfectionism was linked to a powerful millennial expectation that Christ would return to reign on earth. Though this took many forms there was a crucial distinction between the *pre*millennialist belief that the

Second Coming would be a sudden, apocalyptic event presaging the thousand years of Christ's rule and the *post*millennialist view that Christ would come only after a suitable world had been built to receive him. Though both versions had communitarian implications, the former stressed the gathering of a faithful or sanctified Church to await Christ's return. In New England in the 1840s this would take its most dramatic form in the growth of Millerism and the Adventist movement. Postmillennialism, by contrast, inspired social action—the promotion of reform of all kinds, including communitarian movements, that could assist in the creation of a world fit for divine rule.[22]

The ground for community was prepared by uniting these perfectionist and millennialist themes into one argument for moral suasion: by seeking to perfect themselves, men and women could alter the world by the moral force of their example. In 1838 Lydia Maria Child asked Abby Kelley a question that she recognized was as old as Christianity itself: "*Can* individuals living in the midst of a wicked world conduct [behave] precisely as they would if Christ's kingdom had really and universally come, and earth was made a Heaven?" She gave her own answer: "The conviction . . . daily gains strength, that if but *one* human being earnestly and perseveringly sought to reach perfect holiness, that emanation from him would purify the world."[23] Child saw this as a solemn reminder of individual responsibility, but such yearnings also created a widening interest by 1840 in achieving reform through cooperative, communalist means.

The notion of cooperation as the basis of a reformed society had many origins, from ideas about primitive Christianity to views of family life, from the examples of German pietists and the Shakers to the earlier Owenite communities. It drew on the artisan tradition, the labor movement, and—significantly for those who went to Northampton—on the local exchange and reciprocity practiced in rural neighborhoods. But it is also important to note that in the minds of some abolitionists cooperation owed something to capitalism itself. Communitarianism, in this view, grew out of a perception that social organization for material ends could be adapted to higher, moral purposes. As the Massachusetts Anti-Slavery Society's board of managers put it in 1838, "it is a reproach to true Christianity, that while its professors, however widely differing in their political or religious sentiments, eagerly associate together for the purpose of MONEY-GETTING,—to establish banks, build railroads, dig canals, and erect manufactories,—they are slow, almost reluctant, to give each other the right hand of fellowship in carrying out an enterprise of mercy." So communities were partly an attempt to harness capitalism's ability to coordinate human activity to a higher moral purpose and so create cooperative, rather than competitive, social conditions. The abolitionists criticized contemporary society for its tendency to separate material from moral considerations, and so tolerate social evils on the grounds of expediency. Communities would reverse this tendency and place material concerns firmly under moral guidance.[24]

Thus an examination of the communities of this period sheds light on the complex, ambiguous relationship between abolitionism and capitalism that has been the subject of prolonged debate among historians. Scholars have long pointed out that most abolitionist critiques of slavery before the Civil War did not extend to a critique of the conditions of wage laborers in the growing industries of the North. The goal of freeing southern slaves would be achieved when they were legally emancipated, given equal rights before the law, and enabled to join the ranks of "free labor" alongside their white brothers and sisters. But though the free labor ideology was ultimately dominant and had always been supported by abolitionist leaders, it was not held by all abolitionists in the early 1840s. There were men and women who questioned the assumption that "free labor" in itself was a sufficient condition for the moral reformation of society and to whom the competitive labor market was neither a practical nor a moral alternative to slavery. Some abolitionists saw land reform movements as a solution; others considered communitarianism, participating in "one common enterprise" to achieve social reform. The debates they held, their successes and their failures, help explain the conditions in which most abolitionists did, after the mid-1840s, abandon their search for a form of moral economy and accept the logic of market competition.[25]

In this book I use the story of the Northampton community and biographical sketches of some of its members to examine the concerns that motivated them to take part in the communitarian moment and the implications of their involvement. I find that the radicalism of the Northampton community and its members stemmed from an engagement with the structure and problems of society, not a wish to turn their backs on it. As circumstances changed, this engagement contributed to the passing away of the "communitarian moment" of the early 1840s. Radical social and moral reform turned toward more limited aspirations for the future, which helped prepare the ground for the ideological hegemony of American capitalism and the looming confrontation between capitalism and slavery that would be enacted in the Civil War.

CHAPTER TWO

Founders, Origins, and Contexts

On April 8, 1842, seven men met at a little settlement known as Broughton's Meadow, two-and-a-half miles west of the center of Northampton in the Connecticut River valley of Massachusetts, to incorporate their new community, the Northampton Association of Education and Industry. Present were the abolitionists George W. Benson, Erasmus Darwin Hudson, and William Adam; two silk manufacturers, Joseph Conant and Earl Dwight Swift; Theodore Scarborough, a farmer; and Hiram Wells, a mechanic. They gathered at the property purchased for the community, much of which had belonged to a bankrupt silk manufacturing firm, the Northampton Silk Company. The place included about 470 acres of land, a four-story brick factory, a dam and water-power site on the Mill River, a sawmill, several houses, and some small workshops and outbuildings. The meeting concluded several months of preparation and marked the start of a communitarian venture that would last until November 1846. The seven men discussed the community's principles and regulations, which they set down in a printed document for circulation in reform circles, and elected officers from among themselves and their associates to undertake the tasks necessary to start the community. Among these officers were four men not present at the meeting who were nevertheless expected to play a leading role in the association: three more abolitionists, Samuel L. Hill, Hall Judd, and David Mack, and Samuel Brooks, a farmer. The eleven men

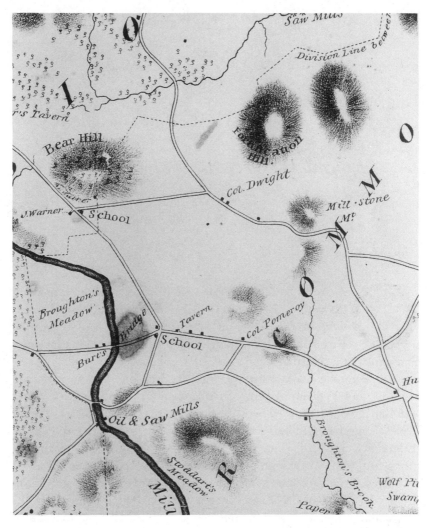

Map of Broughton's Meadow a few years before the Northampton Silk Company's factory was built near the site of the oil and saw mills. From John G. Hales, *Plan of the Town of Northampton in the County of Hampshire* (Boston, 1831). Courtesy of the Forbes Library, Northampton.

present or mentioned at the April 8, 1842, meeting can fairly be regarded as the "founders" of the Northampton community.[1]

The meeting elected by ballot a president, a treasurer, and a secretary, who would head the association's officers and also act under its consti-

tution as trustees, with legal title to its property and authority to represent
it in the wider world. The seven present chose from among their number
Joseph Conant as president and William Adam as secretary. Adam, in
his new capacity, started recording the community's proceedings in a large
journal acquired for the purpose. As treasurer they elected Samuel L. Hill,
absent that day but eventually to become most closely identified with the
community and its local influence. Four men were elected to serve as
directors of the association's stock company; they would represent those
members who invested in the community and would also, for a time at
least, be responsible for most business and financial decisions. Of these,
George W. Benson, Theodore Scarborough, and Earl Dwight Swift were
present at the meeting, and David Mack would soon be coming to Northampton from Cambridge, Massachusetts, with his family. The meeting
also created two bodies to take practical steps in building the community:
a board for admitting new members, and a committee to allocate accommodations for them. To the former they elected Benson and Hiram Wells
from among their number and added Hall Judd and Samuel Brooks from
among those expected to arrive shortly. On the latter committee, Benson
and Wells were joined by Conant. Of the seven men present on April 8,
only Erasmus Darwin Hudson kept aloof from the responsibilities of
office.

Over the next few days and weeks further meetings would draw in new
figures and press on with the tasks of shaping community life and re-
cruiting people to share in it. Though during the next four years some
240 men, women, and children would join the group, by the time the
association disbanded in 1846 only one (Hiram Wells) of those actually
present on April 8, 1842—and only three (Wells, Samuel L. Hill, and
Hall Judd) of the eleven founders—would still be members.

But that all lay in the future. First, we need to understand why the
founders and their families came to be setting up a community at all. To
do so we must examine the overlapping interests and commitments that
brought these eleven men to Northampton, the broader contexts in which
they were acting, and the issues and principles that led them, by the early
1840s, to seek a communitarian solution to the problems they perceived.
What brought them to meet that April day in 1842 so hopeful that they
could change American society for the better?

Founders of a Community

The Northampton Association would assemble men and women with a variety of material, ideological, and spiritual concerns that although often complementary, would at times jostle for priority. Prominent among the interests of the eleven founders were radical abolitionism, nonresistance, temperance, manufacturing, and education, themes significant in the early shaping—even the naming—of the community. Dividing the eleven men into groups allows us to capture the varied importance of these and other influences. That they can be divided into four pairs— each with a dominant and minor member—and three individuals, none of whom can easily be grouped with any of the others, incidentally tells us something about the internal dynamics of the nascent community.

The dominant figure in the first pair was George W. Benson, the minor player his neighbor from Brooklyn, Connecticut, Theodore Scarborough. Of all the Northampton community's leaders Benson would become the most prominently associated with it in reform circles, in part because of his impeccable abolitionist credentials and connections. He was, first of all, linked to the old antislavery movement of the early republic. His father, George Benson (1752–1836), had been a Providence merchant and a founding member, and later secretary, of the Providence Society for Promoting the Abolition of Slavery. During the 1790s Benson senior abandoned his Baptist faith for Quaker sympathies, which much of the family shared. Persuaded by his son to retire to a farm in Brooklyn in eastern Connecticut in 1824, he had devoted the last part of his life to the two reforms, peace and abolitionism, that would play an important part in the lives of his son and his son's associates. He was active in the Rhode Island Peace Society, a founder and vice-president of the Windham Peace Society in 1826, and in 1834 third president of the New England Anti-Slavery Society, the region's crucial early proponent of immediate abolitionism.

Before his father's death, George W. Benson had earned abolitionist laurels in his own right. With his younger brother, Henry Egbert (1814–37), George formed friendships early in the abolitionist campaign with William Lloyd Garrison and other leading advocates of immediatism. In 1833-34 he worked closely with Brooklyn's Unitarian minister, Samuel J. May, to defend Prudence Crandall and her school for black girls in the neighboring town of Canterbury. On visits to the Benson household during the Crandall affair Garrison had courted George's sister Helen, and

George W. Benson, about 1845.
From Charles A. Sheffeld, ed.,
History of Florence, Massachusetts.

their marriage in 1834 cemented the Bensons' position close to the heart
of New England's abolitionist leadership. Partner in a Providence wholesale wool and leather firm after 1831, George W. Benson gave that up
to take overall charge of the farm in Brooklyn at his father's death five
years later and devoted an increasing amount of time to abolitionist activities. He was a local agent for the *Liberator*, became prominent in the
Windham County Anti-Slavery Society, and from 1837, Connecticut
agent for the American Anti-Slavery Society. The Benson house, which
Prudence Crandall apparently called "the asylum of the oppressed," was
an important stop for abolitionist lecturers touring the state or traveling
between New York and Boston. In the late 1830s, under Benson's sisters,

it was the effective headquarters of the Brooklyn Female Anti-Slavery Society. After the Crandall affair and a split in the town's Unitarian church it served to focus a network of sympathetic neighbors and supporters that would, in time, provide many members of the Northampton Association.

The Bensons' seventy-five-acre farm was supposed to support George's mother and sisters and his own growing family of small children. By 1840, he later wrote, it was evident that it could not. Why this was so is unclear: possibly the rolling upland soil was not very productive; more likely Benson's other activities left him insufficient time to devote to farming. At all events he sold it in the spring of 1841 and moved his family to Northampton. He persuaded one of his neighbors, another abolitionist farmer, Theodore Scarborough, to move his family too. At first, they even brought the Unitarian minister, May's successor William Coe with them, but Coe withdrew from the group as the Northampton community was forming. It seems that Benson moved to Northampton intending to invest the proceeds of his farm in the property of the Northampton Silk Company, and that during 1841 he was gathering partners together to go in with him in silk manufacturing. Over the course of the year, as prospective partners were assembling, the manufacturing project turned into a wider effort to promote social change by creating a community of reformers, if not at Benson's instigation, then certainly with his support.[2]

Close counterparts to Benson and Scarborough were Samuel L. Hill and his friend Hiram Wells, though they were artisans, not merchants and landowners. Hill, seventh child of a Quaker farmer and carpenter in Rhode Island, had broken with the Society of Friends when he married outside it, had himself trained as a carpenter, and then tried unsuccessfully to be a trader before becoming a mill overseer in the growing factory town of Willimantic, Connecticut, in the late 1820s. Here, while he advanced in the management of successive cotton mills, he had become a pillar of the Baptist church, but broke with it in the mid-1830s as he developed his sympathy with Garrisonian abolitionism, and never joined a church again. He gained some local prominence as an abolitionist leader, helped found a male antislavery society in 1836 in emulation of the Female Anti-Slavery Society of Willimantic, set up the previous year, and became well known to abolitionists across eastern Connecticut as he took part in their meetings or offered hospitality to traveling lecturers. Wells was a blacksmith who had grown up in the nearby town of Lebanon and later moved to Mansfield to work as a machinist. He also had reform sympathies and,

Samuel L. Hill, about 1850.
From Charles A. Sheffeld, ed.,
History of Florence, Massachusetts.

though less active in the movement, had, with Hill, become acquainted
with the circle of Windham County abolitionists based in Brooklyn. In
1841 Hill purchased a farm at Broughton's Meadow and found Benson,
Coe, and others already negotiating for the Northampton Silk Company
property that lay adjacent to it. Consolidating the two properties, Hill
and Wells joined what turned into the community, bringing with them
a sort of businesslike determination and skepticism that may explain why
they stayed in the association for the duration of its existence, and would
take a leading part in its later transformation. Like the Bensons, though
to a lesser extent, their abolitionist, work, and neighborhood contacts in
the Willimantic area enabled them to recruit members.[3]

Kinship, proximity, and industry, as much as reform or abolition, linked these men to the third pair of founders, Joseph Conant and Earl Dwight Swift, to whom Hill was related by marriage and Wells would have known and perhaps worked with. As New England's household-based rural economy evolved in the early nineteenth century, northeastern Connecticut became engaged in silk raising and manufacturing. The scattered hamlets and rapidly flowing streams of the town of Mansfield emerged as the single most significant center of silk production. Beginning in about 1810, local merchants and mechanics had introduced machinery to process locally raised raw silk, and by the 1830s some small mills were established at water-power sites in the town. Always uncertain and unstable businesses, these silk mills were run by a few families, occasionally reinforced by skilled silk workers from England and elsewhere. Joseph Conant, born in Mansfield in 1792, became involved in 1829 in a venture that would grow into the Mansfield Silk Company, the town's first substantial joint-stock firm in the silk business. Though the company went bankrupt in the mid-1830s it drew others into silk manufacture permanently. Among Conant's assistants was Orwell S. Chaffee, who had grown up on a farm in Mansfield, married Conant's daughter Lucina in 1834, and worked with his father-in-law, until he tried to set up his own mill four years later. Conant also employed Earl Dwight Swift, who also came from a trading and silk-manufacturing family and would marry another of Conant's daughters, Olive, in 1839. The economic conditions of the late 1830s, however, played havoc with the prospects for silk production in Connecticut. When the Northampton Silk Company in Massachusetts, already bankrupt, sought an experienced man to supervise its mill in 1839, Conant took the job and moved north. Olive Conant Swift and her new husband went with him, and were also employed by the Silk Company. In 1840 Joseph Conant took a three-year lease on the Northampton mill from the company's assignees for $1,000 a year and operated it on his own account. In 1841 Benson arrived, probably intending to join him in the business, but as Hill and Coe also became involved during the year, the idea of forming a community began to take hold.

Little evidence survives of Conant's opinions or his stand on abolition, though a claim made much later that he had been involved in the Underground Railroad in Mansfield suggests that he was sympathetic to the cause. The memoir of a Northampton community member indicated that Conant and Swift were happy to go along with the change from silk company to association because they were amenable both to its principles and its potential as a profitable investment. Conant's experience in silk manufacture and his ability to invest in the association made his presence valuable to Benson and the others, and they honored this by choosing him as their first president. From Conant's viewpoint Benson's interest in investing in the mill probably seemed the best chance of surviving in the silk industry at a time of great uncertainty. The formation of the community enabled him to keep his family and its skills together, because he brought into it both of his sons-in-law and their families. Swift brought $1,000 in capital to invest. Chaffee had evidently had difficulty establishing his own firm in Mansfield and probably found coming to Northampton an attractive way of staying in what was becoming a precarious industry.[4]

The business anxieties of Conant and his extended family had little connection with the concerns of the fourth "pair" of community founders, Hall Judd and Samuel Brooks. These men may have had little in common, except in two respects: both were among the few members of the association who came from the immediate vicinity of Northampton, and both lived very simply. We know little about Brooks, but he seems to have been poor. He had owned a very small farm in the nearby town of Hadley, had a mortgage on it, and sold this land in 1842 for no more than he had paid for it. He also had a large family, whom he brought with him into the Northampton community soon after it was founded. Evidently the Brooks family was seeking something the group could not provide, for later in 1842 they left Northampton for the Shaker community at Enfield, Connecticut, where a number of them were still living in 1850.[5] Judd came from a background that rejected extravagance and embraced evangelical religion, temperance, abolition, and nonresistance. He preferred an ascetic life. His father, Sylvester Judd, a Northampton editor and historian, retained a firm republican suspicion of fashion or display of any kind; his brother Sylvester Jr. was a Unitarian minister whose minor transcendentalist writings also evoked the simplicity of a vanishing way of life.[6]

Hall Judd turned these ideas into a set of precepts about diet, dress, and worldly comforts so rigid that even his family teased him about it. A brother told of visiting the family home while Hall was away and sleeping in his bed, "if bed it might be called . . . 'The soft side of a *Plank*' would be *Down* compared to it." On another occasion his mother brought pies to the dinner table and Hall "as usual, denounced all *living* except on Faith and Saw Dust." Hall had worked as a clerk and as a farm laborer in Connecticut and western Massachusetts. His views on slavery and religion got him excommunicated from churches in Hartford and Northampton, but his movements and connections with radical abolitionists had led him to a Connecticut woman, Frances Birge, of principles similar to his. She could, wrote Hall's mother, "turn her hand to any kind of work, she is a good sewer, is economical, is healthy, a thorough Grahamite, her views of dress, and of fashions, and of things which belong to the world perfectly agree with Hall's." Over several months in early 1842, Hall Judd spent time in Northampton discussing reform principles with Benson and his colleagues; and though he was apparently not at the initial meeting, he was clearly regarded as a potential community member. Shortly after its founding, Hall Judd and Frances Birge married and formally joined the association. They were to remain in it to the end.[7]

Though arbitrary in part, this "pairing" of some of the men who started the Northampton community allows us to identify common strands of interest and commitment that led members to join. To differing degrees, abolition, nonresistance, and manufacturing were interwoven in the lives of them all, and for some a commitment to asceticism was a further draw toward community. Their backgrounds and acquaintanceships also overlapped and helped bring them together. Even Conant and his sons-in-law acted together; they joined the association early in its life and would leave together later in 1842 to set up again as silk manufacturers on their own.

Though they also had overlapping interests—in abolition, nonresistance, and education—the three remaining figures among the founders are less easy to group with others. David Mack, Erasmus Darwin Hudson, and William Adam were all strongly committed to social reform, but came from quite distinct backgrounds and traditions. All would make a mark on the life of the community, but their dealings there with one another would be tense, at times even hostile. Their work together would be the result of coalition, rather than personal loyalty. Not only would this affect the character of the community's development but it would help explain why all three men and their families withdrew between 1843 and 1845.

Of Northampton's "founders" David Mack was probably the most enthusiastic about the prospects for communities as instruments of social change. Born in Middlefield, a hill town west of Northampton, son of a merchant who later settled in nearby Amherst, Mack had studied at Yale and then started to train as a lawyer, but abandoned that for a teaching career, and in 1831 became preceptor of a Quaker school in New Bedford. In 1836 he joined the New Bedford Young Men's Anti-Slavery Society. By then he had married another teacher, Maria Brastow, and they later moved to Cambridge to set up their own school for girls. Intellectual interests and reform sympathies brought the Macks to the edges of both the transcendentalist circle and Garrison's abolitionist clique.

In 1841 David and Maria observed with interest the formation of the Brook Farm community. In fact, both signed Brook Farm's articles of association in February 1842 with the intention of joining. By early March, however, they had changed their minds and planned instead to move to Northampton in May. The reasons for the switch are unclear, but a letter sent to Mack from Brook Farm the previous summer by Nathaniel Hawthorne hints at some of Mack's anxieties. Hawthorne was evidently keen to assure Mack of the untruth of rumors then circulating that Brook Farm's founder George Ripley exercised undue power over the members: "We have never looked upon him as a master, or an employer, but as a fellow laborer on the same terms as ourselves, with no more right to bid us perform any one act of labor, than we have to bid him." Mack evidently overcame any misgivings sufficiently to sign up at Brook Farm, but must have learned almost immediately of the proposal to create a new community at Northampton. Possibly the prospect of joining a group where there was no single leader, but a set of elected officers, caused him to change his family's plans. In time Mack would himself serve in several capacities at Northampton, as president after Joseph Conant left and then as secretary and director of education, in place of William Adam. He may even have persuaded Hawthorne to consider joining the Northampton community with him; the author at any rate thought it necessary to write to Mack in late May 1842 to explain that he was not coming after all.[8]

Erasmus Darwin Hudson was drawn to Northampton by his abolitionism and by the connections he had made with Benson, Hill, and Judd, but his career had been different from any of theirs. Brought up and married in the town of Torringford in western Connecticut, he had trained as a physician—indeed, still practiced on occasion—and then become successively a schoolteacher, amateur geologist, and avid temperance reformer. A Congregationalist, his orthodox religious views were unshaken until he became involved in the abolitionist movement in the mid-1830s, first in Litchfield County, then as a founder of the Con-

necticut Anti-Slavery Society. Increasingly sympathetic with the radical
wing of immediate abolitionism, he became a tireless itinerant agent for
both the Connecticut and American Anti-Slavery Societies, using his
lecture tours and his contributions to the Connecticut society's newspaper,
the Hartford *Charter Oak*, to advocate the Garrisonian cause in a state
largely hostile to it.

Hudson had lectured with Benson, valued Benson's home in Brooklyn
as a base and a haven, spoken at meetings organized by Hill, and found
himself in strong sympathy with Hall Judd. On a lecture tour in 1839–
40 Hudson carried a pocket-sized memorandum book to compile comments, for future reference, on the men and women he encountered. All
three men came in for praise: Benson as a hospitable "whole soul reformer," Hill as "a good Christian philanthropist," and Judd as a man of
principle with whom he felt particular affinity. Hudson's move to Northampton followed from Benson and Hill's decision to set up a community.
Indeed, he may, like Judd, have been involved in discussions about it
during the early spring of 1842. But Hudson seems to have regarded the
community more as a home for his family and a base for his work as an
abolitionist lecturer than as something to engage his own wholehearted
commitment; at any rate he had clear notions about the terms on which
he could be content with community life. Much more than Conant or
Swift that day in April 1842 Hudson held himself back from participating
too directly in its business.[9]

Of these ten men, seven were from Connecticut and three from Massachusetts. In both a geographical and a cultural sense the eleventh founder, William Adam, and his family, had traveled much further than the
others to be present at the start of the Northampton community. Adam's
extraordinary story suggests that he was a man of considerable talent,
resourcefulness, and courage who, nevertheless, never quite succeeded at
what he set out to do. Born in Scotland in 1796, educated there and in
England in the classics, theology, and Asian languages, he had sailed to
India in 1817 to join the Baptist mission at Serampore, just outside Calcutta. Two years later he married Phebe Grant, daughter of another missionary, at Calcutta's Anglican church. Despite his early efforts as a
missionary, in 1821 he was himself converted to Unitarianism by a prominent Hindu reformer, Ram Mohun Roy. Scandalized missionaries spoke
of him as "the second fallen Adam." At times supporting himself by
working as a mercantile clerk, he spent the next seventeen years working

against long odds to influence the British East India Company's rule in Bengal.

He assisted in the running of an Anglo-Indian school, but angrily resigned after a disagreement. Having become a Unitarian minister after his conversion, he tried and failed during the 1820s to convince Ram Mohun Roy to accept Christian monotheism. He established a church in Calcutta, with some support from British and American Unitarians, only to see his Bengali brahmin congregation depart for Ram Mohun Roy's new religious society, the Brahmo Sabha, in 1828. Abandoning the ministry, Adam then edited a succession of Calcutta newspapers. Objecting to East India Company policies, he was obliged to move from one paper to another as the government suppressed them. Against the background of a fierce debate about the future of education in British India, he was commissioned in the mid-1830s to study schooling in Bengal and neighboring Bihar. Knowing, even as he set out, that the government had determined to support education conducted in English, Adam spent three years of travel and systematic research preparing reports that firmly advocated the contrary policy of sponsoring education in vernacular languages. As he left India in 1838, it was evident that his recommendations would be ignored. William Adam had apparently failed again.

Yet his years in India gave him connections and ideas that would indirectly pave the way to involvement with the Northampton community. Adam's effort to establish Unitarianism in Calcutta gave him contacts with leading churchmen in Massachusetts. His mercantile work introduced him to Boston shipowners and merchants in the East Indies trade, including members of the Dixwell family, who would provide hospitality and financial assistance to the Adams when they came to the United States. His friendship with Ram Mohun Roy, though often strained (and ended by the latter's death during a visit to England in 1833), introduced Adam to concepts of religious toleration not very different from those later adopted at Northampton. With hindsight, Adam would come to see Ram Mohun Roy's involvement in a successful campaign to obtain a law against *sati* (widow-burning) in 1829 as his own introduction to women's rights. Adam's journalistic campaigns for reform made him critical of governmental power. The work for his reports on schooling gave him a detailed, sympathetic understanding of Asian rural society matched by few, if any, contemporary westerners. Though Adam's background and experience would lead to important differences with New Englanders, his views on equality and religion were close enough to theirs for him to make common cause with other founders of the community. He was the only member of the Northampton community who had considered in some depth how a whole society might be reformed by education. At the same time, he recognized that change through education was gradual, and that radical reform demanded other social changes as well.[10]

William's precarious income and the Dixwells' patronage led Phebe Adam to leave Calcutta for Boston with her children in 1834. He followed four years later with the intention of taking them on to London. Probably because Phebe refused to move, William instead visited England briefly by himself, then accepted a post created for him at Harvard as professor of Oriental Literature and returned to take it up. He disliked Cambridge and his job, but made contacts among Garrison's circle of abolitionists. They completed his conversion to radical abolitionism; he, in turn, captivated them with the prospect that land reform in Bengal, for which he was starting to campaign, could strike a blow against American slavery by producing cheap cotton for European markets. When Adam sailed for England again in 1840—this time with his family—it was as a Massachusetts Anti-Slavery Society delegate to the World's Anti-Slavery Convention held in London that June. There he cemented his alliance with the Garrisonians by supporting their demand that the convention seat the women delegates who attended. When the demand was refused, it was Adam who drafted the radicals' formal protest.[11]

At this point he resigned from Harvard and stayed on in London to become secretary of the British India Society, a group with close abolitionist and free trade connections formed to press the British government for reforms in India. He also edited its newspaper, the *British Indian Advocate*. Adam's knowledge and experience excellently qualified him for this work but he was restless and discontented in England and soon thought of emigrating again. Now, he decided, he would become a farmer. His family was anxious to return to America, but Adam wavered, and even paid a deposit on some land in Australia before acceding to their wish. They set out in the late summer of 1841 with the intention of buying a farm in Pennsylvania, but Adam had also read articles in the transcendentalist journal, the *Dial*, lent him by Wendell Phillips, and this may have given him the idea of joining one of the new communitarian experiments instead. Still undecided, he made inquiries about Brook Farm, but late in the year ended up in Northampton. Having first looked around for land to buy, he decided instead to join Benson and the others in setting up the Northampton community. With the strong endorsement of William Lloyd Garrison, he came highly recommended to the new group. This, his unusual experience, and his status as a "professor" gave him considerable influence. He became an early investor in the scheme and almost certainly played a major part in the discussions over the winter of 1841–42 that preceded the community's founding. His credentials would both help and hinder his acceptance of community life. His cultural distance from some of the American reformers he had joined would lead to mutual awkwardness that ultimately contributed to his departure.[12]

The Communitarian Context

The "founders" of the Northampton community were not "typical" members. The absence of women at the opening meeting signaled an assumption of superiority by men that though challenged, was never fully overturned. Still, the stories we have just outlined, of William Adam and the other ten founders, suggest both the common factors and the diversity of experience that they brought with them. An examination of these stories in the wider context of the kinds of influence—material, intellectual, and ideological—that led them to construct a new type of social organization; an examination of the economy and ideas about business and industry, of abolitionism and nonresistance, and of the effects of those movements on religious experience, will help explain why such diverse groups of men and women as the members of the Northampton Association should have sought to found communities, and why they did so in the early 1840s.

Two sets of circumstances created the immediate context for the interest in communities among radical reformers: the financial panic of 1837 and subsequent depression, and the disputes in the abolition movement that caused it to splinter in 1839 and 1840 into two or three antagonistic fragments. In addition to these general conditions, though, there were particular ideological influences that crystallized efforts to start communities and helped determine the makeup of the group that created the Northampton Association.

The economic crisis in New England both created the opportunity for founding communities and spurred certain men and women to seek to take advantage of it. As they moved to Northampton, George W. Benson and Samuel L. Hill were among thousands responding to the long depression that began in the financial panic of 1837. Trouble began with the collapse of banks and prominent mercantile firms and spread as credit was tightened and other institutions were dragged down. Anne Talbot, sister of a Northampton capitalist, wrote in March 1837 that one of the town's two banks had closed and noted, too complacently, that that left "one here, which I should think was as much as such a place required." Among the activities hit hard by the depression, manufacturing of various kinds was prominent. In the Connecticut Valley region carriage-building, toolmaking, hat-making, and broom-making, along with parts of the textile industry, were forced to shut down or severely to reduce their scale of operation and would recover, if at all, only after several years of weakness and uncertainty. In Willimantic, Connecticut, Samuel L. Hill survived these early years of financial panic, but not untouched; the textile firm he managed was shaken by the failure of one of its backers in 1837, and Hill apparently changed jobs at around this time. Other future members of the community also faced the prospect of ruin as the depression spread.[13]

Newspapers began to fill with articles and editorials advocating farming as a superior, stable livelihood. Many men in uncertain businesses with enough capital to buy land of their own contemplated becoming farmers. Samuel L. Hill moved to Northampton in 1841 for this purpose. When William Adam arrived in town that October, he was still pursuing the plan he had conceived before leaving England: "He is resolved on purchasing a farm," wrote a Boston friend; "he is to work on it himself and be aided by his family." Hall Judd too, tired of clerkships and laboring jobs, had been planning to become a farmer, and had gone to Connecticut in October 1841 to look for a suitable place near Bloomfield. It was already commonplace among reformers to connect the wish to take up farming with a wider desire to influence society by setting up communities. The link had been made most prominently by George Ripley, as he led the movement to turn transcendentalism from philosophy to social action and set up the Brook Farm community. If the plans for Brook Farm had not worked out, Ripley would have taken up farming anyway.[14] When Hill, Adam, and Judd turned from their plans to farm to the effort to form a community, they were following a path already taken by the founders of Brook Farm.

The Northampton community, however, was not primarily the result

of a drive "back to the land" from cities and industry. All kinds of activity—rural, urban, and industrial—had been disrupted by the depression. Many members would be drawn from rural backgrounds. Few, if
any, shared William Adam's expectation that he could take up farming
for the first time at the age of forty-five and make a living at it. The
economic crisis had strongly affected rural areas, and it was characteristic
of the confusion it had produced that Hill and others "returning" to the
land encountered George W. Benson and others trying to leave it. Among
Benson's Brooklyn neighbors who would join the community were the
members of the Scarborough family, which was heavily in debt by the
late 1830s, and the mechanics Enos L. Preston and James A. Stetson,
who had both been obliged to sell property to pay debts.[15] Interest in
setting up communities reflected, not a flight from one sphere to another,
but the hope of establishing a better society capable of providing stable
livelihoods.

The coalescence of the Northampton community around a silk company did not result simply from chance or opportunism. Silk production
embodied the vision that farming and manufacturing in balance with each
other could provide the basis for a healthy, successful form of society.
Cultivating mulberry trees would provide food for silkworms, whose silk
would be the raw material for the manufacture of thread and other goods.
Industries that were inherently unstable even at the best of times suffered
disproportionately in the depression, and silk production in Connecticut
and Massachusetts was particularly vulnerable. But, ironically, as the crisis
had deepened in the late 1830s, farmers and manufacturers placed increasing hope in silk as an activity that could rescue them from financial
difficulty. After interruptions and business reorganizations before and
during the 1837 panic, investors began to speculate in mulberry trees.
Throughout northern Connecticut and western Massachusetts mulberry
cultivation expanded, and in centers such as Mansfield and Northampton
silk manufacturers tried to survive the contraction of credit. The collapse
of the Mansfield Silk Company in 1836 had prompted men such as Joseph Conant and Orwell S. Chaffee to try and restart production on their
own on a smaller scale. Meanwhile, the Northampton Silk Company, set
up in 1835–36 with an unusually large stockholders' investment of almost
$100,000, found itself in trouble as the crisis spread and struggled to
rearrange its business in order to continue in the straitened circumstances
of the late 1830s.[16] When the bubble of mulberry speculation finally burst
in 1839, farmers and manufacturers alike were thrown into further dif-

ficulty. A desperate effort to keep the Northampton silk mills going led
to Joseph Conant's appointment as superintendent late that year, and to
the migration of manufacturers from Mansfield to Northampton to try
their luck in this new silk region. The failure of these efforts and the
stockholders' decision in 1841 to seek a buyer for the Northampton Silk
Company's property prepared the ground for the formation of the Northampton community. In some ways, the Northampton Association's hope
of building a community around silk seemed to perpetuate the inflated
visions of the late 1830s. But the intention was to realize the balance and
benefits of silk production while avoiding the evils of speculation and
competition that had apparently destroyed the business in 1839.

For the depression did not lead merely to instrumental efforts to recoup
losses or earn livelihoods. It also concentrated minds on a wider critique
of the economic practices that led to social injustice. Hill and Benson,
among other members of the community, had had painful experience of
trade, its uncertainties, and the wage system and what they saw as its
elements of unfairness. As former manufacturers and traders, they sought
not to overthrow the existing economic system, but to organize it on more
stable and equitable principles. To them, an association of people living
and working together would have a chance to establish a harmonious
balance between the organizational advantages of a joint-stock enterprise
and the social benefits of a community of equals. It would banish the
uncertainties of speculation and competitiveness. Hill commented, later
in his life, on the motivations of the early members of the Northampton
community: "We expected to work out an improved state of society, and
make ourselves and friends happier—to get rid of the competition so
omnipresent and oppressive."[17]

If they wanted an example of the things they wished to avoid in a
competitive economy, they needed look no further than the story of the
property they were buying in the winter of 1841–42. The Northampton
Silk Company was built on the optimism and plausibility of Samuel
Whitmarsh, a New York merchant who had settled in Northampton and
bought an extensive property there at the end of the 1820s. Whitmarsh
became one of a number of promoters convinced that the United States
was destined to be a major silk-producing nation. Like other enthusiasts
he planted mulberry trees, built a cocoonery to feed silkworms, and pub-
licized his methods. He looked around for investors in a factory that could
process raw silk into finished goods and secured backing from New York

merchants led by the Talbot family, China traders who also owned a house in Northampton. The Northampton Silk Company was conceived on a large scale, but hopes for its success were dashed even before the buildings were complete. The Talbots and others were threatened by the 1837 panic, and the company was only kept going over the next two years to promote interest in silk and so fuel mulberry speculation. Whitmarsh himself faced failure, resorted to dubious tactics to stave off ruin, and was suspected of misstating the value of property and materials. When at length the company went bankrupt, and Whitmarsh was forced out, a local writer recalled that he "had neither cash nor credit to buy a barrel of flour"; at least four creditors sued him. He sought to retrieve his losses in a visionary scheme to establish a silk factory in Jamaica, for which he managed to obtain substantial English backing. With him went his brother Thomas—later briefly a member of the Northampton community—and several young men from Northampton, including the son of one of his creditors, who were to help build the establishment. But this scheme also failed when, owing to carelessness or ignorance, its shipment of imported silkworms died.[18]

Different people drew different lessons from the tale of Whitmarsh and the Northampton Silk Company. At the height of his troubles in 1837, Charles Nicholl Talbot received a letter from his father advising him—with pointed reference to Whitmarsh's overconfidence—that "at your time of life a pull back will serve to give you caution and enable you to avoid engaging with those who however honest, have no doubts." It would be best for Talbot, he continued, "to commence on Mr Girard's rigid plan, 'keep my plans to myself' . . . : study your own interest, consult your own judgment, . . . however friendly you may be to others." That way, the writer concluded, "I seldom went wrong, but the moment I suffered others to influence me, I never succeeded well and often not at all."[19] Such advice led in the direction of single proprietorships, commercial independence, and individualism. Appropriate as this might be for many mercantile activities, it was hardly feasible for manufacturing efforts of much size. The Northampton Association, eventual successors to the Northampton Silk Company, sought instead to promote cooperative ownership and communal social arrangements. These, it was hoped, would permit the concentration of investment that a large factory demanded, but avoid the uncertainties and immoralities of speculative, overconfident business practice.

Abolitionists Divided

Economic depression and business crises formed part of the web of connections that brought the Northampton community together. Another was the crisis that faced the abolition movement. It was this crisis much more than economic concerns alone that had thrown crucial leaders and members of the community together in the first place and had helped define their place in the wider reform movement.

Historians of abolitionism have devoted much attention to the schisms that nearly destroyed the movement at the end of the 1830s; it is necessary here only to provide a broad outline of the issues before looking more carefully at their influence on the founders of the Northampton community. The campaign for the immediate abolition of United States slavery expanded rapidly in the early 1830s. To its early supporters among the black community were added the considerable weight of white abolitionists inspired by the evangelical revivals and the urge for social action they created. The insistence that slavery was not merely an institution to be reformed, but a "sin" to be expunged, was both the core of their campaign for immediate abolition and the entry point for the argument that northerners as well as southerners were implicated in its evils. During the mid-1830s antislavery societies were founded across New England and other parts of the North, sustained not only by indignation at chattel slavery itself but also by the political success of the South and its sympathizers in banning the distribution of abolitionist tracts and curbing debate in Congress and other public forums. Their early organizational success had several consequences for abolitionists. It provoked popular, often violent opposition in the North; it raised questions about the denial of equality to northern blacks; and it attracted strong support from women as well, whose concerted action in local and national antislavery societies itself started to bring into question widespread assumptions about the gendered bounds of public behavior. In addition, Garrisonian abolitionists in particular, critical of the political system's complicity in the crimes of slavery and increasingly suspicious that the United States Constitution was protecting slaveholders, became wary of political action as a means to effect abolition. Moral suasion and renunciation of all contact with those seen as complicit with slavery became the heart of their strategy. Their disputes with colleagues who held other views were to shatter the movement.

Gender and politics were the rocks on which the united immediate-abolitionist campaign of the 1830s broke apart. Evangelicals, led by Lewis Tappan of New York and supported by many clerical members, brought part of the split about by walking out of the 1840 annual meeting of the American Anti-Slavery Society in protest at its policy of permitting women to speak on public platforms and the appointment of Abby Kelley to its executive committee. At the same time the Garrisonian champions of women's participation were also challenged by groups seeking to form a separate antislavery political party. This would, in their view, entail a compromise with the Constitution and so signal complicity with slavery; it would also exclude women, because they could not vote.

Together these two splits left the radicals in an embattled state. They retained control of their national organization, the American Anti-Slavery Society, and of the state societies in Massachusetts, New Hampshire, and Ohio where they were particularly strong. From these bases they proclaimed their adherence to what they called "old-organization" abolitionism. But they faced opposition from "new organization" abolitionism at the national and state levels, from Tappan's new American and Foreign Anti-Slavery Society, which curbed women's public participation, and from the advocates of independent political action, who formed the Liberty Party in 1840. Abolitionist publications and correspondence from 1839 to 1842 provide ample evidence that these splits and the often subtle differences of opinion and alignment that they entailed occupied an increasing proportion of reformers' time and attention. The "old organization" abolitionists (loyal to Garrison) took particular pains to distinguish themselves from both Tappanite evangelicals and political abolitionists, whom they regarded as tainted with "new organization" and "third partyism." Contemporaries and historians alike have often asked what these disputes had to do with the movement's ostensible purpose, to free slaves.[20]

Historical interpretations of these disputes have tended, until recently, to consider their role in the movement's own strategies or their more general impact on antebellum history. Aileen S. Kraditor, for example, argued that Garrisonian policies and tactics did further the movement's overall purpose of ending slavery. A more skeptical school of thought dismisses the abolitionists' splits as petty sectarian wranglings among a small group of men and women whose influence was insignificant. A third type of argument, succinctly expressed by Ronald G. Walters in his study *The Antislavery Appeal*, suggests that the abolitionists' divisions should not be overemphasized because they merely masked the more fundamental patterns of agreement between radicals, evangelicals, and Liberty Party advocates that were ultimately to draw the various factions closer together again in the 1850s.[21]

But for our purposes the wider implications of these disputes are less important than their effects on the men and women who took part in them. There is little doubt that they took them very seriously indeed; otherwise they would not have filled newspaper columns and countless letters writing about them. Both the radicals and their opponents were convinced that the debates over women and politics, and the other issues that followed from these, presaged fundamental social change. As an unsympathetic minister had written at the prospect of the Grimké sisters' appearance to lecture at Fourth of July celebrations in Newburyport in 1837, "A man . . . might as well attempt to stem the current of some mighty river or the fury of a hurrican[e] as to oppose the Abolition torrent which is now sweeping over the northern portions of our land and threatening to destroy and prostrate whatever it cannot carry along with it," and he expressed himself opposed to "everything which is ultra and wrong."[22] The splits in the abolition movement were highly significant in creating the radical "moment" of the early 1840s, and in several ways they helped shape the context in which communitarianism grew up.

Recent studies of the abolitionist movement that emphasize personalities and group culture have implied that the splits of the late 1830s and 1840s can be attributed to a built-in proclivity for instability and dispute. Undoubtedly there were psychological and structural conditions that fostered fragmentation among these reformers;[23] nevertheless, there is an impersonality about such interpretations that overlooks two important aspects of events. First, abolitionists disputed with one another and broke apart their organizations not just because their personalities disposed them to it, but because they were fighting for what they recognized as real issues of principle—principles, moreover, that were as deeply held on the conservative or evangelical side of the split as they were on the radical side. Second, the splits over women's rights and politics caused considerable pain to men and women who found ranged against them friends and colleagues with whom they had once shared hard campaigns. Horace Cowles, who had been active in western Connecticut, wrote to George W. Benson early in 1841 expressing regret at the break in the antislavery movement and the silence of more than a year that this had caused between them; however, he also ended his letter with a condemnation of Garrison and his followers' positions on women's rights and third-partyism, which, given that it was addressed to Garrison's own brother-in-law, was presumably not an effort to strike a compromise. At the same time Benson was criticizing attacks made on Garrison by Reverend Nathaniel Colver and his "new organization" allies: "No stone will be left unturned . . . to destroy his [Garrison's] reputation. Judgeing them by their conduct I should think they more earnestly desired [that] than the emancipation of the slaves."[24] Many among the abolitionists who came to the Northampton community were deeply embroiled in the movement's rifts and were preoccupied by them between 1839 and 1841.

Connecticut was the scene of particularly bitter conflict. With local exceptions, such as in the Bensons' own Windham County, immediatist abolitionism had been slow to take root, and there was no separate state antislavery society until 1838, five years after the founding of the Massachusetts society. No sooner did the movement gain ground than it split apart, and Garrisonians largely lost control of the state's main antislavery societies and newspapers to their opponents. Adherents to "new organization" captured the Connecticut Anti-Slavery Society and its organ the *Charter Oak* and cast off Erasmus Darwin Hudson, Benson, and others who remained loyal to Garrison. Hudson revealed his disappointment at the rift when, shortly after being removed from his post, he recorded a visit to Hartford in his diary: "Called at my former home the Anti Slavery Depository!—It is now a gloomy place! The anti slavery spirit . . . has fled—a bitter Sectarian, anti woman, anti Garrison-time serving, *popularity seeking* spirit has taken full possession!" The only thing that cheered him up was meeting his "good warm hearted brother" Hall Judd.[25] Even Windham County, where considerable support for Garrison remained, proved uncertain and divided. Local societies, including the Brooklyn Female Anti-Slavery Society, supported by the Bensons and their neighbors, ceased to function. In February 1841 Garrisonians had called an eastern Connecticut antislavery convention to meet the following month in Willimantic, and Benson claimed that "in this section of the country the cause never looked more promising, the people are almost wholly united in the life giving principles of old organization." But the convention proved his optimism misplaced, showing support for plans to organize a third party and condemning Abby Kelley's participation in the American Anti-Slavery Society's executive committee. When the Connecticut Anti-Slavery Society met in Hartford in May, and Kelley rose to speak, she was denied the right to do so on the grounds that the meeting's invitation to "all persons" did not include women. Garrison supporters were losing ground rapidly in the state as a whole, to which Kelley would refer in a letter to Benson as "your inhospitable region."[26]

Against such a background of dissension and defeat these abolitionists, their families, and some of their friends decided to search for somewhere else to move to, a search that would lead them to set up the Northampton community. Four founders of the community, Benson, Hudson, Samuel L. Hill, and William Coe, had been prominent at the Willimantic convention; six men and women who would later join it were among the signers of a protest against the Connecticut Anti-Slavery Society's silencing of Kelley. One of them, Susan Byrne, treasurer of the Willimantic Female Anti-Slavery Society (Working), also wrote to Garrison to criticize the "disorderly conduct" of Kelley's opponents. She linked the campaign for women's rights to demands for radical social change: "We have not forgotten the taxes which caused revolutionary war, [nor] . . . the aristocratic feeling that keeps the laboring people destitute of knowledge." But the pain of the abolitionist split was an inducement to members of the many small groups of Garrisonians across Connecticut to gather together for mutual support. When Samuel L. Hill said that the Northampton community was intended to "make ourselves and friends happier—to get rid of the competition so omnipresent and oppressive," he was referring not just to wider economic and social conditions, but also to the strife he and his abolitionist colleagues faced at the beginning of the 1840s.[27]

So a mixture of material and ideological circumstances led reformers to Northampton. But to understand more fully why they chose to form a community and sought to construct a new way of life we must look further at their beliefs and at the practical issues those beliefs had posed for their position in the abolition movement in the late 1830s. For some abolitionists the split between old and new organization was much more than a debate over the tactics and strategy of achieving reform; it was a cultural struggle that engaged them in a fundamental reevaluation of society at large.

Nonresistants

For none was this more so than for the groups of men and women, many of them supporters of Garrison, who by the late 1830s had identified themselves as "nonresistants" and were ready to extend antislavery reform into a full critique of existing society, government, and institutions. Following Christ's injunction to "resist not evil," they rejected any recourse to the use of force, and relied on the power of moral suasion to carry their arguments. There was, of course, a lengthy tradition of Christian nonviolence evident in America from the seventeenth century on among Quakers and other sects. Quakers had contributed to the growth of peace societies in the 1820s, and in time this involvement led some of them to embrace abolitionism. Two factors helped strengthen the abolitionist peace movement and turn it toward nonresistance. First, popular opposition to abolition, which grew as it did in the 1830s, demonstrated the realities of a society many of whose citizens were intent either on using violence themselves, or on acquiescing in its use, to defend the sin of slaveholding. Second, as they refined the theoretical underpinnings of their attacks on slavery, some immediatists—including Garrison—came to see that slavery was only one manifestation of "the ancient and universal recognition, contrary to Christian teaching, of the right of coercion by some men in regard to others, . . . that the only irrefutable argument against slavery is a denial of any man's right over the liberty of another under any conditions whatsoever."[28] To work against the authority of any institution backed by force or the threat of it therefore became both a realistic practical action and a logical principle. The formation of the New England Non-Resistance Society in 1838 marked the merging of abolitionist and peace principles and a radicalization of the two movements. Nonresistance was a crucial strand, both in the splits in the antislavery movement and the subsequent creation of utopian communities.

As the historian Lewis Perry has shown, radical abolitionists of the late 1830s adopted a particular form of nonresistance. They did not follow its conservative version, which counseled passive submission to authority. Nor, though it was fundamental to their principles, did they limit themselves to the practice of nonviolence. They went further, condemning all institutions based on force and rejecting the legitimacy of existing governments, churches, and other organizations in any way implicated in the coercion of other human beings. To abolitionist nonresistants several sets of convictions came to fit together. Not only should war, capital punishment, and other forms of governmental coercion be rejected, but participation in government at any level should be avoided.[29] Not only should Christian fellowship with slaveholders be avoided, but efforts should be made to reform existing churches to bring this about, and connections broken with churches that refused to banish them. Not only should "all persons," men and women, be free to speak out against sin, but organizations that curbed that freedom should be spurned. As nonresistance grew among New England immediatist abolitionists in 1838 and 1839, it played a powerful and logically consistent role in the radicals' rejection of evangelical and political antislavery. The splits in abolitionism over women's rights and plans for a new political party were underpinned by nonresistance principles.

Their opponents termed the nonresistants "no-governmentists," claiming that they were willing to attack all existing institutions in any way implicated in the use of force. Many abolitionists condemned nonresistants, as they condemned other advocates of women's rights, for bringing "extraneous" issues into the antislavery movement and diverting it from its true purposes. One logical outgrowth of nonresistance was, obviously, a form of radical individualism or anarchism that rejected all kinds of organization whatsoever and placed individual men and women in atomized relationships with one another and in direct, unmediated relationship with God. Those who called them "no-governmentists" or "no-organizationists" feared the social disorder and lack of control that might flow from this position. But, as Perry has pointed out, Garrison and his nonresistant allies rejected these labels. Though they attacked existing "human government," they sought to establish the "government of God" and social institutions that could embody it. Their arguments contained a strong streak of perfectionism, inspiring action to build a better way of life. Nonresistance in this form led not to a rejection of institutions as such but to a search for new social organizations uncorrupted by existing evils.[30]

Many of the founders and early members of the Northampton community were connected with nonresistance. At least twenty, including Benson, Hill, Hudson, Judd, Mack, and Scarborough, had attended nonresistance meetings, contributed to the Non-Resistance Society, or actively advocated its principles; others, such as William Adam, were sympathetic. It may be significant that William Coe, the Unitarian minister who at first joined Benson, Conant, and Hill to purchase the silk company property in 1841 and then relinquished his place to Adam, had expressed reservations about nonresistance and never embraced it. Meanwhile, it was as nonresistants that residents of Northampton who observed the group's preparations identified them. After meeting William Adam in December 1841, Hall Judd's father noted in his diary that "he and some other nonresistants have purchased lands in and about Broughton's Meadow" and wrote a few weeks later of Hall that "a few of his non-resistant brethren have planted themselves . . . near the Silk Factory."[31] These men and women were among numbers of nonresistants for whom community appeared a sensible outgrowth of their criticisms of existing institutions. Various strands in their reform and religious experience led them to set up a new social structure with particular ways of realizing the ideal of perfect government on earth.

The nonresistance principles of key founders and members of the Northampton community were not just abstractions. They had been forged and reinforced by harsh practical experience, and were all the more powerfully held for that. Their view that northern society rested on violence was rooted not just in political theory, but in the treatment they often saw meted out to free blacks and escaped slaves, and in the hostility they met in their own work as abolitionists. Benson had become acquainted with mob violence, some of it officially sanctioned, during the Prudence Crandall affair and had subsequently faced down threatening crowds on more than one occasion. In 1835 Samuel L. Hill had confronted a mob led by a fellow deacon in his own church, an incident that led him to leave the church and adopt nonresistance.[32] Itinerant lecturers like Erasmus Darwin Hudson frequently faced disruption, threats, and actual violence. At Harwinton, Connecticut, in August 1838 rioters released a herd of pigs onto the meeting ground while Hudson was speaking. More seriously, having spoken at a Baptist meeting house in Georgetown that November, Hudson awoke the next morning to find that his horse had been attacked: "My *old grey* had been in *bad hands* during the night and was badly sheared—her tail was all cut off." Word then arrived that the meeting house had been blown up. He did not believe this at first, but went and "found it too true." Someone had put twenty-five pounds of gunpowder under the pulpit he had lectured from and set it off. Three years later (the "old grey" evidently having gone to greener pastures), another of Hudson's horses suffered for his actions. After an argument with some Universalists at Clinton, Connecticut, Hudson found the animal's mane cut off, its tail trimmed, and two-thirds of one of its ears missing. Having spent some time cheering "Old Dick" up, Hudson and five others sewed back together the remnants of his buffalo robe, which the attackers had also shredded. At Newtown a week later the traces to his wagon were cut. Hudson wrote of these events as trials heroically overcome, but they both reinforced an emergent critique of society and the need to rely on the minority of stout souls who would assist the cause. The people who gave Hudson shelter, helped repair his torn robe, or "[did] not flinch or grumble" when their meeting house exploded were scattered members of an abolitionist community some of whom might be gathered in a single place to further the cause. Evil and its agents would be countered by the moral power of men and women gathered to "uphold the right."[33]

"Come-Outers"

Many evangelical and other conservative abolitionists also strongly opposed nonresistants' condemnation of existing churches and the ministry for alleged implication in the sin of slavery. As radical abolitionists sought to make their churches free of the taint of slaveholding, and to use churches to propagate the antislavery campaign, they often confronted popular and institutional objections to their efforts, and by the late 1830s an increasing number were following the biblical injunction to "come out" from among sinners and break their links with the churches, or set up new ones. As one radical editor asked, how could men and women work for social reform "while we cling to those systems and arrangements, the influence of which is destructive to the peace and happiness of our fellow beings?"[34] Upholders of denominational orthodoxy condemned what they saw as "infidelity" to the word and authority of God. Nonresistants and "come-outers," for their part, attacked what they saw as a "priesthood" intent on retaining its own power over the minds and actions of its followers. As three members of the Northampton community argued in 1843, "the highest and purest form of worship is that which gives to every man the utmost liberty of speech, consistent with the exercise of a spirit of love and brotherhood"; therefore no gathering that reserved the right to speak to "a distinct body or order of men" like the clergy could be truly Christian.[35]

To these nonresistant abolitionists nothing was of greater concern than their argument with the churches. Because it was widespread and constant, ecclesiastical hostility seemed to them more pernicious even than political opposition; the Massachusetts Anti-Slavery Society reflected this view in 1844 when it attacked the Liberty Party for diverting attention "from a corrupt church and clergy to the less guilty state." If abolition was to be brought about by moral suasion, obstruction by politicians who were inherently likely to bow to expediency mattered less than opposition from clergymen who should have been leading the fight against sin. But this was more than a view that the churches should supply moral leadership; it conveyed, too, a conception of society that emphasized the importance of local communities, in which religious gatherings were a more immediate and regular source of moral influence than politics or other public activities. Protesting and withdrawing from churches that opposed abolition appeared to be an effective tactic for ordinary people committed to the cause.[36]

"Come-outerism" took two forms, only one of which concerns us here. Some of the men and women who withdrew from the churches over slavery formed themselves into smaller groups, continued to worship together and sometimes turned these groups into new church organizations. These "come-outer sects" contributed to the endless fragmentation of American Protestantism that some commentators have seen as its perpetual institutional condition.[37] But other "come-outers," perhaps because of their wider acquaintanceships in the abolitionist and nonresistance movements, saw withdrawal from the churches as the first step away from sectarianism in general, as the start of a movement that might unite all Christian reformers in a nondenominational fellowship and abandon the authority of churches and ministers altogether.

Nonsectarian "come-outerism" was an important source of inspiration (and members) for the Northampton community. It united people from several religious traditions, Quaker, Baptist, Congregationalist, Unitarian, and others. The founders of the Northampton community carved different spiritual paths to the same point. Samuel L. Hill had become an active member of the Baptist church in Willimantic, Connecticut, soon after his arrival there at the end of the 1820s, when it was the only formally organized church in the new factory village. He served as the church's clerk and then its treasurer, but in 1835 broke with it: not only had he become a nonresistant, opposed to the bearing of arms, but he had also become convinced that water baptism, the use of visible bread and wine at communion, and the payment of regular salaries to ministers were unscriptural.[38] Erasmus Darwin Hudson underwent a less radical, but still profound change in the second half of the 1830s, from orthodox Congregationalist to doctrinal liberal. In his diary for 1835 Hudson described the last illness of Samuel Woodward, a physician who was an unbeliever, with the mixture of awe and smugness of the righteous regarding the death of an infidel. Woodward "could not think that there would be an eternal punishment," wrote Hudson the day before the older man died. "Oh God! will he not be fearfully surprised?" By 1840, Hudson had added marginal comments to this diary to mark the repudiation of his old beliefs. "What a change of my own mind," he wrote. "Much [was] written in this book under the influence of *educated bigotry*—contrary to the natural spirit of the writer—Evangelical heresy." Hudson's "natural spirit" had turned him into an eloquent critic of slavery and an implacable opponent of the sectarianism, "priestcraft," and doctrinal tyranny of the conventional churches. Although Hudson and his wife did not formally break their connection with the Congregational church in Torringford until the end of the 1840s, their expressed criticisms of the churches were indistinguishable from those of many who had "come out."[39]

Some individuals moved from sectarian to nonsectarian "come-outerism." In Bloomfield, Connecticut, which was Hudson's home in the late 1830s and early 1840s, several nonresistants had withdrawn from the local church to worship together, and were excommunicated for their pains. Hall Judd worshiped with this group when he was in the area. In 1842 and 1843 several of its members left for Northampton, turning their allegiance to a small, sheltered group into commitment to a larger, more embracing, nondenominational community.[40] Hudson, Hill, and others were also in touch with a further group, in the small town of Chaplin, Connecticut, that fought a long battle over abolitionism and women's rights within their Congregational church before being forced to give up. Chaplin's antislavery movement, active and close-knit, had cooperated closely with the church until the abolitionist split of 1840 set Garrisonians and Tappanites—including the minister—at odds. According to Joseph C. Martin, one of the radicals, the minister acted to stop revival meetings at which women could speak and in March 1841 preached what Martin called the "Frog Sermon," in which he compared the Garrisonians to the three unclean spirits ("like frogs") in the book of Revelation. They were a "disorganizing" influence, refusing to follow the "old way"; their arguments against civil government represented "infidelity concealed under the mask of philanthropy and religion"; and their criticisms of churches and ministers were the work of "the man of sin." For two more years Martin and his friends fought the minister and sought to get the church to condemn slavery. Failing at this, they "came out" from it in 1843 and were then formally excommunicated. A few months later, Martin and several others moved to the Northampton community.[41]

These "come-outers" turned the charge that they were sectarians back on their clerical accusers by proclaiming their tolerance for the beliefs of others. Rather, it was the churches, they countered, with their resistance to the opposers of sin and their restrictions on "free speech" and women's rights that were guilty of sectarianism. This argument embraced a general attack on practices, such as observing the Sabbath, that nonresistants associated with the arbitrary exercise of clerical power. Their meetings, such as the convention "to discuss the origin and authority of the ministry," held at the Chardon Street chapel in Boston in November 1840, drew furious criticism from evangelicals and others who labeled it an "anti-sabbath convention," and correctly perceived in it a root-and-branch assault on existing organized churches. Among the participants were George Ripley, who had left the Unitarian ministry and was about to found Brook Farm, and at least five future members of the Northampton community, including David Mack.[42] Opposition from churches and their ministers to radical abolitionist principles lay at the core of many men's and women's experience of the splits of the late 1830s and early 1840s. To George W. Benson it was one of the main reasons for giving up his Brooklyn farm and his family's dedication to Windham County abolitionism. Though "fully persuaded on the whole, that the principles we love and have advocated, are beginning to make some impression on the public mind, sectarianism is the hindrance to this peoples advancement in Truth and holiness," he wrote early in 1841.

At first sight Benson's solution appeared to be a straightforward rejection of institutions: "Man cannot be free while laboring to build up a sect or party, he must be left untrameled to follow truth withersoever it may lead, before he can attain to a perfect man in Christ Jesus."[43] There were indeed nonresistants who drew this conclusion. But Benson's own abolitionist experience had helped leave the way open to a different conclusion, that institutions consistent with true Christian principles were possible and should be supported. As his own Windham County Anti-Slavery Society had resolved in 1840, while corrupt organizations were not worthy to be preserved, "we cannot . . . be hostile to any institution which is not inherently corrupt." Abolitionism itself provided a model of uncorrupted organization. William Adam, writing about the American Anti-Slavery Society in 1840, noted that "the principle on which this Society has based its operations is that all the members of civil society irrespective of religious and political distinctions may harmoniously co-operate" in pursuit of abolition. Adam's references to nondenominational,

harmonious cooperation directly prefigured the efforts he, Benson, and
others were soon to join in as they created a community at Northampton.[44]

The divisions in the abolitionist movement of the late 1830s and early
1840s therefore went much deeper than disputes over tactics. They reflected fundamental disagreements about the makeup and conduct of society itself. The four themes we have identified—economics, abolition,
nonresistance, and nonsectarian "come-outerism"—helped shape the
lives, not only of its founders, but many of the other men and women
who would join the Northampton community over the next few years.
Few were unaffected by any of them. In many cases several themes overlapped, or were joined by and reinforced further concerns with moral
reform, temperance, diet, and health. Of the eleven "founders," for instance, at least five—Hudson, Judd, Benson, Hill, and Mack—are known
to have campaigned for or expressed sympathy with temperance principles, and others may have done so in ways that went unrecorded.

The Logic of Community

By 1840 reformers in general were becoming gripped by debates over
communal organizations. Late that autumn Margaret Fuller wrote that
"one thing seems sure, that many persons will soon . . . throw off a part,
at least, of these terrible weights of the social contract, and see if they
cannot lie more at ease in the lap of Nature."[45] Reform journals of all
kinds published a constant stream of material about plans for communities and discussed their advantages and disadvantages. Abolitionists and
nonresistants shared this interest fully. It was from these discussions that
the idea of forming a community at Northampton would arise, and
through them that the abolitionist critique of slavery would turn into a
wider critique of American society in general.

There were several parallel developments. Albert Brisbane's works on
the ideas of the French utopian Charles Fourier were starting to circulate
in intellectual, radical, and labor circles. Even as they were promoting
direct imitation by American devotees of the rapidly growing Fourierist
movement, they also inspired critical debate among moral reformers attracted by the community idea but who rejected the secular and materialist
bases of Fourier's program. Discussions in the transcendentalist circle,
coupled with a growing sense of the need for social action, prompted

George Ripley and others to set up the Brook Farm community at West Roxbury, outside Boston, in 1841.[46] Meanwhile, the Universalist abolitionist and nonresistant Adin Ballou had published plans for a "Practical Christian" community that would not only put basic Christian principles into operation but could satisfy the demand of many New England reformers that such ventures be founded on moral, not materialist grounds; by 1841 these plans were evolving into the Hopedale community at Milford, Massachusetts.[47]

Talk of communities became widespread among radical abolitionists. In 1839, Erasmus Darwin Hudson defended the principle of "associated action" as a means of achieving social change. Two years later he was praising an article on phrenology by a member of Ballou's universalist church, pondering the Old and New Testament promises of "the coming of the Kingdom of Christ," and predicting that God was "testing the religion of the day and bringing out the pure gold from the dross." Even a hesitant communitarian such as Hudson drew inspiration from a variety of the influences that were to shape the movement. "What say you to a little social community among ourselves?" wrote William Lloyd Garrison to George W. Benson early in 1841: "I think we must be pretty bad folks if we cannot live together amicably within gunshot of each other." He noted that Benson's former business partner in Providence was proposing to set up a small farm community. Later in the year the Lynn abolitionist James N. Buffum wrote that the nonresistant campaign for change in the churches was bringing forward concepts of tolerance, duty, and common interest that led logically to associations to bring about widespread reform.[48]

The Bostonian abolitionist and nonresistant Edmund Quincy went further, writing that "cooperative associations" were "one of the marked tendencies of this age" and "a most encouraging sign of an earnest purpose to search after and to remedy the cause of the evils which prevail in this disjointed world." To the "co-operative principle," Quincy wrote, we owe "whatever is best in our social and domestic institutions," and he expressed optimism that communities would succeed in furthering "the advancement of the highest individual and social interests of man." As he was writing, Brook Farm, Hopedale, and other communities of various kinds were being established or mooted, but Quincy was not put off by the existence of simultaneous efforts in different places, made "without concert" or coordination. Rather, he saw that as a sign that history was on the side of the communities, "that there is an inexorable need that thus urges men to forsake the institutions which their fathers had builded for them, and go forth in search of new homes." The only matter for debate, he felt, was the overall influence of community ventures. Were they, as their critics suggested, merely efforts to withdraw "from danger to congeniality," which would leave the lights of reform hidden under a bushel, or were they "the concentration of the hosts of light to do more effectual battle with the armies of the aliens"?[49]

Some comparisons with the other main nonresistant community, at Hopedale, suggest that from its inception the Northampton community was intended to fulfill the second of Quincy's purposes, "the concentration of the hosts of light to do more effectual battle." Hopedale, like Northampton, grew out of abolitionist and nonresistant principles, but its origins were in a particular religious group, six or so restorationist Universalist ministers led by Hopedale's founder, Adin Ballou. These men resolved in 1838 to live in a way that would be "perfect in all possible respects" and attempted to carry out their resolve in the Hopedale community three years later. Membership was open only to those subscribing to a religious test. Men and women prepared to accept and follow its precepts could join Hopedale and seek to live as perfectly as possible, to make the community "an outward manifestation" of the kingdom of God eventually to be realized within all individuals. Hopedale was intended to be the first of many such communities to which, as Lewis Perry put it, the regenerate would withdraw, leaving the unregenerate under the government of worldly tyranny. Ballou's restorationist beliefs (that all would be saved, but only after a period of punishment for their sins) embodied a conservative fear of social chaos. The Hopedale community would offer a bulwark against this, and an example of social order. The community was regulated by a series of rules, many of them highly specific, which Ballou modified from time to time in an effort to achieve a workable ordered society. These principles and the rules to be followed marked Hopedale out quite specifically as a place separate from the world. Though it maintained constant links with reform movements and other communities, its religious separation was also to keep it distinct from Brook Farm and Fourierist groups with whom cooperation and even mergers were periodically contemplated.[50]

Northampton's approach, also strongly influenced by nonresistance, was different. There was no single leader, never any individual with as strong a role as Ballou in defining and influencing the community's shape and development. Though Northampton had rules and regulations, they had more to do with the framework within which decisions would be made, and less with prescribing what those decisions would be. Northampton's founders were not only a diverse group of individuals, but less pessimistic than Ballou about the ability of human beings to live together in harmony. Above all, they desired no religious test for membership, and never prescribed one. Instead they pursued the radical abolitionist ideal of a society in which people of all religious views could associate in a nonsectarian organization. In this sense, therefore, Northampton was conceived more as a "concentration of . . . light" than a withdrawal of the perfect from the world.

"This Desert Where No Water Is"

Even the community's location underscored this hope. As we have seen, it had strong roots in Connecticut—seven of its eleven founders, including four of the seven abolitionists among them, were from there—and Connecticut had just proved a desperate disappointment to the Garrisonians. But Benson, Hill, Hudson, and their friends were hardly "withdrawing" to a more hospitable region when they moved to western Massachusetts. Rather, they were setting up an outpost of Garrisonian abolition and nonresistance in an area strongly disposed to disapprove of it. Samuel L. Hill's son would later comment that radical abolitionists like his father were in "decided conflict with the respectability of the northern towns and cities." Nowhere was this more true than in Northampton, Massachusetts.[51]

Northampton, originally settled in 1654, was one of the oldest towns in western New England, and tended to pride itself on its political and religious conservatism. Old families traced their colonial forebears and maintained their connections among a regional elite based on business, land, law, and the Congregational Church. The town still had many farmers who tilled the rich meadowlands of the Connecticut River valley, but it was also a commercial center, with merchants and small manufacturers in a variety of trades; by 1840 less than half its population of 3,750 primarily supported themselves by agriculture. It was the Hampshire County seat and a base for the lawyers, judges, and minor functionaries who congregated around its courts. It was also starting to become a tourist center, its three hotels catering to visitors who came to enjoy the romantic scenery of the mountains that rise close by. In addition to north-south road and river connections, and good east-west roads, there was the new (though short-lived) canal to New Haven. In the mid-1840s the railroad would reach the town from Springfield. The population had risen only slowly during the 1830s, but over the next decade Northampton would experience more rapid growth, based on manufacturing, transportation and immigration. The place still recalled its former position as one of the bastions of New England Federalism, and by 1840 the Whig party was firmly entrenched. There was also a vocal Democratic minority, and a new pattern, derived from the Antimasonic and Workingmen's politics of the late 1820s and early 1830s, of political challenges to the major parties that would prove valuable to the Free-Soil movement of the late 1840s.[52]

The radical reformers who came to take over the former silk company property out at Broughton's Meadow found little welcome in Northampton. There were strong veins of anti-abolitionist feeling and of racism betrayed in lack of sympathy, or worse, for the plight of slaves and free blacks. There was support for the American Colonization Society, which asserted that blacks were inferior and should be denied citizenship. Like many towns, Northampton listed black residents separately at the end of its annual tax lists. When reformers started an antislavery society at the end of 1835, at least one of the town's two newspapers expressed violent opposition to the movement, and meetings were periodically disrupted. After David Lee Child moved onto a farm in the town in 1837 to grow sugar beets in an experiment to promote reduced dependence on slave-grown sugar, he helped promote abolitionist activities. A copy of a hand-bill he had issued in 1838, calling citizens to celebrate the anniversary of the August 1 emancipation of slaves in the British Empire, was nailed to his door with the word "persons" crossed out and "NIGGERS" inserted. Northampton also had significant southern connections. Members of several of its leading families had married southerners or moved to the South to live. Southern visitors came to its hotels, and a sprinkling of wealthy families from the South had settled there, all of whom found abolition repellent. Tradesmen and hoteliers, watchful for their businesses, also found it offensive. Few Whigs or Democrats among the town's political leaders were inclined to disagree.[53]

Though Northampton had its antislavery society, which grew rapidly and was quite active in the mid-1830s, its members, like most of the abolitionists in the surrounding region, attached themselves to "new organization" or political abolitionism in the splits at the end of the decade.

The few remaining Garrisonians were isolated or, like the master carpenter Moses Breck, obliged to adapt their views in order to be able to work with evangelical abolitionists.[54] Northampton was strongly attached to orthodox evangelicalism. It had been Jonathan Edwards's town; one of its two Congregational churches was named after him. The Tappan brothers were born and had grown up there, and though they had left, there were still connections with them; one of Northampton's leading abolitionists was their nephew, who, like several of his colleagues, was a prominent local merchant and pillar of one of the evangelical churches. Hostility to a public role for women was strong. The traditional view had just been restated in a forthright pamphlet by the minister in neighboring Westhampton, who argued that women were bound to keep silent whenever their pastor or any of their brethren were present.[55] The character of local religion and abolitionism made Northampton peculiarly unreceptive to the founders of the new community in its midst; as Garrisonian abolitionists, as nonresistants, as advocates of women's rights, and as nonsectarians they stood opposed to the town's more conservative traditions. The orthodox took a narrow view of the community; one woman, asked to describe it in 1843, simply wrote "they call themselves 'community people' or 'come outers'. They are some thing like Quakers—do not believe in keeping the Sabbath."[56]

We can get a good idea of what Northampton was like for a radical abolitionist from the letters of Lydia Maria Child, who lived there intermittently between 1838 and 1841 as she and David Child struggled with the sugar-beet farm. For a short time after she arrived in town she was optimistic. Two-thirds of the people, it was claimed, were sympathetic to abolition, and there was polite interest in the sugar-beet experiment. But she quickly came to feel that this sympathy was formal, not strongly felt, and that "Orthodoxy has clothed most of the community in her strait-laced garments." Child's attempts to raise abolition issues in conversation quickly led to her ostracism by leading families, whose conservatism she gauged when she heard a Springfield minister denounced for his extreme abolitionist views, and then discovered that the man was a colonizationist.

Child privately criticized Northampton abolitionists who regarded peace in their churches as more important than agitation to end slavery. Roxana Starkweather, for example, was "just such an abolitionist. . . . The supposition that the Presbyterian church would have ten less members . . . would at any time have rendered the emancipation of the slaves a doubtful measure in her eyes." She attributed their weakness in part to the influence of a former merchant with southern connections, Thomas Napier, a church deacon whom Child portrayed as a "rich slave-auctioneer" and pious hypocrite. Napier, their next-door neighbor for a while, "prays much louder than he talks, for the sake of being heard better, either by God or his neighbors." David Child would play his accordion to muffle the sound of the man's voice and its "tone . . . of whining expostulation." More important, Napier was said to contribute $250 a year to the salary of his minister, who "in return preaches against all reforms, and puts as many obstructions in the way of reformers as possible." There were, she added, "many abolitionists belonging to that church; but they never open their lips—so highly do they value 'the peace of the church.' "

Child saw religion and materialism at the heart of the radicals' weakness. "Calvinism sits here enthroned," she wrote, "with high ears, blue nose, thin lips and griping fist." Though she and David worked hard to obtain signatures on petitions to Congress, she quickly became despondent: "I have never been so discouraged about abolition as since we came into this iron-bound Valley of the Connecticut." Her chief solace lay in the support of Northampton's Unitarian minister John S. Dwight, at whose ordination in 1840 George Ripley had advocated "the kingdom of God on earth." But Dwight was soon to leave the town, to follow Ripley out of the ministry and into the Brook Farm community. In 1841, as Child herself was about to leave for New York to edit the *National Anti-Slavery Standard*, she could write, "I wish George Ripley had stated his plan [for Brook Farm] before we came here, to this Desert where no water is."[57] Shortly afterward Benson and his colleagues started to prepare their own community in a climate that would be no more hospitable than it had been for her.

Preparing for Community

Because the association did not keep records until its first formal meeting there is little precise documentation of the preparations made before April 8, 1842. We know that there were discussions over several months among some of the founders, but letters, deeds, and memoirs provide only glimpses of their plans. During 1841 the economic and ideological context we have been discussing, and the widely canvassed prospect that communities might be effective instruments of moral and social reform, induced the founders of the Northampton Association to turn their private endeavors into a cooperative venture.

George W. Benson moved his family from Brooklyn, Connecticut, in the spring of 1841, probably to the house at Broughton's Meadow they were to occupy for almost a decade, near the Northampton Silk Company property. One of his daughters recalled that after the sociability of Brooklyn, the Bensons were relatively isolated for the first few months, and the child lived a "lonely life" until the community got going. Samuel L. Hill and his family also arrived sometime that year, intending to settle on a fifty-acre farm just to the west of the silk company estate. But before he could complete his arrangements for farming, Hill later recalled, Benson and others "brought forward the idea of forming the Community Association," and Hill added his land to the community's property. This switch from planning business partnerships to forming a community cannot be dated exactly, but it was almost certainly before October 1841. That month Benson and Hill, together with Joseph Conant and William Coe, purchased the silk mill and estate from the silk company trustees.[58]

By the end of October the Adam family had also arrived. They made arrangements to have a house at Broughton's Meadow fitted up for them—work that would take until December. As he reached Northampton, William Adam still had plans to farm, but within two or three weeks he had been convinced to act on the idea that had been planted in his mind earlier in the year and join the effort to form a community. Boston friends who visited in mid-November reported that Adam had invested "with four others" in "the great silk farm," and that although Phebe and her daughters were "desponding" at the prospect, William was going around "in a perpetual excitement." Either then or later, Adam bought out William Coe's share in the venture for about $2,000, though the deed formalizing this arrangement was not executed until February 1842. Meanwhile, Adam read Vattel on natural law, with its discussion of community property, and its argument that the poor had inherent rights to subsistence. He and Conant also took legal advice, probably on the group's plans to draw up articles of association.[59]

Adam was one of the authors of a "Preliminary Circular" issued in February 1842, announcing the new community and opening the recruitment of members. This was one of the final stages in the preparations that would lead to the April 8 meeting. Shortly after it was issued, David and Maria Mack, who had just signed the Brook Farm articles of association, changed their plans and opted instead to move to Northampton.

Hall Judd also became involved about this time, and Erasmus Darwin Hudson must have been drawn in too, though precisely how and when is not clear. The April meeting, in addition to instituting the community, marked the completion of its legal arrangements. Once they had been elected to office, Adam, Conant, and Hill formally sold their portions in the silk company estate to Benson, and so consolidated the property once again. Immediately Benson sold it back to them, this time not as individuals, but as the trustees of the Northampton Association of Education and Industry. They were now embarked on their effort to change the world.[60]

A patchwork of sources have enabled us to retrace some of the steps that led to the April 1842 meeting. But to interpret these steps and to understand the community's progress once it was under way, we need a broader overall view of what the founders were doing. Were they following some kind of blueprint for an ideal society, already formed in their minds and agreed between them? Or were they proceeding in an ad hoc manner, to see where each step would lead them? The answers to these questions will not only help us locate the Northampton Association in the wider history of "utopian" communities, but will help explain the developments that were to take place within it over the next four years.

Only one of the founders gave his own view of the matter. Samuel L. Hill left two brief memoirs of the community, one of which appeared in 1867, twenty-five years after the founding, and the other in 1908, just over twenty-five years after his death in December 1882. Both stress the community's ad hoc character. Hill notes that he, Benson, and others had originally come to Northampton for their own private purposes and only adopted the community idea as their plans developed in 1841. Even as the community was starting, he remembered, they were improvising, not following a preconceived plan. This is what he meant by his remark that "we expected to *work out* an improved state of society."[61]

There are reasons for doubting this claim. By the time he made it, Hill was a successful manufacturer who might have wished to disassociate himself from organized socialist or Fourierist theories that had become discredited. He did not deny the abolitionist and religious influences on the group, but by the end of Hill's life abolition was respectable and toleration more tolerable. Hill's memoirs dwelt neither on the reasons that might have led them to a community venture nor on the previous connections between members of the group. Perhaps the community was more thoroughly planned and less accidental than Hill implied?

The evidence does suggest a more complicated picture than Hill's version of events. But his claim for spontaneity is significant, because it fits with the abolitionist, nonresistant, and "come-outer" origins that would help shape the community's character and development. The founders would provide a framework for community, but not the precise rules under which it must be conducted. They would leave details to be drawn in by members, a challenge that was taken up repeatedly in the next few years. Following their consciences and the principles they had learned in their struggles over slavery, women's rights, and the churches, they would work toward a new form of society. By doing this, Hill wrote, and by educating their children in the new community they were forging, they would "ultimately revolutionize the old system."[62]

CHAPTER THREE

"They Will Soon Convince the World":
Shelter, Base, and Mission

The members of the Northampton Association expressed their principles in language similar to that of many utopian communal groups in the 1840s. Early in 1843 they declared that "association" together provided the best means of enacting "the principle of equal brotherhood, the all-embracing law of love so emphatically taught by true Christianity." They rejected the "distinction of rights or rewards" made in ordinary life "between the strong and the weak, the skilful and unskillful, the man and the woman, the rich and the poor" and sought a social equality that would ask "only of all honest effort according to ability." Existing society could not support these ideals, because it was divided at all levels by the evils of "competition" between individuals and classes, between capital and labor, between slavery and freedom, between political parties, and between churches riven by denominational rivalries.[1]

These references to equality drew both from abolitionism and from the wider language of radical social and labor reform of the 1830s. Equality of men and women implied an assault on the patriarchalism that had traditionally subordinated women's effort to men's authority. Critics of utopian socialism would later mock the naïveté of claims to seek the abolition of conflict between labor and capital, and had this aim stood alone it might be taken merely as bourgeois fantasy. But the juxtaposition of economic conflict with other forms of political and social division makes ideals like those professed by the Northampton community more radical than that. The critique of "competition" was shorthand for the types of conflict that proceeded from the exercise of power at all levels of society. Only by overthrowing social institutions and building new, equal ones would exploitation be ended. One of the members' favorite texts came from Paul's Epistle to the Galatians: "There is neither Jew nor Greek, there is neither bond nor free, there is neither male nor female; for ye are all one in Christ Jesus," and they envisioned a comparable cultural equality, based on racial and religious toleration.[2] The purpose was to create a type of social organization that could express the millennial hope for the gathering of all people into a heaven on earth. Practices, behavior, language, and habits associated with privilege and exclusivity would be shunned, so that members could be "peaceful, happy and active fellow-laborers together" and "bring mankind into harmony and union."

A Blueprint for Community?

Ever since the mid-1840s there have been writers who have been misled into referring to the Northampton Association as a Fourierist community. It was not. Its members were advocates of moral suasion, many of whom criticized Fourierism for its materialism and inadequate reliance on moral influences. John Humphrey Noyes was largely correct in 1870 when he classified Northampton, along with Hopedale and the early years at Brook Farm, as "an independent Yankee attempt to regenerate society."[3] But like Samuel L. Hill's picture of the spontaneous character of its origins, this tells us less than it might about the influences that guided the community's founders, whose thinking did not just spring up out of nowhere. The Northampton community had features in common with other communities of the 1840s and characteristics that would lead it to develop in distinctive ways.

Common influences and unique characteristics were each apparent in two important documents produced by the founders early in 1842. The first was the "Preliminary Circular," signed by Joseph Conant and William Adam, adopted at a meeting of "the owners of the Northampton Silk Factory estate" on February 15, 1842, which announced the "projected Northampton Association of Education and Industry" and outlined the principles that the founders hoped to promote there. The second was the association's initial constitution and articles of association, ratified at the April 8, 1842, meeting, which guided the community during the first few months of its existence. Many of the organizational aspects of community envisioned in the two documents were identical and were common among contemporary communities. But the principles stressed in its constitution differed significantly from those in the "Preliminary Circular." The shift, which occurred in the space of a few weeks, tells us much about the influences on the founders and their views about how to make their experiment work.[4]

The organization adopted in April 1842, and outlined in both documents, was intended to reconcile capitalism with the ideal of social harmony by using a joint-stock structure as the basis for communal institutions. Unlike Shaker communities, some Owenite groups, and the "no property" community that would be formed at Skaneateles, New York, by the abolitionist John A. Collins in 1843, Northampton was not based on common property. Like Brook Farm, Hopedale, and the Fourierist communities, it would be owned by shareholders who were not required to relinquish their own property beyond the amount of their investment. Yet unlike some Fourierist groups, Northampton was organized to ensure that control was retained by its members, not by outsiders. Only residents could vote in its deliberations. In addition, there would be a formal division between the Stock Company, consisting of resident members who were stockholders, which would exercise financial control, and the Industrial Community, consisting of all resident members, stockholders or not, which would run day-to-day operations. The two bodies would overlap, but the power of stockholders would be curbed by the general membership. Provisions for dividing earnings were also intended to equalize the rights of members and stockholders. Though they differed in some respects, the Northampton community's initial arrangements put it broadly in line with other contemporary joint-stock communities; they were a variant of a common type of "blueprint" for harmony and equality.[5]

The principles set out in the Preliminary Circular were also based on other community theories. The document developed three lines of argument. First, radical social change was necessary in order to overcome social ills: "when existing institutions are found inadequate to promote the further progress of society," communitarian groups could lead the way forward to fulfill God's designs for humanity, and bring about equality and cooperation. Second, human beings should be brought into harmony with one another and with nature, to promote "progressive culture and the high development of all the powers and faculties of our nature." Communities would do this by combining work, domestic life, and education, to make a "union of spiritual, intellectual and practical attainments." Third, life in community would be superior to the "separate and conflicting action" of existing society, where social ranks, based on "invidious distinctions," divided "culture, skill and labor" from one another, separating intellect from action and making it barren, dividing labor from "speculative pursuits" and turning it into degrading drudgery. Work, freed from these constraints by new social arrangements, would become a source of "health, education and happiness."[6] Bringing together work, learning and spiritual development and emphasizing human harmony with nature were particular concerns of transcendentalists, whose ideas influenced Adam and his colleagues through articles in the *Dial*, contacts in Boston and Cambridge, and the example of Brook Farm. Fourierist theories, imported to the United States by Albert Brisbane's *Social Destiny of Man*, published in 1840, also guided the Circular. Though it did not refer directly to Fourier's concept of "attractive industry" and envisioned nothing like the complex and regular movement between tasks that characterized his labor system, the document suggested that the Northampton Association would be divided into departments and subdivisions, each with a leader, not unlike the "groups" and "series" in a Fourierist phalanx. It emphasized overcoming the "drudgery" of labor, proposed special rewards for doing unpleasant tasks, and promised a division of profits between labor, capital, and skill. Though differing in detail from Brisbane's model, all these points reflected Fourierist influence.[7]

None of this means, though, that the community was primarily transcendentalist or Fourierist in inspiration. Borrowed concepts appeared in the Circular only in abbreviated and selected forms, filtered through the concerns of moral-suasion reformers who also emphasized self-control, "personal accountability," and "self-conquest." Moreover, between the publication of the Circular and the drafting of the constitution a few weeks later, moral-suasion arguments had gained prominence and the influence of Fourierism and other community theories had (except in one or two matters) diminished.[8]

The constitution bore much stronger signs of abolitionism and nonresistance than of a desire to copy blueprints for an ideal society. As a result, it was more radical and hard-hitting than the Circular. Differences between the two documents were signaled in their opening sentences. Where the Circular proposed a cooperative association because existing social institutions were "inadequate," the constitution condemned "existing social arrangements" for helping to promote society's "evils." Where the Circular proposed reuniting the separated spheres of work, education, and spiritual achievement, the constitution condemned the division of society into classes, one of which pursued frivolities and the other was consigned to a desperate material and moral struggle for existence.[9] The constitution went further. Organizing a community could begin a root-and-branch reordering of social, religious, and political institutions. It would provide a path by which to avoid "warlike" and violent governments, to scrap unprincipled political parties, and to build a religious life no longer divided into sects or tyrannized by churches, creeds, and "superstition" about forms and rituals. All these themes were hallmarks of radical abolitionism and nonresistance. The constitution also specified, where the Circular had not, that the "family relation" between husbands and wives, and between parents and children, was engraved in "the Laws of Nature and the will of God" and would be inviolate. All, however, would have "equal rights," regardless of "sex, color or condition, sect or religion," and freedom of conscience and expression, subject only to respect for the "equal rights" of others to the same. "Fair argument without praise or blame" was the only legitimate means of "controlling the opinions or belief of another." There should be no rules or creeds, merely discussion. All should have the right of "self-improvement in knowledge." The constitution embodied the application of nonresistant, moral-suasion principles to community organization.[10]

Nor did this focus on moral suasion signal a retreat from concerns with material questions regarding work and its rewards that were central to the purposes of Fourierists and others. Echoing labor reformers of the 1830s the constitution proclaimed that labor required a just reward and that community members had "the exclusive right of enjoying and disposing of the fruit of their labors." Combined with the commitment to "equal rights" and arrangements that gave members a voice in the conduct of community affairs, this gave scope for working people to influence the terms on which rewards for labor were distributed. And so it would, in practice, prove.[11] Instead of following a blueprint that claimed, like Brisbane's, to "solve" the problems of labor by establishing a "correct" form of community organization at the outset, the abolitionists and nonresistants at Northampton left such matters to be worked out in the actual practice of community life.

Moral-suasion principles entailed building a community around the scruples and consciences of its members rather than according to a preconceived design. The constitution asserted that the association's purpose was to *search* for a proper path to social change, that it would need to experiment in order to find it, and that the effort was justified even if it did not succeed in the end. The measure of success would not be conformity to a plan, but whether the community could realize the goals of achieving "mutual benevolence and friendly offices, . . . living in peace and amity towards all" and uniting members' "spiritual, intellectual and practical attainments."[12] Early practical arrangements did not entirely match this ideal. Only when members took a hand in reforming them did it come closer to fruition.

Right from the start, the need for flexibility was evident. The opening meeting had elected trustees and stock directors and created committees to handle admissions and accommodation, but other departments remained to be created and the new bodies had to start improvising procedures almost as soon as they met. A meeting of the Industrial Community a week after the founding created lumber, agricultural, and mechanical departments; others would be formed over the next few months. As early as April 17 a general meeting of the association was asked to approve changes to the constitution to modify arrangements for expelling members. Another meeting a month later approved further changes relating to the replacement of officers, the voting rights of stockholders, and the power of the trustees.[13] Throughout the summer, new by-laws, constitutional changes and procedural decisions were made or debated as members encountered fresh issues. Experience was sought from other communities. In May, William Adam was asked to prepare "a course of Lectures on Social Economy" about "the principles and practices of the Association," and given funds "to visit the nearest Shaker and other communities" to gather information about them.[14]

Gathering a Community

As members figured out how to function as a community, their numbers grew rapidly. By April 8, 1842 there were already nearly thirty people—founders and their families—gathered at Broughton's Meadow. New arrivals quickly doubled this; by the end of the month at least fifty-nine people were in residence. Numbers would rise to sixty-eight by late August and eighty-three by the end of the year. By the spring of 1844, the number would reach 120. Who were these people and how did they come to be at Northampton?[15]

Studies of utopian communities rightly attach importance to the ways members were recruited and admitted. It has long been a commonplace for instance, among critics of Robert Owen's New Harmony community in Indiana in the 1820s, that membership was offered to any of the hundreds of men and women who flocked to the place, without sufficient discrimination between those who were suitable and those who were not. For Owen, however, whose environmentalist theories held that all behavior was the product of circumstance, no person could be "unsuitable" for community, because the environment of community life itself would have a reforming effect; indiscriminate admission was, in other words, both consistent with his philosophy and an opportunity to demonstrate its validity. Partly as a consequence of the failure of New Harmony and in order to avoid its mistakes, partly as a result of their rejection of environmentalism, most non-Owenite communities in the 1840s took care to regulate admission and screen out unsuitable applicants. (By the end of the decade the North American Phalanx had even introduced an application form to be used by prospective members.) Hopedale would consider for full membership only those who could satisfy its religious test. Northampton, though it welcomed men and women regardless of religious affiliation, was also careful to regulate membership and at first put this in the hands of the small admissions board created by the founding meeting of April 8, 1842. The committee soon established features of the admission system that were to last throughout the community's existence.[16]

The admission procedure was a pragmatic mixture of personal and institutional steps and did not follow a rigid path. This mixture of formality and informality makes the process difficult to follow precisely in the surviving records. The constitution was sent to be printed up as a circular to help in recruitment. In September 1842 it also appeared in the *Liberator*. It quickly produced at least one applicant: James D. Atkins, a printer at the university press in Cambridge, who read it and decided to join. But many potential applicants probably heard of the community by word of mouth or from brief references in the reform press; many copies of the printed constitution were sent to people after they had made initial inquiries.

Though most people who became resident in the community were formally admitted to membership, there were others whose status was not easy to determine. There were probationary members, men or women "invited to reside with us," boarders, pupils at the school, and a few whose places were supported by charitable subscriptions. Only full members could vote at community meetings, and after 1843 only they could receive distributed shares of any annual profits, but others had the right to speak at meetings and enjoyed other privileges of membership without distinction. There was even a provision, made during an early shortage of suitable full members, for probationary members to be elected to office as departmental directors and to enjoy full membership while they served.[17]

A key formal point was the decision to admit someone to full membership. At the start this was the business of the admissions board; from 1843 on it would be by vote of the whole community. The moment could be reached in a variety of ways. Some individuals, especially the spouses and children of members, were often voted in quickly and with little formality. From time to time men, women, or families from outside the group, who were known to and well regarded by a number of members, would also be admitted in this way. More frequently, however, various steps were taken before voting was conducted. People who applied on their own initiative, in person or—more commonly—by letter, were usually asked to visit the community for a short period, given its hospitality, and encouraged to talk with members. The same usually went for those who were introduced or encouraged to come by an individual already in the group. If there was mutual agreement that the outcome of the visit was favorable, one of three courses of action could follow. Unusually, the applicant's case might be brought up at the next admissions meeting for a decision whether to admit to full membership. More often, admission would be probationary, usually for one year, at the end of which, if mutually agreeable, there would be a formal vote on full admission. Alternatively, the applicant could be invited to stay for a shorter period, perhaps a month, as a "boarder." At the end of the agreed period, the application might come forward for a vote on admission to probationary or full membership. In a few instances, spouses (men and women) evidently lived at the community with member families for months or years before they themselves joined. There were small numbers of hired workers. Finally, between 1843 and 1845 there were pupils at the school, other than children of members, who were accepted as boarders for an annual fee of one hundred dollars.

As we might expect, the membership that emerged from these procedures broadly reflected the economic, ideological, and religious influences discussed in Chapter 2. In occupational terms members represented roughly a cross-section of contemporary New England society, but they were not drawn proportionately from across the spectrum. Of the occupations of fifty-nine male members for whom evidence can be traced, twenty-one (36 percent) were professionals, merchants, or had been proprietors or managers in substantial manufacturing enterprises. Another twelve (20 percent) were clerks, laborers, or factory operatives. In other words, just over half the membership were from occupations at the top or bottom of the social scale. The remainder of the membership, twenty-six men (or 44 percent), were artisans or farmers who represented the group of "independent" producers, many of whom were adversely affected by recent economic changes and the depression. Compared with Brook Farm in its early years, for instance, the Northampton community was attractive to members of relatively modest social status, though there was no equivalent to the rush of artisan members who joined Brook Farm after it adopted Fourierism in 1844. Admission was occasionally granted to people—especially men—with skills that were particularly needed, but skill was rarely the sole criterion of acceptability. Most artisans had reform or family connections too.[18]

This range of backgrounds is also reflected in evidence about the property and wealth of members. The fourteen families who came to the community from the Connecticut towns of Brooklyn, Mansfield, Windham, and Chaplin will serve as examples; together they accounted for seventy-one (30 percent) of the known residents. Their wealth varied considerably, from the moderately prosperous manufacturer Joseph Conant to the unsuccessful craftsman Enos L. Preston, who after the depression had no taxable property at all by 1840. Most of those from the farming and small manufacturing districts of Brooklyn, Chaplin, and Mansfield owned some land, and several of the artisans among them had small farm acreages along with their workshops. In Brooklyn, Theodore Scarborough and George W. Benson both owned substantial farms in 1840: Scarborough was taxed on two houses and 172 acres of land, Benson on one house and 73 acres. In Mansfield, Joseph Conant and his sons-in-law Chaffee and Swift each had farmland in addition to their manufacturing interests, and the mechanic Hiram Wells had a building and 20 acres of land in 1838. For those from the factory village of Willimantic, the situation was slightly different: Samuel L. Hill slowly built up his real estate holdings in the 1830s from his earnings as a factory manager, but apart from owning a couple of cows was not involved in farming. His assistant William Haven probably owned little more than his family's house, if that. Both had relied on their jobs in manufacturing, and Hill, at least, had moved in order to end this reliance.[19]

But the overall position of these Connecticut members was modest. None had dominated their neighborhoods; none were able to invest such large sums in the Northampton community that they could dominate it. Theodore Scarborough, the wealthiest member of the Brooklyn contingent, ranked only twenty-fifth out of the 323 taxpayers in the town in 1840. George W. Benson ranked fiftieth. In Chaplin, Joseph C. Martin and Austin Ross, with holdings of 23 and 45 acres respectively, each paid only half or less of the average amount of tax paid in the town during the late 1830s. Several members, propertied and poor alike, had suffered reverses during and after the 1837 panic. Conant, Chaffee, and Swift all had their tax assessments scaled down in 1838 and 1839 because of debts. Martin was increasingly in debt by 1841. In Brooklyn, James A. Stetson was taxed on his workshop in 1837, but had lost that by the following year and retained only his house. For most of these families the economic uncertainty of the late 1830s had threatened or interrupted the pattern of family accumulation of property that those in such mixed farming and manufacturing regions had come to expect.

The age profile of members confirms, in turn, that a search for economic security during the crucial phases of family formation may have encouraged many to apply to join the community. Ages at joining are known for 174 of the members of the association (about three-quarters of the total). The community attracted relatively young people, particularly those in families with children. Sixty-six members (38 percent) were aged between twenty and thirty-nine when they joined, over one in four were under ten, and another one-fifth were between ten and nineteen. The elderly, by contrast, were hardly to be found; only four men and two women were aged fifty or more when they arrived, and most of them were members of families that included younger people. Community life seems to have been particularly attractive for families as a means of providing education for children and, perhaps, as an attempt to secure mutual support and cooperation with others during the period of childrearing that was the most demanding phase of the family life cycle. Seven women and two men had been widowed, and six of these nine brought children with them.[20]

The community's occupational, wealth, and age profiles suggest that its vision of a more equal, reformed society was as attractive to those already heavily engaged in trade or capitalist manufacturing as it was to those who, like Brook Farm's artisans, were seeking to resist greater involvement in it. They were neither just those who had fallen on hard times, nor just those who were achieving moderate success in rapidly changing economic conditions, but both. The successful and the not-so-successful were equally alert to the difficulties of a competitive economy and attracted by the vision of harmony that cooperative effort in a community framework promised to let them fulfill. Yet quantifiable data about members' lives provide only one aspect of the complex set of considerations that explain the community's composition. Ideological and personal factors were more significant. The admissions process was crucial in determining the community's character, because like any formal system of selection that can be run informally when the operators wish, it became an effective means of excluding those people felt to be unsuitable and including those assured of a general welcome.

Few new members had previously lived in a communal group. The former slave Sojourner Truth had belonged to the New York sect known as The Kingdom, remaining loyal to it during the scandals that led to its breakup in 1835. Susanna Bassett, who came to Northampton with her family in 1844, had already stayed for a time at Brook Farm.[21] More significant than prior community experience was the climate within abolitionist and nonresistant circles after the rifts of the late 1830s and early 1840s that led reformers to seek out community solutions. Particular links among such groups were important in determining who joined up at Northampton. Broadly speaking, the community was dominated by two overlapping networks: one based on ties in the abolitionist or nonresistant movements, the other based on ties among neighbors and kinship groups.

Among subscribers listed in the *National Anti-Slavery Standard* during the summer of 1841 to a "one dollar pledge" campaign for emergency funds to sustain the American Anti-Slavery Society, were twelve men and women who would later join the Northampton Community. At least thirty-seven individuals or family groups who joined the community, well over half its total membership, had identifiable abolitionist connections or sympathies; twenty or more of them were also nonresistants. Early joiners included the shoe dealer Joseph S. Wall of Worcester, a former Quaker who had for a while edited a nonresistant paper, the Worcester *Reformer*. He had conducted this largely as a vehicle for the writings of the Lynn abolitionist and debarred Quaker nonresistant William Bassett, whose wife's sister, Eliza Boyce—also a nonresistant—Wall had married in 1841. Wall himself died late in 1842, but Eliza returned to live in the community and doubtless encouraged Bassett and his family in their decision to join in 1844. William and Susan Parker, who had sons named after leading abolitionists, moved to the community from Nantucket in 1842 and would stay until the end. There was the Hayward family of Salem, who had been active in antislavery societies there and remained loyal to the Garrisonian faction when the movement split; they also supported the Non-Resistance Society. For Samuel A. Bottum of Mansfield, Connecticut, and his family, an interest in silk manufacture and abolitionist sympathies coincided to bring them into the community for a period. William Haven was a former assistant to Samuel L. Hill in the Willimantic mills, had helped him found the Willimantic Male Anti-Slavery Society in 1836, and came to Northampton with his large family. There was the group from Chaplin, Connecticut, who had been struggling for abolition and women's rights in their Congregational church. A steady trickle of abolitionists would continue to join over the years: Susan Byrne, a founder of the Willimantic Female Anti-Slavery Society; Abner S. Meade, a shoe cutter and abolitionist of Danvers, Massachusetts; two sisters, Lucy and Harriet Hayden, who had been active in Bath, Maine; Emily Farwell, whose father was an active abolitionist in Cambridge; Elisha L. Hammond and Eliza P. Hammond of New Ipswich, New Hampshire, who were well known to Garrison and his circle; and the itinerant lecturers James and Louisa Boyle, from Ohio, whom Erasmus Darwin Hudson drew to the community in early 1843. When Sophia Foord, a teacher from Dedham, Massachusetts, arrived in May 1843, she quickly contacted her fellow abolitionist Robert Adams of Fall River, who was expected to join, urging him to come soon: "Again and again have I been desired to request your presence." Personal contacts, developed in the abolition movement, were a vital part of the process of gathering members.[22]

Obviously it was significant that Benson was Garrison's brother-in-law. The Garrisons spent a summer living at the community, participating in its meetings and its forays to abolitionist events in the region. Two of the Garrison boys were pupils at the community school. After Garrison had left Northampton in 1843 at the end of his summer's stay, he sent greetings to twenty-two members of the community by name. From time to time he would recommend members or ask the community to accept a destitute reformer as a boarder. But Northampton was by no means an extension of the "Garrison clique." For one thing, Garrison's suggestions were not always accepted. More important, the community played a role in the movement that, if anything, contrasted with and complemented that of the Boston group, rather than coinciding with it. While the Garrison clique helped focus and sustain prominent abolitionists and urban activists in the movement, the Northampton community helped to do something similar among the poorer, less prominent Garrisonian sympathizers in Connecticut and other rural parts of New England.[23]

Though the numbers involved are too small, and the people too widely and unevenly scattered, to permit statistically valid conclusions, explicable variations in the "supply" of abolitionist members to the community can be identified. A look at several centers in the Boston area and in Essex county sheds light on the circumstances that promoted or restrained community membership. Though members came from Boston and its immediate vicinity, their numbers were disproportionately small considering the city's size. A number of abolitionists there contemplated joining soon after Northampton was founded, but few materialized. Probably the very strength of abolitionism in Boston was a disincentive to move to Northampton—why join a distant movement when abolition activities were so healthy right at home? Lynn, another stronghold of radical abolition, provided only William Bassett and his family and one other member; again, the abolitionist community was strong at home.[24]

Smaller abolitionist groups in the towns to the north of Lynn, however, were much more affected by the splits in the movement at the beginning of the decade, and where these splits occurred recruits were more commonly found. Salem, Marblehead, and Danvers between them provided several members for Northampton. The Anti-Slavery Society of Salem and Vicinity broke its connection with "old organization" in 1840 and renamed itself the Salem Abolition Society in token of its "new organization" affiliation. This isolated radicals such as Josiah Hayward. Hayward seems at first to have found a home by joining in his wife's work with the Salem Female Anti-Slavery Society, which remained with the "old organization," but even this group was split, and the prospect of moving to the true Garrisonian community at Northampton, which the Haywards did early in 1843, was probably more attractive than remaining in Salem's divided territory. From Danvers, at least two abolitionists went to the Hopedale community and others either moved to or maintained close connections with Northampton. Further north though, in Ipswich and Newburyport, members were not to be found. Ipswich's society seems to have gone almost wholesale for "new organization." Though Newburyport's abolitionists divided, the majority of those who remained loyal to

Garrison appear to have been older people, not highly active in the movement, and not likely to be attracted to community schemes more suitable for younger individuals or families.[25]

The willingness of the Northampton and Hopedale communities to admit known reformers quickly into their membership probably helped keep radical abolitionism alive during the early 1840s, particularly in localities where it was under strong pressure. Acceptance was not automatic, however. Northampton rebuffed some abolitionists, and members made it clear when they felt a particular individual was unsuitable. Erasmus Darwin Hudson, away on a lecture trip in 1842, was anxious to know whether an application had been received from his fellow campaigner Oliver Johnson, whom Hudson now regarded as "used up." He felt Johnson should be declined: "He's not to be admitted. . . . I think they should be pretty careful who they admit."[26]

To fulfill its design of becoming a model for a nonsectarian society the community hoped to draw in men and women from different religious traditions. The founders, as we have seen, themselves represented some variety: George W. Benson's family had moved from the Baptist Church toward Quakerism; Samuel L. Hill had moved from the Quakers to the Baptists, before leaving churches altogether; William Adam was a Unitarian who had once been a Baptist; Hall Judd and Erasmus Darwin Hudson came from orthodox Congregationalism. The members they attracted added to the mix. The religious backgrounds of thirty-one individuals can be identified or inferred. Of these, nine were Unitarians, seven Congregationalists or Presbyterians, five were Baptists, and four Quakers; the remainder were a Methodist, a Universalist, a Shaker, two from other Christian groups, and one, Calvin Stebbins of South Wilbraham, Massachusetts, a freethinker, whose "house was a natural resort for ministers but he agreed with none of them." As might be expected there was a bias toward denominations that had been most subject to liberal theological influences and to debates on slavery and reform, but such a mixed gathering for religious purposes was still rare in New England, and the community could rightly claim that it was putting its nonsectarian principles to the test.[27]

All the main themes that we have identified—economics, reform, and religion—influenced the family of William Bassett of Lynn to join the Northampton community in 1844, after a seven-year struggle with financial difficulties and institutional resistance to radical principles. Bassett's story illustrates how radical social reform could appeal even to someone of conservative background. He was a member of a staunch Quaker family, son of a merchant, and closely connected with the town leadership of Lynn in the 1820s and 1830s. He was a rising shoe merchant in his own right, one of a group of Lynn entrepreneurs who were reorganizing the shoe trade, taking control of manufacturing out of the hands of artisans, putting out work to rural binders, and running the finishing processes in their own central shops.[28] Bassett also followed in his father's footsteps as a leading member of the Lynn Quaker meeting. Until about 1836, by his own admission, Bassett took part in decisions to exclude abolitionist speakers like Garrison and Henry B. Stanton from Quaker meeting-houses. But he became increasingly troubled by this and by Quakers' reluctance to renew their public condemnation of slavery. Having joined an antislavery society early in 1837, he faced censure for belonging to an association outside the Society of Friends. This initiated a running conflict, conducted verbally and in print, that was ultimately to lead to his disownment. In 1837 Bassett published a pamphlet defending his membership in antislavery societies. In 1838 he attacked Quaker meetings that segregated seating for white and black members, and the same year demonstrated his increasing attachment to Garrisonian abolitionism by becoming a founding member of the New England Non-Resistance Society. By 1840, as exclusion from the Society of Friends was imminent, Bassett had teamed up with his wife's brother-in-law Joseph S. Wall to produce the Worcester *Reformer*, largely to publish his own abolitionist, nonresistance, and nonsectarian writings.[29]

Financial troubles now caught up with him as well. Bassett lost his position in charge of a large shoe workshop, worked for a while as the overseer in another shop before losing that job also, and by the early 1840s was coming to think critically about the injustices of an economic system that seemed no fairer to wage workers than it did to slaves. The *Reformer* ceased publication, and in 1842 Wall and his wife moved to the Northampton community; though Joseph Wall fell ill and died there late that year, Eliza Boyce Wall remained a member for over three years. Still active in Garrisonian circles in Lynn, Bassett evinced increasing interest in joining the community himself, inquired about membership in 1843, and early the following year prepared to move to Northampton with his family. In a letter written as he was about to set out, he expressed confidence that he would find, in community life, a true reflection of the social, religious, and economic principles that he had espoused over the previous few years. As he had written after his expulsion by the Quakers, he had been "cast out of one of the 'little cabins' of sectarianism" into "Christianity itself." Joining the community, he hoped to be joining with others who had "come out entirely from the dominion of man, into a place where the mind had room to expand . . . knowing no bounds but the universe—accountable to no being but God."[30]

Black Members

Still, although the community's ideals were expressed in general egalitarian terms, the actual process of assembling a membership followed patterns shaped by existing social contacts and conditions. For instance, the community espoused the principle of racial equality and, in some cases, the ability to take rapid, informal decisions about admitting residents led to the arrival of black members who contributed to the community's abolitionist connections. But the overwhelming majority of members were white. Recent studies have emphasized that in the wider movement black abolitionists often faced condescension and outright racism from their white colleagues. Communities were no different. Many had no black members at all. There were a handful of black Shakers. Brook Farm, other Fourierist groups, and Owenite communities had few, if any, and Carl J. Guarneri has recently documented evidence of open discrimination among some Fourierists. Hopedale had one black resident, but she left after a short stay.[31] Northampton was unusual among predominantly white communitarian groups in having black members over a considerable period of time. Did this mean that it was an exception to the general rule?

Some evidence points to this. Three black residents, David Ruggles, Sojourner Truth, and Stephen C. Rush, remained at the community over several years. Ruggles and Rush both wrote letters praising it during their stay, and the *Narrative of Sojourner Truth* published a few years later expressed affection for the group and regret at its collapse in 1846. Black visitors such as Frederick Douglass and Ruggles's former amanuensis, Henry Richards Crummell, also commended its atmosphere of freedom and equality.[32] But it is also evident that the community's appeal to potential black members was limited. Only four stayed for more than very brief periods. Why was this opportunity to build a rare biracial community not taken further?

Few black men and women appear even to have sought to join the community; aside from the four who did become residents only two further inquiries from prospective black members can be traced with certainty. A partial explanation lies in the community's tendency to recruit from rural areas and small towns where black populations were small, and in its comparatively weak appeal to Garrisonians in large centers like Boston and New Bedford, where black support for "old organization" was strongest. Moreover, to most black activists communities appeared as diversions from the central issues of slavery and equal rights. During the early 1840s they were engaged in protecting escaped slaves and free blacks threatened with kidnap or capture, and in campaigns for civil rights for black people in the North. By the time some gains were made in the latter direction in 1843, with the end of segregation on Massachusetts railroads and the repeal of a law against interracial marriage, abolitionist interest in communities was waning, and black abolitionists were increasingly concerned with establishing an independent voice within the movement.[33]

Black men and women who did move to the Northampton area in the 1840s were more closely linked to evangelical than to Garrisonian abolitionist networks. Few, if any, were guided toward the community, to which the evangelicals were hostile. Northampton's black population rose from 58 in 1840 to 152 in 1850; even in a decade of rapid general expansion the black community grew from 1.5 percent to 2.9 percent of the town's population. There was some natural increase, an influx of local migrants from larger black communities nearby, such as Springfield and Hartford, and a small, but significant, number of former slaves from the South, who were settled in the town with help either from the black community or from church networks. The prominent Northampton "new organization" abolitionist John P. Williston was among those taking part in this work. Some migrants were settled at Broughton's Meadow, adjacent to the community, perhaps because it was a secluded place where land was inexpensive. But though the black population was literally expanding around it, the community was largely cut off from the process.[34]

The three black men and one woman who did belong to the community were all exceptions who proved the rule. Two of them, together with others who remained only for very short periods, were former slaves who had been assisted by Garrisonian groups. Even in the early 1840s, before escapes from slavery and rescue attempts attracted wide public attention, and before the strengthening of the federal fugitive slave law, assisting refugees from the South was a secretive business, especially when pursuit was feared. We can never know how many escaped slaves were brought to the community or the houses of members in the course of their journeys north. We do know that it happened. In May 1843, Sophia Foord wrote that an ex-slave had been staying temporarily and had moved on, and that another was expected shortly. The latter was almost certainly Stephen C. Rush, who arrived that month, was shortly afterward invited to stay and was elected to full membership six months after he arrived. Rush remained in the community until 1846. Another black resident, George W. Sullivan, born in Baltimore, possibly arrived the same way, by what Foord referred to as the "rail road under ground," though his name, unlike Rush's, did get entered in the membership register.[35] Garrisonian contacts in Rhode Island and southern Massachusetts helped bring Rush, Sullivan, and others to the community, but the Northampton area was so much less significant in Garrisonian than in evangelical circles that such contacts were comparatively few in number.

The community's two northern black residents, David Ruggles and Sojourner Truth, each came there for particular reasons. Neither was typical of contemporary black abolitionists. Ruggles, born in Lyme, Connecticut, in 1810, had been one of New York City's most active abolitionists in the 1830s, a delegate at the founding convention of the New York Anti-Slavery Society and a supporter of the city's first black high school. He became best known for his work between 1835 and 1839 as secretary and agent of the New York Committee of Vigilance, helping escaped slaves to freedom, fighting for the rights of free blacks, and protecting fugitives from recapture. Despite threats of lynching, several assaults (including being kicked down a stairway in 1838), and a period in jail, Ruggles assisted at least six hundred people, including Frederick Douglass on his flight north from Maryland, and was something of an abolitionist hero.[36]

In the late 1830s, however, Ruggles began to have troubles. A dispute over his failure to keep proper accounts became mixed up in the wider abolitionist split and led to his departure from the vigilance committee in anger at the imputation that he had misused funds. He started a newspaper, the *Mirror of Liberty*, which he used to defend his position, but his long-drawn-out campaign seems only to have alienated much of the New York abolitionist community, black and white. Rifts were deepened in September 1840 when he helped organize, in New Haven, a national convention of black men that many abolitionists criticized as racially "exclusive in character." Worse still, his health declined and he became virtually blind. Ill and with few allies left, he was obliged to accept hospitality and support from Garrisonian contacts near New York. Garrison and others helped arrange for him to move to the Northampton community to recuperate, with some financial support from donations. In November 1842 a specially convened meeting of the admissions board invited Ruggles "to come amongst us and remain with us as a member, without being admitted until better acquainted." There is no record of any further formal step to admit him, but this may not have been necessary; as his stay lengthened he seems simply to have become regarded as a full member. Others later recalled his presence at meals and companionship with children. Ruggles himself wrote articles supporting the community, at one point denying a report that he was an "employee" and explaining that he had been accepted as part of a community of brothers and sisters working for the sake of humanity.[37]

Sojourner Truth, too, seems to have been rapidly accepted after she turned up at the suggestion of Springfield friends late in 1843 at the end of several months as an itinerant preacher. Like Ruggles, she was not formally admitted, but she certainly lived as a member, spoke at meetings, and voted. Born around 1797 and brought up as a slave in the Hudson Valley, Isabella (or Isabella Van Wagenen as she became known) took her freedom when New York finally abolished slavery in 1827, and subsequently went to New York City. Her life there revolved around domestic work, and the religious commitment that would draw her to The Kingdom in the early 1830s and, later, to leave the city in 1843 to walk the highways spreading the word of God. At this point she started to use the name Sojourner Truth, though she would not abandon her old name entirely for several years. An interest in communities and a search for a new place of rest led her to Northampton toward the end of the year.[38] She would remain for the rest of the community's existence.

Ruggles and Truth shared a degree of isolation from the main channels of black abolitionism. In Ruggles's case this was due to his disputes with former colleagues, his poverty, and his failing health. Sojourner Truth, though she had belonged to sects that opposed slavery, had not previously been active as an abolitionist speaker. Their appearance at the community was fortuitous, not inevitable. They, together with Rush and Sullivan, were present not so much because the community attracted black members, but despite the networks and contacts that were overwhelmingly likely to steer black abolitionists away from the group into other neighborhoods or activities.

Sojourner Truth. From *Narrative of Sojourner Truth* (Boston, 1850).
Courtesy, American Antiquarian Society.

Those Who Did Not Join

Comparable considerations applied to white applicants. Whereas the informal aspects of the community's admissions policy helped make the group inclusive and bound it to the wider abolitionist and nonresistant communities from which it sprang, formal exercise of the policy enabled members to control entry to the group, whether to exclude particular individuals, to fit the size of the group to its limited accommodations, or to select members whose skills or material resources the community from time to time needed.

Interest in joining was by no means limited to those who actually came to Northampton and were invited to remain. The wider enthusiasm for communities in the early 1840s, the dissemination of the Northampton Association's constitution and the publication of visitors' accounts of the community all attracted inquiries from men and women who were considering applying for admission. At least 180 written inquiries were made by or on behalf of people who did not, in the end, join. Others made personal visits or sought admission through friends or acquaintances connected with the community. Of the letters of inquiry few survive, but the association's records contain copies of the letters successive secretaries were instructed to send in reply to them. These letters to nonjoiners reflect the existence of a wide pool of interest in radical and community reform, from which the actual membership of the group was only selectively drawn.

Enthusiasm for "community" was no guarantee of admission. Letters and personal calls came from a succession of people who were traveling the country looking for an ideal community to join. An example was a young man called Stephen Young, who convinced by the early 1840s that "competition . . . [was] repugnant" and "cooperation attractive," set out to find a suitable place to settle. He headed for the Sylvania Association in Pennsylvania, but heard that it was full, tried a Swedenborgian community that turned out to be breaking up, and then joined up with another man to travel to the Northampton community. Here too, though they found "noble men and women," there was no room for new members. Young subsequently went to the North American Phalanx for a period, before leaving there to settle at Brook Farm. Here, evidently, he found what he was looking for, though he was forced to leave again when Brook Farm disbanded. Young's companion, A. L. Smith from Rhode Island, also joined the North American Phalanx for a period, before withdrawing to run a vegetarian hotel in New Hampshire.[39]

A comparison of the occupational characteristics of males identified from among the unsuccessful applicants to the community with those of male members suggests that there was no striking difference in social status between those who joined and those who did not. There was a slightly lower proportion of professional men, merchants, and manufacturers among the nonjoiners and a slightly higher percentage of artisans; if this is significant at all, it may reflect the community's wish to encourage members with capital and to reject those whose skills were already well represented in the community. The chief reasons for excluding people were practical and economic. Letters to inquirers repeatedly explained that room was scarce, capital short, or skills not presently needed. Shortage of accommodation was a chronic and recurrent problem: residents had to live either in the six or seven houses located on the community's land or leased from adjacent property owners, or in the upper two stories of the silk factory, which were turned into a community boardinghouse with sixty to seventy residents. On the other hand, when withdrawals depleted the community in the winter of 1843–44, but the rise of Fourierism in New England had helped revive interest in community life, it was possible to find replacements to fill available space without too much difficulty. The number of residents fluctuated over that winter, and fell as low as 106. In early April it was rumored that seventeen new people were to arrive within the next few weeks, and though this proved to be exaggerated numbers did rise again to 120 by the end of the month and stayed high during the first part of the summer.

Accommodation was not the only concern, however. In April 1843, after one year, the number of residents exceeded one hundred for the first time and would not fall below the hundred mark until November 1844. Throughout the community's existence, but particularly during this most crowded phase, members were also anxious only to admit people able to make a material contribution. Workers with skills in particular demand were encouraged, others put off or referred to other communities. Families with many young children were also discouraged. People with capital to invest, in the form of cash or usable equipment were, on the other hand, urged to press their applications; this was particularly so in the expansion of early 1844. Requests from leading abolitionists or local reformers to take in destitute individuals were usually rebuffed as well, though in one or two cases room was made for people whose support was guaranteed by outside contributions.

Yet even in difficult times, key factors that shaped the membership, such as abolitionist sympathies, could override these material constraints. Compared with those of members, relatively fewer of the nonjoiners' names crop up in lists of abolitionist leaders, society members, or contributors. More striking, though, is the tendency for nonjoiners to come from different localities and to lack family connections with the core groups of members within the community. Kinship and neighborhood were crucial in determining membership, and the absence of such links strongly influenced which prospective applicants either failed to follow up on their inquiries or were turned down in the formal process of application. Among unsuccessful applicants, kin connections were rare or nonexistent. Taken as a group, they were much more geographically scattered or isolated than the membership.

Kinship and Neighborhood

Indeed, most black abolitionists, like many others in the movement, stood outside the networks that were most likely to bring them into the community. Having abolitionist and nonresistance sympathies was important, but to join the group it also helped considerably to have kinship or neighborhood ties to someone who was already a member. The role of kinship and neighborhood was very significant in shaping the character of the community, its ideology, and its progress. This underscores how for a significant number of members, belonging to the community was less a break with a previous way of life than a means of putting existing ties to work for the cause of reform.

It is useful here to compare the Northampton community with Brook Farm, whose mixture of individual and communal living arrangements it most closely approximated among the Massachusetts utopian communities. Anne C. Rose counted ninety-nine men, women, and children who signed the Brook Farm articles of association between September 1841 and January 1845. Of these fifty-four (55 percent) had kin living in the community, but forty-five (45 percent) were there as unattached individuals.[40] At Northampton the proportion of people with kin in the community was significantly higher. Of the 240 known residents, no fewer than 185 (77 percent) had kin with them; only fifty-five (23 percent) were single and unattached to families. Notably, however, among unattached individuals at Northampton the proportion of women was almost double that at Brook Farm, 30 percent against 18 percent. Compared with its most similar companion community, therefore, Northampton was significantly more oriented toward kinship groups and women. At Northampton, as at Brook Farm, most of the kin groups were married couples or parents with their own children. But to a much greater extent than at Brook Farm there were also extended and complex kin connections among members. Frances Judd, already married to Hall Judd, eventually brought her own parents, two sisters, and a brother into the community. Calvin and Sarah E. Stebbins had two nephews with them as well as their own two children. Mary Ann Smith of Bloomfield, Connecticut, had an uncle or aunt among the group that arrived from the town of Chaplin in

Roxana Maria Gaylord Hill, second wife of Samuel L. Hill,
with their children Arthur G. Hill and Emily K. Hill, about 1845–46.
Courtesy of the Forbes Library, Northampton.

1844. When the community sought an extra mechanic that year, they found B. F. Whipple of Charlestown, Massachusetts, who was brother-in-law to Eliza Preston Hammond.[41]

For some individuals, kinship ties reached across the community. Samuel L. Hill had with him not only his own wife and children, but also his widowed sister-in-law and her four children. Hill's wife, Roxana, was the younger half-sister of Joseph Conant's wife, Pamelia, so Hill was related by marriage to Conant, and indirectly to Conant's sons-in-law Earl Dwight Swift and Orwell S. Chaffee as well. George W. Benson was part of a chain of kin relationships that included no fewer than twenty-eight members of the community, almost one-eighth of the total. In addition to his wife and four children, he had a cousin, with *his* wife and two children, and the families of two of Benson's wife's siblings, totaling three adults and fourteen children. These extended kin connections were crucial in the formation of the community. Kinship helped give the Northampton community a distinctive character. One of Benson's daughters remembered her family's initial isolation at Broughton's Meadow coming to an end as the community got started: "The brick mill became a place of residence for families, and uncles, aunts, and cousins, besides others, began to arrive, and my lonely life was relieved by companions of all ages." For her community was closely identified with a sense of extended kinship.[42]

Kinship overlapped with, and was reinforced by, neighborhood ties. Of all the members whose places of origin we know, 56 percent came from just nine localities in Connecticut, Massachusetts, or New York, and 80 percent were from just sixteen places. The single largest supplier of members was Benson's town of Brooklyn, Connecticut, from which virtually the whole Garrisonian connection decamped to Northampton between 1841 and 1843. Following Benson and his family were several members of the neighboring Scarborough family, farmers and abolitionists. In 1843 Benson's brother-in-law James A. Stetson arrived and soon sent for his wife and six children. Mansfield, Connecticut, with its silk manufacturers, was another important source of members, as we have already noted. But there were smaller neighborhood groups from elsewhere. Hill's acquaintanceships in Willimantic produced a succession of new members over several years. Hudson's temporary home at Bloomfield, near Hartford, was another early source of recruits, and Chaplin, Connecticut, near Mansfield, would supply several families from 1844 on.

Abolition, kinship, or neighborhood were, therefore, three vital links between the members of the Northampton community. Only a small proportion of the total did not apparently have at least one of these connections. Many, such as the Bensons, the Hills, and their relatives, had all three. What effects did this have?

Above all, it enhanced the stability of the membership. Studies of utopian communities that tend to focus on the institutions or their leadership often miss their essential fluidity. Thirty-six of fifty-nine utopian communities established in the United States between 1841 and 1849 lasted for two years or less. But many longer-lived communities also had mobile populations of members, and Northampton was no exception. Most residents stayed less than two years—in other words for periods comparable with the survival time of most utopian communities. Of the 240 people, including members, boarders, and pupils, who were resident at the Northampton community for at least one month during the community's fifty-five month existence, no more than 120 were present at any one time. There was sufficient turnover to replace the whole membership over the community's life.

Closer examination, however, reveals a clear distinction between residents who stayed for relatively short periods and those who remained for a long time. Over a quarter of the total number of residents remained for six months or less, nearly the same number for between six months and one year and another sixteen percent for between one and two years. These were mainly men, and a few women, who had come to work in exchange for board or who had been admitted as probationary members for fixed periods. Of one hundred men, women, and children who stayed for twelve months or less, twenty-five were single men, another nine were single women, and thirty-two were in married couples or families without other kin or neighbors in the community. Of this total of sixty-six individuals, only twenty-three (just over one in three) had known connections to abolitionism. In other words, the community's shortest-term residents tended to be those for whom the ties of kinship, neighborhood, or abolition were weakest. Most of the exceptions were special cases. Among the short-stay families who did have kin or neighbors were the eight members of the Conant, Chaffee, and Swift silk-manufacturing families, who left *en masse* in the autumn of 1842, and the five Birges, who only arrived within a year of the community's demise.

The mean length of stay for all residents was about nineteen months. Only ninety-six individuals (40 percent of the total) were present longer than this average stay, but unlike the short-term residents the majority of this latter group did have kin, neighborhood, or abolitionist ties. Of these long-term residents, only ten (just over 10 percent) were single or widowed; the vast majority belonged to married couples or families. Sixty-two (64.6 percent) had neighbors or kin other than their immediate family present in the community. So personal ties distinguish long-term residents from the majority of more transient members. Of thirty-four individuals or family members who did not have kinship or neighborhood ties, twenty-eight (82 percent) had identifiable abolitionist sympathies or connections. All five "single" women among them did: Sojourner Truth, the teacher Sophia Foord, the widowed Eliza Boyce Wall, Mary Ann

Smith from abolitionist circles in Bloomfield, Connecticut, and Lucy C. Hayden, the abolitionist from Bath, Maine, who stayed in the community after her sister Harriet married and departed in 1844. Three out of the four single men were also abolitionists: David Ruggles, the ex-slave Stephen C. Rush, and Charles May, a former naval officer and teacher who was brother to Reverend Samuel J. May and Abigail May Alcott. Charles May, in fact, twice came close to having his kin with him at Northampton. George Benson tried unsuccessfully to persuade Samuel to join in late 1844. A year earlier, when the Fruitlands community was at the point of collapse, Charles had secured approval to bring his sister and her children out to join him, but Abba Alcott—doubtless fed up with communities—decided to move to Concord instead, and so saved Northampton from a later appearance in one of Louisa May Alcott's stories.[43]

Purely at the level of demography, then, there was a division within the community between short-term, poorly connected residents and long-term members with ties not merely to the community as an institution, but to the ideals and social contexts that helped form and shape it. The community's key organizing factors, abolitionism, kinship, and neighborhood, were therefore also keys to its own ability to sustain and renew itself.

Rural Neighborhoods

The importance of kinship and neighborhood ties also reflected strong links with rural regions whose economies combined farming with small-scale shop-based manufacturing. In the 1830s such regions had already become important sources of rank-and-file support for the abolition movement. Studies by Judith A. Wellman for New York and John L. Brooke for Massachusetts, among others, suggest that popular moral reform—including anti-Masonry, temperance, and abolition—grew well in areas of small-farm and small-shop production and exchange, which had been under great economic stress in the decade before the Northampton community was founded.[44] Their milieu, in turn, provided the community with an important source of values and assumptions that underlay its search for radical social reform and helped shape its ideological character.

Evidence about members' places of origin or previous residence does not initially suggest that such regions were very significant in the community's makeup, especially if children are excluded from the analysis. Of 133 residents who were sixteen or older the year they moved to Northampton, 126 came from identifiable places in New England or New York State. The community was drawn from places of widely varied size and character. On one hand, ten members came from Boston, another two indirectly from New York City. On the other, five came from Chaplin, Connecticut (whose population in 1840 was 794) and one from Easthampton, Massachusetts (population 717). But over half those joining came from towns with more than 2,500 people, over a third were from places of 5,000 or more; only a quarter were from towns of fewer than 1,500. Urban or urbanizing places were as frequently a source of members as rural areas. A comparable pattern appears in the workforce structures of the places people came from. Almost 30 percent came from towns less than one quarter of whose workforce was in agriculture, and fewer than 15 percent came from places where agriculture occupied more than three-quarters of the working population. Altogether ninety-three (73.8 percent) came from places where manufacturing occupied at least one quarter of the workforce. So at first sight it seems that urban activities, not rural, dominated the backgrounds of community members.

Yet a significant proportion of members came from places where both agriculture and manufacturing were important. Altogether, nearly three-fifths of members were from places where the economy was still balanced between the two activities and where they continued to be closely integrated in household-based and small-scale workshop production. Fifty-eight individuals (46 percent of the total) were from towns where at least one quarter of the workforce was in agriculture and at least another quarter in manufactures and trades; another sixteen (12.7 percent) were from agricultural towns where manufactures provided at least 10 percent of employment. Such places included Mansfield, Connecticut, where small silk factories relied on raw silk produced in local households, and Brooklyn, where farming and skilled workshop-based trades were carried on side-by-side, by-employments were common, and where families periodically shifted emphasis from one occupation to another as they accumulated property and land. In other towns, like Worcester and Canton, Massachusetts, abolitionism throve in the small-shop culture of shoe-making, machining, and other trades, and links to a sizable local farming population had still not been broken. Altogether more members of the Northampton community came from towns with small-scale, mixed economies than from larger urban or manufacturing centers. Fewer than one-quarter, for instance, came from towns where, taken together, professional and commercial occupations accounted for more than one-tenth of the workforce. Small and medium-sized working communities were the most significant sources of the community's members.[45]

This picture is reinforced when we consider the backgrounds of those who stayed in the community longest. In the same way that kinship, neighborhood, and abolitionist ties helped explain the distinctions between long-term and short-term residents, places of origin were also unequally represented among the two groups. Though those who stayed for nineteen months or more came from a range of places, and rural origins were common among those who remained only a short time, the overall pattern is clear. None of the long-term residents came from Boston, only two from New York City, and only a handful each from growing urban and commercial centers such as Cambridge, Massachusetts, and Norwich, Connecticut. The majority came from the middling and small rural farming and manufacturing towns that supplied so many members: Brooklyn, Mansfield, Chaplin, and Bloomfield, Connecticut, and New Ipswich, New Hampshire, and from larger but still workshop-based centers elsewhere, such as Northampton and Worcester, Massachusetts. Because these people tended to provide the stable membership of the community, rather than its more transient residents, towns like these and their values played an important role in shaping the practices and attitudes of its members. Though some of its leaders had been associated with commerce, factory production, or other activities outside this milieu, and even though abolitionist activity in many senses broke the bounds of parochial and provincial-minded cultures, there are signs that the values of small-farm, small-shop, face-to-face communities and transactions provided Northampton's members with a model for imagining a new society that could avoid some of the evils that the commercial, industrial, competitive culture were introducing.

The relative strength of abolitionism in rural areas that were economically diversified and had expanded their ties to the marketplace has often been taken to confirm the conventional argument that abolition and capitalism went hand-in-hand.[46] But this deduction glosses over a more complex picture. Precisely because such regions had experienced relatively rapid economic change, they had also faced the dislocations that it entailed. If the demands of producing for growing markets had not already done so, the panic and depression of the late 1830s placed considerable strain on common patterns of economic life in such areas, which were often based on small-scale production and informal, face-to-face negotiation for work, food, and other goods. The calling-in of debt and the threat of economic hardship compromised personal ties, creating embarrassment and anxiety. It is not surprising that in these circumstances, some men and women should have contemplated the advantages of a system in which cooperation would replace competition and the social obligations of kinship and neighborhood could be protected from the peremptory demands of economic need. Along with its abolitionist and nonsectarian principles, and entirely congruent with its commitment to nonresistance, the community held up a vision of an economy based on moral principles that owed much to its roots in small-farm, small-shop regions. Parallels between the communities of the 1840s and the values and practices of rural neighborhoods were not lost on contemporaries. Samuel Griswold Goodrich of Connecticut even claimed that "a sort of communism or socialism . . . prevailed in our rural districts long before Owen or Fourier," and that "these pretended inventors were mere imitators."[47]

This rural vision shaped the community's attitude to lawyers and to the law. The 1842 constitution urged members to settle their disputes by negotiation and arbitration, and not by seeking the assistance of the state by resorting to legal action. Later rules stipulated that any member who took legal action of any kind would be deemed to have withdrawn from the community. It is significant that though merchants, manufacturers, ministers, and teachers joined the community, no lawyers did. There were several grounds for objecting to the use of the legal system. Resort to the law epitomized competitiveness, elevated antagonism above harmony, and used formal rules and procedures to handle issues that should be determined by a moral sense. Some members had been repelled by their encounters with the law; David Mack, for instance, had embarked on a legal career as a young man but found making "the worse appear the better cause" objectionable. But the suspicion and distrust of law was also grounded in the values and experiences of rural economic life, where recourse to the courts was regarded as a breach of "neighborhood," and only properly undertaken in particular circumstances. Anxiety about the growing litigiousness of nineteenth-century society and the compromised personal ties that this implied underpinned the community's determination to avoid the courts at all costs. Nothing but direct, honest relations should take place between individuals in a community of Christians.[48]

Shelter, Base, and Mission

Communitarians confidently asserted their importance to the wider antislavery and human rights movements. Even after the 1846 fire that severely damaged Brook Farm's prospects, George Ripley wrote of his community as "our little germ of social unity," still certain that it could lead to substantial social change.[49] Critics were skeptical. How would building communities in Massachusetts free slaves? Was this not just another sign of the radical abolitionists' propensity for finding distractions from the main purposes of reform? Did it not signify the movement's weakness, and a sectarian spirit of withdrawal into irrelevance?

One way of weighing the contradictions in a community's ideology is to consider the purposes members themselves attached to its existence and to their presence there. At Northampton the heavy cultural baggage of abolitionism, nonresistance, come-outerism, economic dislocation, and neighborhood and kinship ties make such an assessment complex, but there were strands in the intentions and experience of members which make certain purposes identifiable. Much communitarian language referred to the process of withdrawing from the world; the pain and upheaval in their recent lives made this an appealing prospect for many abolitionists. To others, though, the shelter of community served only to provide a base for continued reform efforts, for ventures into a hostile world that so evidently needed redemption. Finally, there was the view that the existence and activities of the community were reforming, even potentially "revolutionizing" in and of themselves.

Elements of withdrawal were clearly evident, and consciously realized by men and women who moved to Northampton in the early 1840s. We have already seen that the abolitionist split battered isolated groups of radicals, especially in Connecticut. Two out of every five of the Northampton community's members whose origins are known came from just six towns in Connecticut affected by these disputes. Small groups in Bloomfield, Chaplin, and elsewhere had become isolated in their own neighborhoods. They removed, with their pain and chagrin, to Northampton in an effort to reestablish their lives among like-minded sufferers. Elisha Hammond was said to share his beliefs with just four women in New Ipswich, New Hampshire, before he moved to Northampton in 1844. From Bath—"the Gibraltar of pro-slaveryism in Maine," according to Lydia Maria Child—came the sisters Harriet and Lucy Hayden, two of the town's few Garrisonians. Reaching the community could be a release and a relief. After she arrived in 1843, Sophia Foord's first comment to a friend was "I am at length located in the looked-for haven." Sojourner Truth apparently found at Northampton "the quiet resting place she had so long desired."[50] Quite apart from the refuge that Stephen Rush and perhaps other escaped slaves found in it, abolitionists often referred to the community as a "retreat," as a "paradise" withdrawn from the turbulence of "the world." For all these people it served as a sort of Garrisonian lifeboat in western New England, helping sustain the movement in its leanest years, before campaigns against the Constitution and the Mexican War began to revive it.

But communitarian and millenarian language often contained references to shelter and "gathering" that pointed not to retreat but to regrouping for renewed action. So the community was not only a shelter but also a base. Erasmus Darwin Hudson was reluctant to become heavily engaged in running the place because he was not as concerned with building a community as such, as he was with having a place for launching abolitionist campaigners into hostile territory. He was critical of the Shakers of Alfred, Maine, whom he visited while on a lecture tour in June 1842, who "believe[d] their example is sufficient," and did little or nothing to spread the word about their principles. In September he wrote that the Northampton community should put agents into the field, "to preach godliness and its collaterals," nonresistance, antislavery, and temperance, and he expressed the fear that its members' concern to benefit the world was secondary to their own convenience.[51] Hudson negotiated terms that enabled him to maintain his post as a lecturing agent for the American Anti-Slavery Society and left his wife and children behind at Northampton as he conducted extensive lecture tours throughout New England and as far away as Pennsylvania. In early 1843, partly at Hudson's instigation, James and Laura Boyle were brought to the community from Ohio; James Boyle, too, spent time away on lecture tours, sometimes in company with Hudson. Periodically, on forays into Connecticut for reform conventions, they were joined by George Benson, William Adam, and younger members.

For Hudson, Northampton was a temporary haven for rest from harsh labor, and with Boyle's arrival imminent he became enthusiastic that its role could be extended in this way. Abby Kelley, the movement's most prominent woman lecturer, wrote to Hudson from New York State early in 1843 that she might come to Northampton: "I am exceedingly like a wilted cabbage leaf—so thoroughly exhausted. . . . I shall want to rest the

sole of my foot, and, more especially, the crown of my head, pretty soon."
Hudson, excited at the prospect of attracting Kelley to the community,
attempted to persuade her to become a member, and put forward his
vision for its potential contribution to the wider movement: "I think we
will make this a Moral Reform depot—for antislavery, non-resistance,
holiness, etc., and then go forth, east, west, north and south to work—
making this head quarters."[52] Kelley did not come, but Hudson's practical
vision of the community as a base for reform activity did not immediately
fade.

Had it limited itself to the role of sheltering a few lecturers and refugees, however, the community might still have remained vulnerable to
charges of irrelevance. Instead, many members believed that they were
engaged in a mission of wider significance. In keeping with the strategy
of moral suasion that they were seeking to uphold they saw this engagement as taking two related forms. On one hand, they took action to
advance the reform causes they were engaged in. On the other, they saw
this action and their very presence as moral "testimony" whose influence
could itself advance the cause.

So members of the community played a role in local reform efforts,
injecting a radical abolitionist agenda into the prevailing Tappanite atmosphere. They organized or attended abolition meetings in Northampton, on some occasions managing to cooperate with local leaders at public
meetings for visiting lecturers, on others provoking refusals from churches
and ministers for meeting places for their activities. On July 4, 1843, a
group from the community, accompanied by William Lloyd Garrison,
wishing to hold an antislavery meeting in town, were denied the use of
either town or church meetinghouses and ended up convening in the main
street, where Garrison lectured from a tree stump. But local organizations
reluctant to have Independence Day disrupted by radical attacks on slavery
and the Constitution, were willing enough to permit meetings to take
place when hallowed public events were not so threatened. Community
members joined local abolitionists and took leading roles in a succession
of meetings in Northampton Center during 1843 and 1844: conventions
to support the escaped slave George Latimer; a large meeting on August
1, 1843, to mark the tenth anniversary of emancipation in the British
empire; public lectures by Frederick Douglass in April 1844, accompanied
by performances from the Hutchinson family singers—all of whom stayed
at or visited the community; and a meeting of Northampton's black citizens in August 1844, chaired by David Ruggles and addressed by Ste-

phen C. Rush. A meeting in September 1844 to protest against the Torrey and Walker cases involved local cooperation on several levels: Ruggles again took the chair, the meeting appointed Rush and a local black abolitionist Desdemona Freeman its secretaries; there were addresses by community members, including the student Giles B. Stebbins, and—in what was probably her first public antislavery address—Sojourner Truth spoke "on the practical workings of slavery in the North." The meeting was shared with "new organization" abolitionists, including even the Baptist minister Nathaniel Colver, one of the men held most heavily responsible by Garrisonians for the splits of the late 1830s.[53]

All these activities served the proclaimed purpose of testifying in the cause of human rights. And the community's existence itself furthered this testimony. According to his own account Stephen C. Rush was illiterate when he heard news of the Latimer case and determined to flee Maryland for Massachusetts in the spring of 1843 to gain freedom. After over a year in the community, during which he learned to read and write, Rush sent William Lloyd Garrison, in a letter for publication in the *Liberator*, one of the most eloquent brief statements of its wider purpose. "We are here," he wrote, "to honor liberty and to denounce slavery. To assert the right of man and to testify against oppression. To invigorate the love of freedom and to deepen the detestation of Tyranny to proclaim the dictates of eternal justice and to rebuke the wrongs done by man to man." Outside sympathizers with the community, anxious to defend it against hostile critics, also painted its achievements in universal terms. B. C. Bacon, in an account published in June 1843, asserted that "this Association surmounts the difficulties incident to their new state so rapidly, that they will soon convince the world that society, with its legion of evils, is not past redemption."[54] Bacon captured the dual character of the moral-suasion argument. To withdraw from "the world" is not to turn one's back on society, nor even to disengage from it, but to take a position from which one can work to redeem and transform it.

A Cultural Assault

Of course societies do not usually take redemption lying down. Forged as it was in the struggles between radical and other abolitionists in the late 1830s and early 1840s, the Northampton community inevitably formed part of the small, but insistent radical challenge to the wider middle-class cultural hegemony of evangelical and orthodox denominations that the historian Charles Sellers has recently branded "Presbygationalism."[55] Though the community's location in Northampton appears to have been fortuitous—because of the availability of the silk company's property, and the interest of manufacturers in it—it is hard to imagine a more likely place at the beginning of the 1840s for embattled old organization abolitionists to irritate their evangelical opponents.

In the dominant view, moral-reform campaigns such as abolition and temperance were expected to focus on particular issues for social and individual improvement, essentially within the existing framework of society. Abolitionists should attack slavery, not digress into other issues. Temperance reformers should attack alcohol and promote the self-discipline of individuals, who alone could ameliorate their own weakness and their low standing in an unequal society. Respectability and advancement would follow from individual self-improvement and from a personal search for salvation under the guidance of churches and ministries. The aim of reform was to restore society to order, not challenge its fundamental assumptions.

The Northampton area and most of its reformers well exemplified this "Presbygational" program. Its leading abolitionists were closely connected to the evangelical wing of the antislavery movement; in the birthplace of the Tappans, Tappanite ideals were propounded by Tappanite followers, including some of the Tappans' own relatives. Reformers, led by the manufacturer John P. Williston from the First Church and the merchant William H. Stoddard (a nephew of the Tappan brothers) from the Edwards, worked closely together, binding most of the town's abolitionists in support for the "new organization" American and Foreign Anti-Slavery Society. Only a few, more radical abolitionists stood outside this religious connection. Seth Hunt, the local abolitionist most sympathetic to "old organization," who became the community's most dependable ally in the town, was one of the very few locals prepared to identify himself as a freethinker. With these exceptions, reform was strongly associated with orthodox and evangelical Congregationalism.

This broad consensus was also amenable to the gradually emerging movement toward political abolitionism. Western Massachusetts became an important source of support for the new Liberty Party; one of the party's early gubernatorial candidates, Lucius Boltwood, came from nearby Amherst. Naturally, at the level of political campaigning, opposition to third-party efforts from the established Whigs was fierce. After the 1844 elections, and as part of the tide that would start to sweep the Liberty Party toward reincarnation in the Free-Soil movement, J. P. Williston joined with the Williamsburg manufacturer Joel Hayden to finance the *Hampshire Herald*, a third-party newspaper published weekly in Northampton. In 1848 when the new Free-Soil alliance converted one of the existing Northampton papers to its views, Hayden and Williston stopped producing the *Herald* and put their weight behind the wider cause. Hayden would be elected as a Free-Soil lieutenant-governor of Massachusetts in the 1850s, before the collapse of the Whigs and further political upheaval propelled evangelical and political abolitionists alike into the nascent Republican party.[56]

Reform principles and religious practices kept the Garrisonians at the Northampton community firmly outside these local developments. The community's form of campaigning, its cultural assumptions, its attitudes to religion and politics challenged other reformers. This challenge was embodied in its own forms of worship, which were explicitly nondenominational and free of a ministry or other formal religious leadership. There was no creed or religious test for admission. There were no religious services, but there were weekly meetings, held on Sundays, at which religious matters were discussed and the community's principles were celebrated. Summer meetings were held out of doors, often under the branches of a large pine tree, which to sympathizers and opponents alike became a symbol of closeness to God and nature and of the rejection of artificial institutions. Participation was open to all who wished. Visitors as well as members could speak. Religious pluralism, the equality of speakers, the absence of ministers: all constituted an affront to the theology and culture of established denominations. Even the Society of Friends, whose practices this most resembled, had institutional rules and authorities. The Northampton community's principle of attacking the authority of ministers was extended from community meetings to its educational program for children; by 1844 some members were even starting to ask whether the attack had not been taken too far.[57]

The community's local reform efforts also included events that fostered the confrontation with evangelical reform and the wider evangelical culture. Successive meetings were held in the community and in town in late 1842 and early 1843 to pass resolutions in support of Thomas P. Beach, who had been jailed in Newburyport for disturbing the peace at a religious meeting, and to advocate the right of free speech in the proclamation of reform ideals. Beach himself evidently attached great importance to the

Northampton community resolutions in his favor, because he devoted much of an issue of the newspaper he printed while in jail to a report on them.[58] The Beach and free-speech resolutions were public expressions of the community's opposition to conventional churches and ministerial authority, a product of its nonresistant roots and part of a campaign to attack local ministers, which lasted through much of 1842 and 1843. Erasmus Darwin Hudson, for instance, wrote that he had attended a local church—he called it "the meeting of a neighboring sect"—in July 1842, and made public remarks about "living prayer," which "created some squirming." As he was attempting to recruit James Boyle (successfully) and Abby Kelley (unsuccessfully) to the community, Hudson envisaged that the three of them would hold conventions across western Massachusetts "to tear up the stony ground. I never was in a region more completely priest-ridden than this."[59] Had the community merely kept to itself it might have provoked no reaction; as it was, it was a persistent thorn in the side of the local churches.

Hudson, Adam, Boyle, and others took the campaign further afield. In February 1843 they led a convention in Connecticut of "new covenant believers," called to gather support "for free religious inquiry, independent of the power of the priesthood, or the prejudices of the people." Proclaiming that Christianity was purely spiritual and that "perfect love to God" consisted in "impartial and equal love to man," the convention condemned all human impositions on the life of the churches: the "seventh day sabbath," prophets and ministers, "temple worship" (that is, church buildings themselves), creeds and covenants, and the "carnal ordinances of water [baptism], bread and wine [communion]." Religion as it existed, the convention decided, was "not saving us from sin"; therefore it was not Christian.[60]

To no one's surprise, this kind of thing upset people. "The . . . Community is in bad odor in this vicinity," wrote Hall Judd's father early in 1843, "on account of their religious practices and principles."[61] Even sympathizers noted that its attacks on the churches had gained it a widespread reputation for "infidelity" and disorder. Members were criticized for "sabbath-breaking" and dismissed as "disaffected community croakers." Garrison wrote that he and they were regarded as "fanatics and incendiaries" in the locality. James Boyle stoked the fires on July 4, 1843, by speaking at the tree-stump meeting in the middle of Northampton "of the clergy of the place, and the religionists of the day, in the most withering terms," while Garrison claimed that "religious bigotry reigns with despotic sway over the minds of the people, and inflames their prejudices." The radicals' attack on religious conformity was always closely linked to their wider political agenda. Local editors criticized the New Covenant convention for advocating the withdrawal of northern states from the Union, and particularly attacked William Adam—a British subject—for associating himself with this argument. In lectures and correspondence throughout the early 1840s, James Boyle argued that antislavery, moral, and religious reform and political change were all linked together. The United States had become conservative, he wrote, and had wrongly renounced its original "ultraism." It was time to return to the principles of the Declaration of Independence and apply them to making a better world.[62]

Foremost among these principles was equality. The Garrisonian assault on dominant cultural assumptions took the form, not least, of advocating race and gender equality and of putting principle into practice by violating existing taboos against activities that crossed racial and sexual boundaries. It is worth examining the apparent public implications of some community practices, and the reaction they provoked.

The radicals asserted that women had the right to participate equally with men in public meetings. This was the most explicit ground of division between them and the evangelical abolitionists. The insistence of many ministers (not least the Westhampton pastor Horace Chapin) that the equality of women was contrary to scripture provoked nonresistants and come-outers to attack the clergy. They were often excommunicated for this, and several excommunicated radicals subsequently joined the Northampton community. Disagreement over women's rights was prominent in the disputes in Chaplin, Connecticut, for example, and may also have figured in the divisions in Bloomfield which led Erasmus Darwin Hudson's family and others to move to Northampton. Several community practices embodied the principle of women's equality, at least symbolically. Women members held equal rights with men to speak and vote at meetings. Community women appeared on platforms at public antislavery meetings in Northampton; at least six were present at one of the Latimer conventions in early 1843. Above all, the fact that community religious observance took the form of informal meetings without ministerial leadership indicated that women could act, as men often did, as spiritual leaders. All this constituted a challenge to accepted orthodox or evangelical practice, where women's roles—particularly in public—were more circumscribed.

Religion and race had also become intertwined in abolitionists' attacks throughout the late 1830s and early 1840s on the practice in many churches of seating black worshipers in separate pews or sections of meetinghouses. William Bassett had attacked the Society of Friends for tolerating this injustice, and David Ruggles had also joined the chorus of criticism.[63] Pursuit of the campaign against separate pews maintained a local and religious dimension to the broader argument for racial equality in transportation, education, politics, and other arenas that black and white abolitionists advanced in the 1840s.

The career of Sojourner Truth at the community combined the assertion of an active role for women with the potential for equal participation of blacks and whites. We know that she arrived in Northampton late in 1843 after several months' itineracy as a preacher; here she had been following in a long tradition of women exhorters, a dying tradition, but one not yet forgotten in the 1840s. Her own later testimony suggests that she continued this work after settling in the community; a famous story, presented in the *Narrative of Sojourner Truth*, of her using her power and wit as a speaker to forestall the threat of a physical attack by a crowd refers to an incident at a Northampton area camp meeting in the months after her arrival. In the community, too, she spoke at meetings, participated in funeral services, and served on public platforms. Letters and memoirs also suggest that other members accorded her personal authority as a source of wisdom and advice. Possibly because she was only just beginning, at this stage of her life, to engage in public activity that was not explicitly religious, she does not seem to have attracted much hostility or criticism.[64]

Black men did, however. The Stetson family kept as a memento a stone thrown at Frederick Douglass when he spoke at a meeting in Northampton town hall in 1844; the next year, a meeting of black citizens provoked the printing of burlesque programs, posted around the town to ridicule the event.[65] David Ruggles and Douglass became the focus of insinuations that reveal how opposition to the community was couched in gendered terms, themselves inscribed on images of race. A hostile description of a visit to the community published in Lewis Tappan's *Journal of Commerce* in 1843 made these connections explicit. The writer criticized as "Wild, insane, *brutal*," the (white) male leaders of the community, who would take "refined ladies" (presumably also white) "and compel them to live in the woods, to meet and associate with the vulgar unionists *of all colors* that make up these Associations." In the dining room of the community boarding house, he had seen, seated opposite "one of the accomplished

and lovely daughters" of a member, "a large *male negro*!! This alone would
have turned a much stronger stomach than mine." Revulsion against the
community's principles of racial equality were here expressed as fears for
the respectability of white women and children, victims of the "men, or
rather, the *maniacs*" who were in charge.[66] In 1844, the Boston *Atlas* again
couched racial fears in sexual terms by reporting that during a visit to the
community (which "comprises all colors, from jet black to pure white")
by the Hutchinson family singers, young Abby Hutchinson "was gal-
lanted to her hotel by one of its members, and he a huge *black man*!"[67]
Shortly afterward the Newburyport *Watchtower* condemned the Northampton community, in terms that clearly alluded to its assaults on
conventional race and gender boundaries, as a group of "extreme Abolitionists, Come-outers, broken down politicians, *negroes*, ladies and
children. They are a Non-resistant, and we think a non-compus Community."[68]

When the Whig *Hampshire Gazette* refuted the insinuation in the Boston *Atlas* story about Abby Hutchinson, it did so by claiming that she
had been driven in a carriage shared with other whites.[69] Ruggles and
other abolitionists rejected such evasions. They took the opportunity to
reiterate the principles of equality which they saw animating the community and as part of its own wider attack on convention. The *Salem
Register*, attacking the writer in the *Journal of Commerce*, condemned "he
who stigmatizes as *brutality* this practical recognition of the equality of
man, irrespective of color."[70] Ruggles, in a letter to the editor of the
Albany black paper, the *North Star* in 1844, praised the community as
"this promising Home for Humanity . . . founded on the high idea of the
EQUAL BROTHERHOOD OF THE RACE." Noah Jackman of North Attleboro, rebutting the criticisms of the *Watchtower*, pointedly contrasted the
racial equality of the Northampton community with "the Jim Crow cor-
ners" of several Newburyport churches. By exposing the prejudice and
hypocrisy that underlay the attacks on the community its defenders carried forward its effort to question and to alter conventional attitudes to
gender and race.[71]

Shifting Ground

The community's assault on dominant assumptions was strongest in
the early 1840s when it was most in tune with the wider abolitionist

campaign. By 1844 the rifts between Garrisonians and their opponents were beginning to take new shapes. The attacks on churches and ministers and the charged debates over women's roles began to die away. The overt confrontation between radical and evangelical abolition, of which the existence of the Northampton community was a potent instance, began to be overtaken by the parallel dispute over politics. To their old criticism of the United States Constitution, and the five-year resistance to proponents of an antislavery third party, the Garrisonians added, at the American Anti-Slavery Society's annual meeting in May 1844, the specific call to work for disunion. This proceeded logically enough from older positions on politics, voting, and the repudiation of any contact with sin. It also reflected the decline in importance of evangelical abolitionism. The American and Foreign Anti-Slavery Society was increasingly a spent force as a distinctive body. Nationally and locally, many of its adherents gave their attention to the other, more powerful, arm of "new organization," the Liberty Party and the nascent free-soil movement. J. P. Williston's partnership with Joel Hayden to form the *Hampshire Herald* was the sign of this shift in Northampton, and Williston himself acknowledged the inspiration of Joshua Leavitt, the leading evangelical abolitionist to move to a third-party position at this point.[72]

Though many nonresistants supported it, the adoption of disunionism marked the decline of nonresistance as a vibrant unifying strand in radical abolitionism and reduced the cultural resonance of the nonresistance campaign within northern society itself. Disunion certainly kept the radicals outside the mainstream of political life, and in many ways continued to embody the wider social criticisms that nonresistance, women's rights, and the communitarian movement had entailed. But in some respects it shifted the ground of debate toward technical political questions and away from wider cultural issues. A campaign for disunion did not challenge existing social structures or cultural assumptions as directly as putting women on public platforms or denying the authority of churches and ministers did. However much Garrisonians continued to rely on moral suasion rather than political action to achieve their ends, disunionism offered a political, not a social or moral-reform solution to the evils of slavery.[73]

Along with these shifts in strategy, in the mid-1840s abolitionists turned their attention back to the South, after a period of concentrating on the North. The economic depression, the congressional gag-rule and other measures, the schisms in the abolitionist movement, the struggles in the churches, and the campaigns for the rights and protection of free blacks and fugitive slaves had all tended to emphasize a concern with northern society. Disunionism and the campaigns against Texas annexation and the Mexican War once again focused attention on the character of southern society, the conditions of slavery, and the South's political power.

Both shifts made the role and challenge of communitarianism suddenly problematic. Social criticism might continue, but it was no longer so directly linked to the main concerns of abolitionists. For many of the communities active in the mid-1840s, this did not pose insuperable difficulties. Hopedale could continue to fly the flag of nonresistance because this was at the heart of its religious creed and would remain so regardless of its importance in the abolitionist movement. By early 1844, Brook Farm was undertaking its transition to Fourierism. Fourierism became the focus of much of the communitarian interest in New England between 1844 and 1846, and though Fourierists had strong links with abolitionism, their movement stood on its own. The Massachusetts communities, including Northampton, held a series of conventions in 1844 in the hope of reaping the benefits of the excitement Fourierism was creating, but the Northampton Association got relatively little from these.

Northampton faced a particular problem. Its connections with radical abolitionists and its more incidental attachment to nonresistance exposed it much more than either Hopedale or Brook Farm to the risk of seeming irrelevant after the shift of abolitionist policy had occurred. The founders and members of the Northampton community were trying to realize a new vision of northern society for an America from which slavery would be expunged. This mattered a good deal as long as the crises in abolitionism kept the movement focused on the North. From 1844 onward the community's role in the abolitionist movement became weaker and it appeared more as a self-contained institution, withdrawn from "the world." The "communitarian moment" of the early 1840s, which had inspired its creation and given its efforts wider meaning, was passing.

"To Live in the Common Cause:"
Life in Community

The "communitarian moment" brought together men and women of diverse backgrounds and experience. Though many of their ideals overlapped, there was much room for discussion about how social harmony, equality, and spiritual freedom could best be realized in practice. Because Northampton did not try to follow a prescribed blueprint, and because its principles were democratic, evolving a stable form of community life took time and considerable debate. Certain living arrangements, religious practices, and productive activities were more or less set early on, but some of the founders' crucial assumptions about community were challenged by other members in the weeks and months after April 1842, and it was not until 1843 that a stable framework for community life had been worked out.

Debate centered on the economics of community and the relationship between money and authority. Several of the founders had commercial and manufacturing expertise. Samuel L. Hill, Joseph Conant, Earl Dwight Swift, and Hiram Wells had all helped run factories or workshops. George W. Benson had been a merchant as well as a farmer; William Adam had worked as a mercantile clerk and had close links with Boston merchants. These men saw the community they created in 1842 as an extension of the joint-stock principle from the spheres of investment, work, and production into domestic, spiritual, and ideological concerns. Though they created patterns of authority different from those in a conventional business, as substantial investors in the community they designed it to give them some of the power that stockholders exercised in a capitalist enterprise. But others, including Erasmus Darwin Hudson, David Mack, and Hall Judd, had different views of business; Hudson envisaged a society in which, except for local exchanges, most trade would become unnecessary.[1] Though accepting the joint-stock principle as a basis for community, they sought to alter the balance of power within it to further a more radical social vision. With the support of other members, this group would bring about a transformation of the basis of community life.

Transformation was possible because there was no absolute conflict between the two groups. The community's strong roots in mixed farming-and-manufacturing regions and in kinship and neighborhood ties made for broad agreement that trade should be governed by personal considerations and that antagonistic relationships should be tempered by negotiation, not force. Through their encounters with the issue of slavery and the economic conditions of the 1830s, all had come to question the efficacy of existing capitalist institutions in the North. All intended their community to overcome competition and to put a curb on commerce. In 1842 they began to debate the capitalist wage and profit systems as well.

Questioning Capitalism

An increasing orthodoxy among historians holds that abolitionists were sympathetic to capitalism. This interpretation has much to be said for it. Leading mercantile figures were prominent supporters of abolition. Many abolitionists were confident of the superiority of "free labor" over slavery and employed concepts of individual freedom and moral responsibility to endorse the wage system. Leaders often distanced themselves from critiques of the inequalities in northern society: as Garrison, Wendell Phillips, and others argued, "Poverty is not slavery."[2] But this emphasis has flaws. It attends to the opinions of prominent abolitionists, rather than to those of than the movement's rank-and-file, and focuses on the emergence in the late 1840s of a "free-soil," "free-labor" consensus more than on the broader range of views that existed up to that point. The Northampton Association was one of many places in which discussions of capitalism and its faults took place in the early 1840s, and it crystallized an abolitionist vision critical of capitalism as well as of slavery.

As some abolitionists were aware, the authority of employers in the

workplace meant that wage workers were far from "free". A Lynn abolitionist noted in 1841 that wage workers who were obliged by their employers to carry out tasks against their consciences were subject to a form
of slavery.[3] The abolitionist critique of slavery as robbery could also be
applied to an inequitable wage system. Slaveholders, Erasmus Darwin
Hudson wrote in 1841, were "real robbers and thieves, who claim other
men as chattels, and forcibly take from them their honest earnings."
Within a year he was saying the same about the owners of a large cotton
factory he visited in New Hampshire on one of his lecture tours. The
"avails of labor" were "going into the wrong hands, . . . not into the pock-
ets of the laborer—but the sl[ave] holder and capitalist." The "business
operations of the day" were "all thieving and robbing—as bad as coun-
terfeiters," and Hudson speculated on "the effects on . . . the whole concern" if "the law of love The Golden rule [were] strictly applied."[4] To
Hudson, Mack, and Judd the effort to construct a noncompetitive, cooperative community at Northampton was itself a critique of an economy
based on wage labor and private profit.

However, most of the founders saw the community as a means to improve the emerging capitalist system by reinjecting moral considerations
into it. Benson and Hill, by their connections with abolition and nonresistance and their experience of the economic depression, were drawn
to scrutinize the moral implications of markets and the wage system.
"Association," by combining capital, could potentially make a more stable
basis for business, while at the same time avoiding the confrontations
between labor and capital that had emerged in the 1820s and 1830s. In
a famous essay, "The Laboring Classes," published in 1840, Orestes
Brownson had argued that this conflict would not be solved without revolution. Brook Farm and the Fourierists, and the nonresistants at Hopedale and Northampton, all sought to resolve it peacefully. Their view of
community extended the paternalist efforts of the boardinghouses of the
mills in Lowell, temperance reform, and the attempts by factory owners
to create what Anthony F.C. Wallace called "Christian industrialism," by
forming an inclusive society that would bring workers into harmonious
cooperation with employers, rather than trying to regulate them at arms'
length.[5] Northampton's leaders believed that communal institutions provided the best moral environment for the growth of social harmony. Seeking to humanize capitalism, they rejected the labor market as a model and
sought to construct a new framework in which to operate the wage system.

The initial structure of the Northampton community embodied this view. Membership, with the privileges of association, would be offered on the basis of equality to all who were admitted. But the distinction, laid out in the Preliminary Circular and adopted in the 1842 constitution, between the "Industrial Community," to which all belonged, and the "Stock Company" of members who had invested capital, reflected the assumption that capital conveyed certain privileges. Each member voting on day-to-day issues in the Industrial Community had one vote, but those making business and financial decisions in the Stock Company had up to ten votes according to the size of their investment. Precise arrangements for the terms on which food, accommodation, and other necessities were to be provided for all members were not at first settled. They were to be determined by meetings of the members and stockholders as the community became established and would quickly become the subject of controversy.

Unlike some communities, such as Robert Owen's at New Harmony, where the land and buildings remained the property of an individual, the Northampton Association was a legal entity whose property was owned by all the members and vested in the board of trustees (president, treasurer, and secretary), who were subject to annual election by the membership. No individual could, in his or her own right, exercise control over it; nor could any outsider obtain controlling rights, because trustees had to be chosen from among the resident members. Still, Northampton did not have "community of property." Members were not obliged to renounce their own possessions. Any contributions of money or goods they made were voluntary and could be valued and entered on the association's books as subscriptions to its capital stock. Members who resigned could take the equivalent value of their stock with them; the initial rules merely required ninety days' written notice of an intention to withdraw it. Members arriving, therefore, did not surrender any possessions unless they subscribed them. Members leaving were entitled to what they had put in. The only unresolved issue was payment for the work they did while they were in the community.

In setting out the relationships between members and stockholders, these early arrangements modified the conventional distinction between employees and employers without altogether erasing it. But they laid the ground for further fundamental criticism of wage labor and the problems of the free market. There was already a shift in emphasis between the Preliminary Circular and the 1842 constitution; unlike the Circular, the constitution stressed moral as much as functional principles and declared that members were entitled to the products of their own labor. The overlap of members between the Stock Company and the Industrial Community, together with the democratic basis for voting in the latter, gave nonstockholding members a degree of influence in community affairs inconceivable in a conventional joint-stock company. A late-nineteenth-century commentator described the community under this arrangement as "a capitalist subject to an association of workers."[6] Members soon took this opening to strengthen their position further.

The founders' initial assumptions about how work and remuneration should be organized clearly reflected their capitalist frame of mind. They were influenced, no doubt, by the circumstances of having taken over a working silk mill with a handful of women workers, and that their president, Joseph Conant, had already been the mill's superintendent for over a year. They expected that the association would conduct its operations over yearly periods and that at each year's end there would be a division of its earnings. Though the constitution provided that the division would recognize labor and skill, as well as capital, it maintained the conventional assumption that work would be paid for with wages. Yet as various community meetings attempted to put the policy into effect in the late spring and summer of 1842, members worked to shift the system in a more radical direction. At length they succeeded. In doing so they rejected the founders' view that the wage system could support social harmony. Rather, they argued, the community's ideals would best be realized by scrapping wages and adopting a more explicitly communal form of organization. They came to the same conclusion that Charles Lane did when he and Bronson Alcott established the Fruitlands community in 1843: "From the state of serfdom to the receipt of wages may be a step in human progress; but it is certainly full time for taking a new step out of the hiring system."[7]

The Wages Debate of 1842

Only a month or so after the formal organization of the community, members met to decide how they would pay themselves. Immediately, there were serious differences of opinion. Leaders such as Benson proposed that the association should pay its members hourly wages for work done. In the ensuing debate Benson became the chief proponent of the argument that wage payment was consistent with community principles. Hudson, Mack, Judd, and others advanced their different view.

Initial discussions produced no agreement. Women members, apparently expecting the advocates of wages to get their way, met separately and resolved that they would vote to ensure that the rate for men's work and women's work would be the same. Benson and other leaders heeded this move, and when they proposed a wage rate to a meeting in late May 1842, they set it at five cents an hour for all aged eighteen and over, about half the local going rate for male labor. In other words, wages would be equalized, but at the women's rate. The meeting, however, rejected the proposal by a margin of more than two to one, and even more firmly endorsed the principle, put forward by Hall Judd and David Mack, that remuneration for labor should be fixed—in other words, all should be paid equally, not by the hour. The conflict continued into the middle of June, when it was eventually agreed that wages would be paid, but that the rate of compensation should be decided only after the end of the first year's operations. Despite strong opposition in the community at large, the stockholders were for the moment able to sustain the principle of payment by wages.[8]

Erasmus Darwin Hudson was present in Northampton during the early summer of 1842 during a gap between lecture tours; from his journal we have some accounts of these debates to supplement the minutes in the association's records. The first discussion of wages in May produced a variety of views, he noted, and "the true principle of labor and the distribution of its avails appeared to be unsettled in the minds of most of those present." Hudson began to take steps that would eventually lead the community away from the wage system. He argued that current arrangements constituted too little change from those generally prevailing in the economy. It was a "property association," he argued, in which stockholders had privileges greater than those of members, an arrangement he condemned as "the grave of liberty." The Industrial Community, made up of the bulk of nonstockholding members was, he implied, improperly constituted since it was excluded from privileges that should have been extended to all. Instead, he urged, the members in general should have use of the stock, their livings should be paid for out of its avails, and any surplus divided equally among all. According to his journal, Hudson's view was supported by several members, including William Adam, Hall Judd, and Eliza Wall. Opposed by others, whom Hudson did not identify, who "demanded wages," his proposition got nowhere for the time being.

Hudson, fearful that the present arrangements instilled a "domineering spirit," by setting up "rulers and overseers" over the membership, refused to regard himself as a member of the Industrial Community under these conditions, and for most of the second half of 1842 he and his wife formally withdrew from the association in protest.[9] They still took part in discussions, though, and when he was away from Northampton, Hudson kept in close touch with developments. Gradually his viewpoint began to prevail.

The issue was rejoined at a meeting in July at which Hudson was present. It opened with a reading by Frances Judd from the third chapter of Galatians, which George W. Benson immediately followed up with a discourse on civil and racial equality. When Benson had finished, Hudson spoke about equality for women, and then Hall Judd attacked the inequities of "the factory system of labor and wages" in general, and the community's "own system of oppression" in particular. According to Hudson, Judd was supported by other members who were not stockholders, and by the women who worked in the silk mill. Elements of a class struggle within the community emerged. The criticism was too much for the secretary, William Adam, who abandoned his earlier support for Hudson and Judd and joined George W. Benson in rebuking them. Adam went further, demanding that the two men be disciplined for their accusations, and for three or four days the community was in "commotion" over the question. Hudson not only criticized Adam privately for changing sides, but asked rhetorically why there was so much "sensitiveness" to the charge that the community's own arrangements were oppressive. In a letter to his wife that September, he repeated his assertion that its wage and stock system invalidated the claim that the association was a community: its property system was "wrong, radically so," and "if they look at their Constitution they will see what is necessary to constitute a Community." The debate sputtered on.[10]

At some point during the summer members voted to reduce the working day from twelve hours to eleven. In this climate, with the wage system under attack and a decision about paying wages postponed, Joseph Conant and his sons-in-law Swift and Chaffee decided to withdraw from the community. After giving due notice, they withdrew their stock too and set about establishing their own silk mill nearby. Though they remained on amicable terms with it, the Conant group had no wish to be involved in a community that was becoming so different from an ordinary business. Even William Adam welcomed their departure: "Their object in joining us appears to have been from the first, *pecuniary* advantage, not *moral* improvement or *social* usefulness, and we all feel that their departure has strengthened instead of weakening us." In the light of it, he would advocate a by-law preventing members from withdrawing their stock within four years of subscribing, a provision that he later had cause to regret. The departure of the Conant group undoubtedly weakened the ability of the original stockholders to sustain their control over community affairs.[11]

The Changes of 1843

For the rest of 1842 the wage question was left unanswered, as members settled down to the tasks of building their new lives together. But at the first annual meeting of the association in January 1843, it was constitutionally necessary to broach the issue again. Advocates of change, probably led by David Mack, pressed home the opportunity to achieve what had proved impossible the previous summer. In what the historian Arthur Bestor once referred to as a "coup," a majority of members took steps during 1843 to move the community in a noncapitalist direction, arguing that this was necessary to achieve the ideals that the founders had originally set out.[12]

On January 14, just before the annual meeting began, the industrial directors fixed the scale of wages to be paid for the first year's work, awarded individually according to hours worked. Their award was slightly more favorable to members than Benson's proposal of the previous May. Male and female rates were identical, but there was a scale graded according to age, from six cents an hour for those aged twenty and above, down to one cent an hour for children under twelve. The adult rate was comparable with that for women in the surrounding area and about three-fifths the "market" rate for male laborers.[13] Nonetheless, at the annual meeting—actually a series of sessions adjourned from day to day for much of late January—members ensured that the wage system would be scrapped. In a succession of votes they overturned the founders' assumption that the association would operate like a company.

The meeting, and subsequent detailed provisions passed by committees to enact its intentions, moved the association firmly toward a more communal organization. The by-law providing that subscriptions of stock would only be accepted for a minimum of four years was enacted, and an earlier rule that members should not trade or exchange outside the community for their own profit upheld. Control over the admission of members would be removed from the separate admissions board and vested in a ballot of the whole community, meeting regularly for the purpose. Steps would be taken to improve the factory boardinghouse and to make it "a proper nucleus for the community" for all members. During the discussions Erasmus Darwin Hudson and Martha Turner Hudson were readmitted to membership "by acclamation," the reasons for their scruples now removed.[14]

Above all, the old system of annually calculated wages would be replaced by a new system of allowances for subsistence. Weekly sums for food and other essentials and annual sums for clothing, each scaled by age, would be available to all members and probationary members equally. They would be expected to work sixty hours a week, or ten hours a day, if able, but there would be no variation of allowances according to hours worked. At the end of each year, the association's earnings would be reckoned, the subsistence allowances and interest on outside loans paid for, and any surplus divided. Again, new arrangements for dividing profits removed privileges formerly accorded to stockholders. Three-quarters of any surplus would be added to the capital of the association, but not divided among stockholders. The other quarter would be distributed equally to all full members eighteen years and older. These proportions were subsequently adjusted to two-thirds and one-third respectively, but the notion of emulating capitalism's wage and profit systems was abandoned; instead there would be equal subsistence for all and any profits would be equally shared or returned to community use. In April 1843 a community meeting completed the new financial arrangements by enacting an earlier proposal that the community would provide medicines and nursing care to members free of charge.[15]

The 1843 annual meeting decided to enact the changes it made as a set of temporary arrangements to last for the year, and to suspend any existing articles of association that conflicted with them. A new circular announcing them, one that in practice replaced much of the 1842 constitution, was drawn up for general distribution. Its first provision was the effective abolition of the distinction between the Stock Company and the Industrial Community; from now on, the whole association would control matters relating to stock, and all adult members would be equal. As David Mack wrote in the summer of 1843, it was still unclear whether these temporary changes would be made permanent, but he was certain that there would be no return to the old arrangement of a stock company that gave "votes to Dollars."[16]

One critic predicted that the new arrangements at the community would quickly fail because they "open . . . too wide a door to the poor." Opponents at first latched on to their temporary status as grounds for hope that they might soon be reversed. "Management of the stock operations will probably be restored to the stockholders exclusively," reported a visitor in August 1843.[17] But over the course of 1843 it became evident that this would not happen. Instead a further series of meetings in October consolidated the changes by formally revising the association's constitution to reflect them. The chief organizational change, the abolition of the distinction between the stock company and the industrial community, was formalized; stockholders now had no more rights than any other members.[18] Radical abolitionists from outside the community praised the changes it had enacted. Nathaniel P. Rogers enthusiastically endorsed the "young republic" as "a voluntary and kindly attempt of living and getting a living together," an aggregate of individuals "laboring side by side without competition, or rivalry, or selfishness, in the harmful sense." The system, wrote H. H. Joslyn, allowed "each member to labor according to their ability, trusting to their sense of right, and compensating all alike." David Mack explained to an abolitionist inquiring about membership that the "no wage/no interest system" was commensurate with Christianity and "brotherly principle." The guarantee of subsistence and the sharing of profits overcame the need for means of accumulation, because "all were interested in all," and all would work together to obtain their mutual support.[19]

Most of the new practices remained in place during the rest of the community's existence. Changes took place to administrative procedures, and there were repeated attempts to tighten what to some leaders appeared lax control over work and resources. The president, secretary, and treasurer, in addition to acting as trustees for the community, were under the 1843 constitution also constituted as an executive council with powers over business and financial decisions comparable to those of the old stock company. But they gained office through election by the members, not by virtue of their stockholdings, and the general community meeting therefore had some check on their decisions. Though with hard times between 1844 and 1846 the level of provision became poorer, the system of equal allowances for subsistence continued to function until the community ceased.

No one was in any doubt that the community had overturned the assumptions and methods of the capitalist wage and profit systems. As the former Lynn shoe manufacturer William Bassett would write in 1844, shortly after he joined the community, it was "a community of interests—not a community of property"; the rights of capital had been relinquished, because members did not see the justice of rewarding most those who already had most: the most should go to those with least, "for the very good reason that [they] *needed most.*" Bassett concluded, "I have long regarded this movement as one of vast moment, and promising incalculable benefits to the human race." Bassett, whose factory had employed 150 men, set out an indictment of industrial capitalism that could not have been more stinging had it been written by a radical labor leader. "I could not reconcile with my ideas of justice," Bassett wrote, "the inequality that existed between the employer and the employed. . . . [I] became convinced that the evils which I saw and deplored were inherent in the system and that no remedy could be provided but in *its* subversion. I was satisfied that the system of *hired labor* was false and necessarily unequal in its operation."[20] Bassett could conscientiously settle at Northampton precisely because its practices by then accorded with these principles. The 1843 arrangements formed a stable basis for community life.

Life in Community

Even as they adjusted arrangements to secure equality, members faced certain realities that would shape their lives together. They had substantial assets, but also heavy debts. Their land was only of moderate quality, and work was needed to bring it fully into use. They owned a silk factory that had yet to be successful, with machinery that would need constant attention and improvement. They had a rather poor endowment of tools and limited working capital. They were a youthful and active group, but had considerable numbers of children among them; they had ideals about education, but also needed children's labor to help the community get by. These circumstances structured their efforts to build harmony and cooperation.

What did people think when they first arrived at a new community to live? Few, perhaps, were as unlucky as the farm family that moved, with a heavy cartload of possessions, to the abortive Prairie Home Community in West Liberty, Ohio, to find a single rough house, the women and children sleeping in overcrowded upstairs rooms and the men on the downstairs floor. They had "given up the world to come to what was heaven in idea but was subsequently discovered to be *Utopia.*"[21] Even though new members at Northampton or Brook Farm did not face such wretchedness, they did not always find community easy to like at first. Frances Birge arrived at Northampton in the spring of 1842, just as the community was starting, to find that "it seemed to be in a wilderness. A pine grove and ravine were west of it, and the land to the east was covered with mulberry bushes." Sojourner Truth "did not fall in love at first sight with the Northampton Association. . . . [T]heir phalanx was a factory, and they were wanting in means to carry out their ideas of beauty and elegance. . . . [S]he would make an effort to tarry with them one night, though that seemed to her no desirable affair." Actually she stayed for over a decade, until well after the association had dissolved. Margaret Fuller, describing the early days of a new arrival at Brook Farm, captured the sense of what we might call the cultural contrast between community life and the world outside: "The first day or two here is desolate, you seem to belong to nobody—to have a right to speak to nobody; but very soon you learn to take care of yourself and then the freedom of the place is delightful." At Northampton, Sophia Foord found it hard at first to discover how things worked or who did what. How did you address people? How did you behave?[22]

New members and visitors were first struck by the community's surroundings and appearance. Their verdicts varied roughly according to their ideological position. Supporters, such as a Lynn abolitionist who visited in 1844, expressed unbounded enthusiasm for the community: "Nothing short will be adequate to describe the paradisiacal nature of that lovely spot. It is Eden, Jr, to say the least." David Ruggles, unable to see the landscape, painted an eloquent word picture of its sounds in a letter, recounting the rush of water over the milldam, the birdsong, and rustling of the wind in the trees that he could hear as he was led around the community's property. Others were less complimentary. A Pennsylvania visitor saw a place "very wild in appearance." The Mill River was a "romantic stream" but the recently cleared fields, "bristling with stumps, look rather rough." John Finch, an English Owenite who visited in May 1843, found "no proper order or subordination . . . , and everything is dirty and slovenly on the farm . . . and all over the premises."[23]

Skeptics criticized the buildings even more than the site. The com-

A late nineteenth-century view of the former silk factory and boarding house of the Northampton community. From Charles A. Sheffeld, ed., *History of Florence, Massachusetts.*

munity's accommodation included six or seven modest houses, and the upper two stories of the brick factory building, usually called the "factory boardinghouse." Elihu Burritt, "the learned blacksmith," who visited in February 1843 when the area was under deep snow, found "a large abandoned silk factory, thinly partitioned off into rooms [no] larger than cells. . .with unplaned, upright boards, whose open joints were concealed in the inner side by coarse paper pasted over them." The Adam and Benson families lived in their own houses, without sharing with others, and in 1843 Samuel L. Hill gained permission to move his family to a house just outside the community's property. But the majority of members, families, and single people lived in the boardinghouses, or in the smaller houses that also held several families: Hall and Frances Judd, for instance, moved into one of these with two other families when they joined in May 1842. Conditions were cramped. A hostile writer for the *Journal of Commerce* described the factory boardinghouse: its dining room, forty feet long, with two tables of rough boards, where residents served themselves to "as primitive a dinner as one could possibly wish for," and the partitioned rooms on the upper floors, "where they pack in almost as closely as in some of the poorer quarters of New York."[24]

Even enthusiasts could not find beauty or luxury in these conditions; instead they praised the community's plainness and simplicity. The Hutchinson singers found everything in "a plain, simple, rough, pleasant condition," and Nathaniel P. Rogers found the rooms divided "by thin, temporary partitions," adequate "in the infancy of affairs here," and the "accommodating good feeling and. . .fraternal spirit" of the members sufficient to ensure "no lack of convenience or comfort" in the absence of better material provision. Critics and supporters agreed that belonging to the community demanded sacrifices. Burritt claimed he had never seen "a place where more self-denial & sacrifice of personal comfort, rights, & privileges seemed requisite than here." The Lynn abolitionist editor Henry Clapp Jr., though seeing the community as a "mighty channel" for human improvement, remarked that it demanded hard work of its members, that some were probably not up to these demands, and that it "requires *simplicity* to be happy in."[25]

Community life differed markedly from that in comfortable middle- and upper-middle-class households. The Bostonian Esther Dixwell wrote after visiting the Adam family that "their life and arrangements are very peculiar," and when an Adam daughter invited two young Boston friends to come and stay at the community, Dixwell objected: the Adams' house only had bed space for themselves, the parlors were used for schoolrooms, and the family "eat at the public table of the community, which is not a place to introduce people of delicate and luxurious habits."[26] For many members such simplicity was a moral preference, enabling them to resist the "artificial" temptations of society and seek a "true" life without superfluities. If people found these demands testing, that was a measure of the extent to which society had strayed from its true path.

Hall Judd's mother wrote that the members were "a goodly looking people" who "profess to be governed by the commands, precepts and example of Christ and his immediate disciples."[27] Learning to adopt simplicity of language, address, and manners took time and could be painful, but was seen to have good effects. In 1845 the abolitionist lecturer Cyrus M. Burleigh visited Roxcy Brown Nickerson, who had lived at the Northampton community for eighteen months before marrying and moving to Harwich, Massachusetts. "Her residence at the Community," wrote Burleigh, "has done much to free her mind from the artificial fetters imposed on its members by Society. She acts as though she felt that she was a human being." The practical, day-to-day recognition of peoples' common humanity was an essential building block for wider social change. A Northampton member told a visitor in 1844: "The design of this association is to establish equality of rights and interests, to secure universal harmony, peace, and freedom from care, anxiety, dependence, and oppression . . . —to blot out of the human vocabulary the terms, with the ideas they express, of rich and poor, slave and master, hireling and employer, high and low, first class and second class, etc." Daily life in community and the rituals associated with community meetings and other events were intended to express the connections between restraint, morality, and social equality.[28]

Ritual

Work and study occupied six days a week. Regular business meetings, at first of the "Industrial Community," from 1843 of the whole community, were held on Saturday evenings, though sometimes there was no business to transact. Sunday was a day off, but members insisted that this was not "superstitious" sabbath-day observance. On Sunday mornings families and children gathered for instruction, either in the boardinghouse meeting room or outdoors in the pine grove nearby. Some members attended churches in town. Sunday afternoons were devoted to the "free" meetings of adult and youthful members and visitors, where religious and moral subjects were debated. These could combine elements of Quaker meetings, evangelical "concerts" for prayer and singing, abolitionist conventions, lyceum lectures, and debating societies. Members and sympathetic observers took pride in the difference between these meetings and most church services, at which only the clergy and some male elders were permitted to speak. At the community, it was claimed, the principle of "free debate" allowed anyone present to express an opinion.

Defenders of the community implied that these gatherings came closer than many conventional services to the ideal of Christian fellowship. H. H. Joslyn wrote in 1843 that "I had the pleasure of being present at one of their meetings, and was much edified and interested"; B. C. Bacon, describing the Sunday meetings in the *Liberator*, wrote that "I heard nothing of that disgusting gossip about the rise and fall of stocks, the state of trade, the minister's style, the new fashions, and other things . . . which

I have heard from many who defend the Sabbath-day."[29] The meetings were objects of suspicion to the orthodox in the surrounding area, and members took pleasure at besting them in debate. Giles B. Stebbins recalled a visit from the minister of Hadley, the "grave Puritan D.D." John Woodbridge, who attempted to badger a member, Fortune R. Porter, about the danger to social order from differences in belief. Porter, according to Stebbins, gave the minister "a good object lesson in free inquiry" by replying that just as a stick would make different sounds when banged on different parts of a fence, so "you like to hear them and make up your mind which is best."[30]

Discussion could be wide-ranging and searching. Eldad Stebbins of Hatfield, Massachusetts, who stayed in the community in June 1843, attended a meeting where he heard speeches on dietary reform by Sylvester Graham, Mary S. Gove, and the English radical Henry G. Wright (who was briefly a member of the Fruitlands community), followed by a debate in which James Boyle, William Adam, Maria Mack, and a former Methodist preacher named Palmer took part.[31] Outsiders were free to express their views, but were subject to challenge. One Sunday in July 1843 a Mormon "held forth" about his beliefs at the afternoon meeting, but then had to listen while "a member of the Community got up and exposed the fallacy of the Mormon system."[32] This encounter was probably spontaneous. Others were not. When John Finch visited, he acceded to members' requests for a lecture on Robert Owen's theories of the formation of character, and outlined Owen's materialist position, that people were shaped by their social circumstances. According to another visitor present, community members then without exception criticized Finch and upheld their own position, that character depended on individuals' morality.[33]

Nonsectarian, nonresistance principles and avoidance of superfluity also marked more occasional rituals, such as marriages and funerals. Hall Judd and Frances Birge married in June 1842 with exemplary simplicity. A justice of the peace, Oliver Warner, waited in the front room of Hall's father's house in Northampton. Judd and Birge arrived, "in their common dresses," accompanied by George Benson. Hall's father and three others "happened to be present," but his mother "was very busy sweeping, &c. and did not come into the room." The couple sat, Warner "obtained from each a promise to perform their conjugal duties" and "pronounced them husband and wife." The ceremony was over in about one minute. "There was no eating or drinking connected with this marriage," wrote Hall's father, and "Mr. Warner refused his fee, so it cost nothing to anybody."[34] George Ashley's marriage to Eliza Forward at the community one Sunday two years later took longer, but cost no more. Members gathered under the famous pine tree. In due course a justice of the peace, "in the briefest way," obtained the couple's pledges of fidelity and pronounced them legally married, but not before George Benson had given a lengthy address on the duties of husband and wife, explaining (in nonresistant terms) that marriage was "an institution of heaven," with which no human action could meddle, and in which the magistrate had no real part to play. A song by the children and congratulations from everyone closed the proceedings. Sidney Southworth and Harriet Hayden held no ceremony at all in July 1844: they merely gave written notice to the secretary, which he entered in the association's records, "that they had consummated the marriage relation, having found each other of one spirit."[35] Funerals were equally plain. Anne E. Benson, George's sister, was buried in a pine grove in September 1843, after "very simple" services, "such as she desired, and with no one to enact the part of a priest on the occasion." At another burial that year, children filed by and dropped "sprigs and evergreen and wild flowers" into the grave. After Hall and Frances Judd's baby son died in 1845, a crowd of community members and neighbors assembled in one of the houses. A hymn was sung, Sojourner Truth spoke briefly and sang two or three verses, Samuel L. Hill read the twelfth chapter of Hebrews, Hall spoke of "his sorrows and joys connected with this death, the promises of the gospel, etc.," and said a short prayer. Then a man carried the unadorned pine coffin to the grave, near the community schoolhouse, where other members were buried. Everything, wrote Hall's father, as if he had expected the opposite, "was performed in a serious, solemn manner." But there had been one funeral when a remark prompted some children to laugh and a disturbance ensued.[36]

Education

If communities were to transform society, their values would have to be instilled in the next generation. Education was vital. As an article in the *Dial* expressed it in January 1842, "In the true society. . .education is the ground idea."[37] Brook Farm in particular became a center of learning, both for members of its own families and for pupils attracted to the community for schooling. Though the Northampton community's education department never achieved Brook Farm's stature, there were parallels between the two communities' educational ideals. As at Brook Farm, a balance between schooling and work was intended to ensure the mental, physical, and moral development of the children. If this ideal owed something to the transcendentalist goal of "labor and education for all," it also suited the rural farming and artisan families from which many members came. The community sought to correct the widening division in society between mental and manual occupations. As Samuel L. Hill recalled much later, its educational program included "instruction in practical industry, as well as in literature and science. It also included moral and spiritual culture," intended to prepare youth of "good habits, fair talents and useful characters."[38] These ideas derived from the Pestalozzian concept of "learning by doing," from manual labor schools set up to educate and support poor children, and boarding schools that used pupils' labor to enable them to run as "self-supporting" institutions. The founders calculated that by working throughout their schooling the children of the Northampton community would both obtain a rounded education and pay for the cost of it.[39]

Putting ideals into practice took much effort, not least because a significant proportion of residents were children. Nathaniel P. Rogers, who visited in the summer of 1843, wrote that there were thirty to forty children out of a population of just over one hundred. Though it varied over time, the proportion of the community under eighteen never fell below two-fifths of the total, and for a period in 1845 it rose above one-half. Pupils were divided by age into "junior" (roughly from eight to fourteen), "senior," and infant classes. Young boys and girls were taught together, and it is possible that older pupils were also taught in mixed-sex groups. Enlightened ideals and nonresistance principles alike demanded that instruction be based on self-discipline and the inculcation of interest among pupils. Violent disciplinary methods such as flogging were prohibited. Hostile visitors reported witnessing disorderly classes in which children were allowed to do as they wished and teachers were reduced to tears.[40]

For most of the community's first year teaching took place early in the mornings, and pupils spent afternoons at work. Senior pupils went at 7 A.M. to William Adam's house. In his study, Adam taught languages, composition, and "miscellaneous branches" to young men preparing for college, including his own son Gordon, who was, a visitor noted, "a most

unwilling student." In another room at the same hour, Adam's daughter
Phebe held a singing class for younger children.[41] By February 1843,
having acquired some $65 worth of books and moved the teaching from
his own house to a room in the factory boardinghouse, Adam could report
that the education department was "fully organized." By then, it was
teaching over thirty children. Sometime between February and May 1843,
the teaching schedule was reversed; pupils now worked in the mornings
and studied later in the day. That year David Mack took over some of
the college preparation, though Adam still had students. New members
such as Sophia Foord and Emily Farwell took charge of younger pupils.
Seven members clubbed together to hire a German tutor for three
months, and French teaching was for a period provided by the English-
born Fortune R. Porter, who came from New York City to join the community in July 1843; it is not clear who—if anyone—replaced him after
he departed again six months later.[42]

Particularly for young children, teaching differed from that in most
contemporary schools. One of Benson's daughters recalled a system "so
different from the stereotyped training of other young folks of those days."
There were "athletic exercises that the girls, as well as the boys, were
expected to take," and training in sewing, knitting, braiding "and other
useful things . . . while . . . our teacher read the classics to us,—Shake-
speare's plays, Scott's novels, Prescott's 'History of the Conquest of Mexico' . . . and many other . . . books, both prose and poetry." Though
"old-fashioned ways of study were by no means neglected, and we had to
learn our lessons," she had stronger memories of trips into the fields or
to the riverbank: "We were taught botany wherever flowers grew, and we
learned by object lessons many things that city children never knew." Her
cousin George Stetson, aged six when his family came to Northampton
in 1843, also remembered instruction from Sophia Foord on the plain
behind the factory, while "on the banks of the river we were taught to
build the different geographical formations, miniature islands, capes,
promontories, peninsulas, and isthmuses." Benson's daughter recalled her
teachers as having "thoughtful, progressive, intellectual" ideas on education, play, exercise, and work.[43]

By 1843 the school was attracting abolitionist families to apply to
join the community with their children. The Bensons' Brooklyn neighbors James and Dolly Stetson moved to Northampton for this reason.
Word was also passed around in radical circles that the school would
accept boarding pupils, and several abolitionist children, including two

of William Lloyd Garrison's sons, were sent there. The opportunity to work and study among abolitionists also attracted older boys, such as Thomas Hill, and young men, including Giles B. Stebbins, to prepare for college there. Creating the new social and educational environment would take time. Writing in 1844 to the father of a prospective pupil, David Mack explained that "we are anxious to begin with children of not bad habits if possible—for our own children have not been in training long enough to be beyond the reach of disturbing influences." Agreeing to accept the boy for a six-month trial period, Mack was optimistic; if his father had stated it correctly, the boy had "a good basis on which to work, in his 'natural kindness and sweetness' upon which we may hope, with kindness and perseverance to erect a good character." But it would be a delicate process; "should his influence on others be found too strong to be counteracted," he would be sent home again when the six months were up.[44]

Responsibility for children outside lessons fell on a variety of adult members. Parents took care of their own children, but the residents of the boardinghouse in particular evolved various cooperative arrangements for sharing responsibilities. Individual men and women looked after children from outside the community, or whose parents were absent. Some boys and young men worked alongside departmental directors, as quasi-apprentices. Children were often organized to work in groups. Former pupils remembered James Boyle watching boys picking mulberry leaves, and that Samuel Hill frequently kept an eye on children at work. On at least one occasion, David Mack had to organize the "junior class" to bring in the harvest. These instances suggest that supervising children was a common task for men who did not have their own manual occupations. Women, on the other hand, who took charge of girls doing sewing or feeding silkworms in the cocoonery, added this supervision to their own work.

Work

The community proclaimed that work should be intrinsically beneficial to each worker and that rewards should be equal. Each member was asked to select a department in which he or she would work. To avoid misallocations of effort, provision was soon made for members to indicate a willingness to be assigned to departments as they were needed, but the voluntary principle was largely maintained, and over time, increasing reliance was placed on the admission process to obtain skills where they were most needed.

The community's work was demanding. The Adam family rose at half past five in the morning, breakfasted at six, and were teaching classes at seven. Even after the workday had been reduced from twelve hours to eleven, and then fixed at ten on the abolition of wages in 1843, when David Mack wrote to protest the insurance company's insistence that a night watch be kept on the factory building, he stressed that this would be "fatiguing" and that all members retired to bed early after their hard days' work.[45] Periodic crises demanded extra effort. Situated as it was in a narrow river valley, the community was at risk from floods at least three times in its first two years. A sudden freshet in 1842 caused some chaos, though Erasmus Darwin Hudson, absent on a lecturing tour, derived amusement at his son's description of the community's pigs swimming for their lives. In October 1843 there was more serious damage. After two days of heavy rain, the river washed out the entrance to the mill's power canal and breached the canal bank in several places. Throughout a Sunday evening members worked to remove stores, furniture, and machinery from the factory, and it was feared that the sawmill, cut off by the torrent, would be washed away. For several days the silk factory was stopped, "and all hands large and small [were] at work early and late in repairing the damage." William Adam canceled his lessons and "joined one of the working gangs but after one days hard work he found that although the spirit was willing the flesh was weak," and he was forced to give up. George Benson was so busy that he barely had time to eat.[46]

From the early months there was an effort to reduce the employment of outside workers and to rely on the steadily growing number of members. Two skilled men were hired to help start cutlery making, but then left. A local woman was paid to do housework in the boardinghouse from May 1842, but was hired increasingly intermittently as her work was taken over by community members. Six women were employed in the silk mill in 1842 and early 1843, but the number was subsequently reduced to three, and members used instead, although occasional requests for hired help were made at times of strong demand for silk goods. When an English silk spinner called Harding proposed being hired to work for the community at fixed wages in September 1842, he was instead offered membership terms and stayed for a short period. A number of young men were admitted to the community as boarders or prospective members, probably to help provide summer farm labor.[47] Offering membership, or comparable terms, could be a sufficient inducement to obtain small numbers of extra men or boys at a time when local employment was scarce and when many farmers demanded more than ten hours' work on summer days. It became less attractive after 1844, as the economy began to improve and as more laboring jobs in construction and railroad building became available.

The community adopted a gender division of labor largely based on practices conventional in New England agricultural neighborhoods. Women and girls worked mainly at cooking, cleaning, sewing, silk manufacture, and related tasks; the first annual meeting in 1843 described the role of the domestic department as "the providing of females with work." Men and boys did farming, lumbering, metalworking, construction, and other manufacturing jobs. Even in the silk-raising department, which employed both genders, there was a division between boys who picked mulberry leaves and carried them to the cocoonery, and girls who chopped the leaves and fed them to silkworms; in July 1842, for instance, Adam's younger daughter Helen combined schoolwork and running errands with "above all, preparing mulberry leaves for the silk worms at the Factory."[48]

There is evidence that men sometimes helped with domestic work, but women rarely crossed the line the other way to do jobs specifically regarded as "men's work."[49] Given that only about three residents in ten were adult men and that some of them were absent on community or antislavery society business, the gender division of labor created shortages in areas where women were not usually allowed to work. It was no coincidence that when, in the summer of 1843, as the demand for labor "outdoors" increased with the progress of the season, it was the lumber, mechanical, and silk-dyeing departments, quickly followed by the agricultural department, that complained to the community business meeting that they were short of workers. Volunteers were sought to carry out needed jobs, and children were used to help with the harvest. Theodore Scarborough, in charge of the farm, faced with the need to thresh newly harvested grain for the community's use, sought permission in August to purchase a horse-powered threshing machine. Other members, regarding the cash outlay as "inexpedient," at first blocked this, but Scarborough succeeded in having their decision reversed, and he was allowed eighty dollars to acquire a machine.[50] Nothing better illustrates how carefully the community had to balance the allocation of labor to necessary tasks and spending cash on items that either could not be produced or that could save labor for short periods. The pressure of work made it increasingly necessary for the community to draw on the labor of its younger members. Over time, this would conflict with its educational ideals.

There is little doubt that by the winter of 1843–44, the association had established a workable, inherently stable framework for community life. The shift from wage payment to guaranteed subsistence in 1843 did nothing to diminish the community's attractiveness. The number of residents fluctuated from month to month, but rose from eighty-three at the end of 1842 to 113 in June 1843, and to its peak of 120 over the winter and spring of 1844. Had accommodation been available to house the many more who sought to join the community, this number could have risen considerably higher. However, these overall figures disguise a noticeable turnover of members, as some individuals and families withdrew. Tensions and conflicts that arose around all the major areas of activity that we have just surveyed contributed to a constant trickle of departures. There were three important areas of tension: the differences between men's and women's experience of community life; religious tolerance; and a wider set of cultural issues that embraced recreation and education. All led some members to withdraw. In addition, the conduct and experience of community life gave some early members second thoughts about its desirability, and they left too. We shall explore each of these issues in turn. Still, none of them proved fatal; the community continued to grow despite them. These early withdrawals were regarded by many members who remained as an inevitable, even desirable part of settling down to a new way of life. They did not in themselves constitute a crisis for the community.

Gender and Participation

Who benefited from community life? Erasmus Darwin and Martha Turner Hudson withdrew from the community in September 1843 and the following summer prepared to move to West Springfield. They expected their elder son to move with them, but he refused. Instead, he applied to join the community in his own right. Young men felt benefits in the community because it gave them a measure of independence from family control that work in individual households, clerkships, or apprenticeships could not. William Adam's son Gordon, on a visit to Boston early in 1843, expressed his "unaffected contentment" with life at the

Northampton Association. He spent his mornings studying, but afterward "works hard on whatever service he is required," wrote a friend. Whether he was chopping wood, piling boards, or farming, he had companions of his own age, constant change of open-air work, and the right to attend and vote at business meetings; in short, "he feels the consciousness of his independence, and appreciates it." Significantly, though, his sisters were not so happy.[51] The benefits of community were not felt equally by both sexes.

The intention of ending inequalities between men and women was one of the Northampton community's distinctive claims. Garrisonian abolitionists insisted on the equal right of women to speak out in public, and rejected political action to end slavery in part because that would exclude women from the struggle. At the community, Samuel L. Hill recalled, using the language of male antislavery society meetings, "all were invited, including the women, to propose measures and discuss the measures proposed by others." Nathaniel P. Rogers pointedly compared the community with most churches, where women and children were bidden not to speak; here they could express their own views and be free from "the imposition and misleading generally practised upon them elsewhere."[52]

In practice women such as Frances Judd, Maria Mack, Eliza Boyce Wall, and Sojourner Truth did take part in meetings, express their views, vote, and influence community policies. Still, as a description of an autumn 1843 meeting suggests, "free" discussion favored those with most experience of such occasions, particularly men who had given antislavery lectures or participated in conventions. Community meetings could often be deferential, rather than challenging. On this occasion, the meeting started with a period of silence, "broken by a spontaneous effusion of singing." Then William Lloyd Garrison, about to depart from Northampton after a summer's stay near the community, read a passage from the New Testament and gave a valedictory speech. Again, the "impressive silence" that followed was broken by "an out-burst of vocal devotion," and the meeting then moved to resume an earlier discussion on whether the Bible authorized the sabbath and other church ordinances. William Adam argued that there was some authority in scripture, because if "all laws of duty were absolutely written within the hearts of men," there would be no social control but "mere self-will." Garrison and James Boyle argued the opposite. Other members did not get to say a word. Instead, they listened to long speeches, something they were used to from abolition meetings. Garrison's valedictory talk was "very lengthy," and his refutation of William Adam "occupied an immense proportion of the latter part of the meeting (which held near three hours)."[53] "Free discussion" did not in this case include women, the young, or the inexperienced.

The community did take some unconventional steps to recognize women's contributions. Paying the same wages or subsistence to men and women valued domestic work and family duties equally with manufacturing, farming, and other tasks. When Julia A. Wells was made director of the domestic department in 1842, she was credited with seven days' work a week instead of six, in recognition of the fact that her work never ended. To a prospective applicant the next year, David Mack wrote that all adult members volunteered to devote ten hours each day "to productive labor," including "whatever may be requisite for family cares."[54] In theory the community either abolished the hidden "double day" worked by many women in paid employment, or recognized family and domestic tasks as comparable with others.

But scholars have noted that gender equality was a difficult, often impossible, ideal for "utopian" communities to realize. Too many facets of the gendered character of nineteenth-century culture remained unaltered, not least because men found it easier to write declarations of equality than to change their own habits. When we look at women's experiences at the Northampton community, we find that there was a division, between women who clearly disliked community life and those who drew sustenance from it as a source of individual independence.

Carol A. Kolmerten's recent critique of the experience of women in the American Owenite communities of the 1820s and 1840s provides a useful point of comparison for an analysis of the Northampton community. Kolmerten argues that for married women in particular, communitarian groups were the opposite of ideal. At home, middle-class women often had servants to help them with menial tasks, and the domestic sphere was the only place in which most had any autonomy or power. In the name of "equality" communities denied married women these things and, in addition to whatever special or professional tasks they had them do, obliged them to take on menial work without assistance. Married women, Kolmerten suggests, moved to communities only unwillingly, and suffered the loss of whatever privileges and comfort individual family life had given them.[55]

The experience of several married women at Northampton confirms the points in Kolmerten's argument. Soon after the community's founding, for instance, Hall Judd's father noted the situation of William Adam's wife Phebe. It was said that when she lived in India she had had eighteen servants. Now, having reluctantly accompanied her husband to Northampton, she was living in a one-story house with only her elder daughter to help her; during their first winter the health of both mother and daughter was affected by overwork. The daughter worked so hard in the community that she was voted the privileges of an adult member, even though she was underage. William Adam recognized that women undertook severe burdens; writing early in 1843 to answer the charge that the community inadequately promoted women's rights, he noted that there was "a woman among its Directors who has perhaps more onerous duties than any other officer." He was referring to the director of the boardinghouse department.[56]

Maria Mack's story, as later recounted by her daughter, also fits Kolmerten's analysis. When she and David Mack gave up their boarding school in Cambridge to join the community in 1842 it was clearly David's decision. Maria Mack "fully appreciated her husband's high ideals, [but] she took a more practical view of actual life, and it was not without many misgivings that she acceded to his plans." Apart from anything else, she was three months pregnant when David determined that they should sell up and move. Her fears were fully realized. For three years at Northampton she faced "great hardship and discomfort," but "entered without shrinking into the severe labors required of her." Maria had started teaching as a very young woman, and both before and during her marriage had lived in households with servants to do heavy work. Now at the community she "tried. . .hard to fall into the singular life in which she had no faith." Another member recalled that she was known as "Madame Adaptration" because of this determination to get on under adverse conditions. According to her daughter, Maria Mack "nearly lost her life from doing work to which she was not accustomed." In August 1845 she and David withdrew from Northampton to take treatment at a water-cure establishment in Brattleboro, Vermont. It took eighteen months for Maria to recover from the ordeal of community life.[57]

Phebe Adam's and Maria Mack's experiences were not unique. Other couples moved to the community at the husband's behest, with women reluctantly following. Benson's cousin George Thurber and his family came to Northampton in 1842, even though "his wife says she is much attached to Boston." Just before Elisha Hammond set out to join in 1844 William Lloyd Garrison noted the gap between his enthusiasm and his wife Eliza's hesitancy. At least once, the community refused to admit a couple on the grounds that both partners should be willing to belong: "You did not write how your *wife* felt about coming here. We think it is very important that husbands and wifes agree in this matter."[58]

Many women, too, found community life unattractive. Erasmus Darwin Hudson's wife Martha Turner Hudson expressed the wish to move to a house of their own: "O how pleasant to have a little spot to live.. . .For that day I hope & pray." The *Journal of Commerce* claimed that "almost all the ladies" in the community were "unhappy and dissatisfied with their situation." Even sympathizers acknowledged that women in the boarding house "have not found. . .all the conveniences and comforts to which they had been accustomed," but claimed "ameliorations" had been made. After William Bassett had withdrawn from the community in late 1844, he explained his decision as partly influenced by "discontent on the part of my family with their situation." Several women who had joined the community while they were single seem to have agreed that marriage and utopia did not mix. On at least four of the eight occasions that women members married, they left the community at once or shortly afterward to set up their own households.[59]

Kolmerten suggests that single women were more likely to enjoy benefits from community life because it did not similarly rob them of the arena of control that wives could enjoy in individual families. The example of young, unmarried women at Brook Farm, many of whom seem to have been enthusiastic about community life, supports this argument. The letters of Elizabeth Curson, who lived at Brook Farm from 1845 until it closed in 1847 constantly expressed pleasure and contentment, and she was regarded as one of the people who "love the life here." Some single women appear to have found similar contentment at Northampton. According to Olive Gilbert, who set down her life story, Sojourner Truth "gradually became pleased with, and attached to, the place and the people." Two of the Stetson daughters enjoyed it enough to want to return to Northampton after their family had left the community. By contrast, the evidence of Elizabeth Curson's later experience seems to confirm Kolmerten's point; when she returned to community life, as a mother with three children, at the Raritan Bay Union in 1853, she found things quite different: "The associating of families," she wrote, was "very uncomfortable."[60]

The hardships of women such as Phebe Adam, Martha Hudson, and Mary Bassett did play a role in their families' decisions to leave the community. To that extent Kolmerten is correct, but her thesis rests on the assumption that married women entering communities surrendered power that they had exercised in their own families, particularly over servants who worked for them. Part of Elizabeth Curson Hoxie's discontent at Raritan Bay, in fact, was that the community there did *not* prevent wealthier families from hiring their own servants, and so women's workloads were unevenly distributed.[61] Unlike the Adams, Macks, and Bassetts, who came from middle-class urban backgrounds, most women at Northampton were from middling and poorer rural households accustomed to intermixing domestic chores and other productive tasks, cooperating with others, and not relying on servants. Many facets of community life were quite similar to what they were used to in the outside world. Women from such backgrounds lost less status than Kolmerten suggests. Moreover, a few found in the larger arena of the community an opportunity to exercise a degree of independence they could not enjoy at home.

The examples of two other married women, both from rural Connecticut, show that although Maria Mack's experience of hard work was common, her hatred of community life and need for stoic fortitude in face of it were not universal. Frances Judd married Hall Judd when she moved to the community in 1842. Fifty years later, she wrote that the final decision to join the group had been hers. That there were hardships she had no doubt; seven years after the community ended she wrote that "many sacrifices were demanded, much hard labor was required," and that there was "much of trial and discipline," and often "serious inconvenience." Yet she insisted that committed members endured these difficulties, and "much happiness was experienced." Even those "accustomed to good, spacious homes, and every facility for comfortable living"—the middle-class conditions Kolmerten referred to—"were satisfied," according to Frances Judd, "with simplicity, both in diet and dress."[62]

Similar views were expressed by Dolly Witter Stetson, from Brooklyn, Connecticut, who arrived at the community in 1843 after sixteen years of marriage and bearing eight children. She also faced severe burdens, for a while serving as cook to a large group of residents of the factory boardinghouse. But her granddaughter, who collected family memoirs of community life, found strong evidence that Dolly Witter Stetson gained advantages that outweighed the difficulties. A woman of "progressive" views, "she expected to find kindred spirits" at Northampton and apparently did. Indeed, when she returned with her children to a farm in Brooklyn after the community had foundered, she suffered a period of depression and "regretted losing the close contact with the men and women who had stimulated and enriched her life, and whose companionship had been so congenial to her." At least four single women members who married—in other words, half the total—remained in the community for a period afterward, and perhaps did not regard community and married life as incompatible as Kolmerten suggests.[63]

Judd's and Stetson's own self-portrayals, together with other memories of them, suggest that they saw themselves to a degree unusual in nineteenth-century society as independent women, though married and living with their husbands. Despite the burden of work, participation in community debates and decision-making allowed women like Judd and Stetson to practice a degree of equality with men that the wider society rarely permitted. Giles B. Stebbins never forgot the day he and Dolly Witter Stetson debated the biblical justifications for slavery. In training for the ministry, Stebbins expected to win an argument with "a person unlearned, as I supposed, in clerical lore, and that person a woman!" Instead, Stetson put him in his place, and Stebbins could not overcome the feeling of humiliation "that I, one of the lords of creation, should be made to feel so small by a woman!"[64] Frances Judd took pride in the fact that women in the community could, if they chose, vote for decisions against the wishes of their husbands. For Stetson and Judd the commitment to community life meant both the ability to take direct part in a movement for "progressive" reform and the opportunity to live in an environment that did not replicate family life, but was in certain respects superior to it. The sociability of community and the means it provided for maintaining a degree of independence from their husbands made it doubly attractive.

Their remarks about community are further clarified when we reflect on other aspects of their experience at Northampton. Judd's husband, Hall, was chronically sick, and his views about community seem to have diverged from hers. Stetson's husband, James, was often away from Northampton for long periods as the community's agent handling silk sales. These circumstances no doubt reinforced the women's commitment to community as a viable alternative to the pressures and loneliness of family life. Both Judd and Stetson had babies at the community. Young women with small children found advantages in the crowded rooms and common eating arrangements of the factory boardinghouse, where tasks could be shared and assistance easily obtained. For several widows with children too, such as Nancy Richardson and the long-term boarders Ann Paul and Caroline Colt, the community provided a viable means of securing a living and education that did not entail the entire sacrifice of independence usually demanded by residence in a relative's or employer's household.

So women were as likely to wish to remain in the community as they were to press to leave it; however, their toleration for it was finely balanced. Their experiences do confirm a facet of Kolmerten's argument, that communities rarely reevaluated men's and women's roles and obligations. Women like Stetson and Judd found a measure of independence through their own efforts, not because the community radically altered conventional gender expectations. Domestic tasks were accorded equal treatment with other work, but there were signs that men did not always trust women to get on with them unaided. From time to time men, not women, were appointed directors of the boardinghouse. In 1845 inquiries were made about the conduct of departments, and the woman in charge of sewing was asked to submit accounts of daily work done; members of the sewing department protested at the futility and waste of time involved in requiring minute record keeping and at the arrogance of suspecting that the women, who shouldered so much of the daily burden of community life, were not doing their work. Thus although some women could carve out a degree of independence for themselves, most men in the community remained blind to many realities of the life and work that was going on around them.[65]

The problem was that male leaders, including those who had done most to bring about the 1843 changes, viewed the community itself as an extension of the domestic sphere. Community documents emphasized the sanctity of marriage and the family. Like the Fourierist communities, Northampton was keen to rebut any public suspicion of sexual impropriety. Officers inquired into the "morals" of prospective applicants, and in a few cases rejected men and women who planned to move to the community in order to leave their spouses. All available evidence suggests that members practiced monogamy, as they claimed. Rumors to the contrary circulated, and some opponents confidently expected the community to be brought down by sexual scandal, but it never happened.[66] Erasmus Darwin Hudson and others pushed their thinking further, arguing that the "family relation" was the best model for community life itself. Hudson extended the conventional evangelical, bourgeois view of the family as a shelter from the competitiveness and temptations of the market, suggesting that between community members, as between members of a family, there would be harmony, pooled interests, no competition, and no cash payments.[67] But this view was gendered and sentimentalized, steeped in male concepts of the family as an ordered universe protected by paternal authority. It left no room for a vision of women's independence. One of the Northampton community's resolutions in support of Thomas P. Beach, jailed for disturbing church meetings, was that Beach's wife and children had been "deprived of their natural protector." No wonder that for many women the community was an engine of inequality and oppression, and that others struggled to turn it into an opportunity for equality and independence. One evening in 1844 a contentious vote was taken by the membership assembled in the community meeting. Both men and women voted. One woman, who had voted the opposite way from her husband, called on the secretary the next day and asked for her vote to be changed, claiming that she had misunderstood the motion that was put. Fifty years later, Frances Judd still reckoned she understood very well what had happened and wrote with scorn of women who dared not contradict their husbands.[68]

Religion, Culture, and Conflict

At the community's heart were its effort to build a nondenominational Christian society and its concern to build a way of life that would be worthy of moral individuals. Religious experience and cultural issues were therefore crucial to many members and lay behind various kinds of dissension and difficulty. Many argued that the community furthered the cause of reform by liberating its members from the spiritual trammels that pervaded the wider society and which, they knew from the abolition movement, supported the continued existence of slavery. They were attacking the ideological hegemony of existing churches, as part of a search for a new "commonsense" view of the world. The community's nonsectarianism and lack of formal religious leadership contrasted with the hostility radical abolitionists had encountered and were an integral part of its ties to the abolition movement.

For many members joining the community was a further step on a spiritual path they had already set out on when they broke with religious orthodoxy. Sunday afternoon meetings at the community emphasized the radicalism of its nondenominational, anti-ecclesiastical position. Most major denominations susceptible to religious liberalism were represented.

This variety of religious experience posed a dilemma. Members attached high value to individualism of belief and expression, yet the avowed purpose of forming a community was to promote "harmony" and "unity." "We have amongst us the greatest differences of opinions," wrote William Adam, "but. . .we desire as members only those who, notwithstanding all differences, can and will cordially co-operate with us."[69] Frederick Douglass referred to this issue in a memoir of his visit to Northampton written nearly fifty years later: "For harmony, Hopedale had a decided advantage over [Northampton], in that its leaders were of one religious faith, while [Northampton] was composed both of men and women of different denominations, and of those of no religious bias or profession."[70] Where tolerance could be maintained the problem was minimized, but a hallmark of Garrisonians was their rooted objection to association with sin, and dissension over religious issues was a constant danger.

Few members had longer or more turbulent journeys than the abolitionist lecturer James Boyle, born in French Canada to an Irish family, who had once been a Catholic seminarian, but having become a Protestant, moved progressively toward a form of radical perfectionism.[71] Boyle, who had a penchant for rooting out "Devils" wherever he found them, seems to have been a particularly uncomfortable presence among the membership, and it was said that he caused at least two men to leave the community. (Boyle's spiritual independence lasted throughout his life; unwilling to let anyone else speak for him, he even wrote the sermon for his own funeral in 1884.)[72] The pursuit of religious freedom symbolized a deeper contradiction in communitarian movements of this period, that they were group attempts to secure the maximum personal liberty for their members. Hall Judd, regarded by other members as "rigid" and "austere," according to his father, found it hard to get on in the community; had it not been for Frances, he would probably have left. As it was, he kept aloof as much as possible, regarding some members as "infidels" and even many of the professed Christians as "quite too loose for him."[73] For William Bassett, already battered by several years of religious dispute, the conflict was too much to endure, and he withdrew again to avoid it. Explaining his decision to withdraw, Bassett laid greatest stress on religious differences. The community, he wrote, "was constantly convulsed and its peace destroyed by the most violent dissensions.. . .I never met with more painful exhibitions of bigoted intolerance than among those who had there congregated to work out the problem of true social life!"[74] The principles of religious equality and toleration entailed a contradiction.

If all views were valid, but each was sincerely held as a guide to truth, then conflict was almost inevitable.

Tension developed not principally around issues of religious belief as such—where difference was formally tolerated—but over other cultural issues that members were led by their different conceptions of "sin" to interpret in conflicting ways. Though there seems to have been unanimity that no alcohol should be kept or served, and the group occasionally participated in temperance parades in the town of Northampton, there was tension over other issues of moral regulation, such as card-playing. Even sympathetic visitors like the singer John Hutchinson looked askance at young members who played games of "bat-ball" on a Sunday. Frances Judd was later to write of disagreements between a "more liberal party," who tolerated amusements, and "others, owing perhaps to early education," who regarded them as sinful and improper, particularly in view of the general poverty of the community. Allying herself with the latter camp, she regarded this conflict as one of the most serious divisions in the group.[75]

Frances Judd did not name names, but it is a fair guess that among the protagonists in the conflict she referred to were William Adam and David Mack. Evidence from several quarters points to a simmering dispute between the two men, originating in the wages debate of summer 1842 and culminating in Adam's withdrawal from the community in January 1844. Even his friends portrayed Adam as temperamental and intolerant of contradiction. Mack's character emerges less clearly from the sources, but we know that he had a strong vision of how a community could be shaped and a commitment to realizing it. But this was not simply a personality clash. It was grounded in issues of culture, education, and authority that were central to the community's purposes. Adam's withdrawal, the most significant since that of the Conant group over a year before, marked the culmination of the changes that Mack and others had supported since the community's first summer.

Undoubtedly Frances Judd would have counted the Adam family among the "more liberal party" in cultural issues. Their British and colonial background distinguished them from many of their New England colleagues. Unlike most other members, they attempted with mixed success to sustain their contacts in Boston elite society, and in fact Adam was quietly receiving a small subsidy from two Boston merchants. Early on, the Adam daughters also courted disapproval by seeking social contacts among leading Northampton families.[76] David Mack, though less stern than some of his more ascetic associates, came from rural New England roots and was no libertine. Soon after he arrived at the community, Mack proposed that formal religious instruction be included in the school curriculum. This was rejected, probably on the grounds that it could lead to the instillation of a creed, which was just what the community was trying to avoid.[77] But after that, Mack seems rarely to have been out of step with majority feeling in the community. Instead, it was Adam who grew more isolated.

The overt rivalry between the two men concerned education and culture. Adam added the directorship of education to his duties as secretary in May 1842. The Adam daughters offered music and dancing lessons as part of the curriculum, and by the following winter objections were mounting to the dancing, in particular, as "mischievous and useless." In the spring of 1843 the debate over dancing broadened into one about the school in general. Adam was regarded as too academic in his approach. He also seems to have been a formal, rather dry teacher: classes he set up in Boston after his withdrawal from the community failed, according to friends, because "they have been dull & uninteresting."[78] At least once before in his career Adam had walked out of a job when he was criticized. Now, in April 1843, he resigned as director of education because of "some dissatisfaction to his mode of teaching" and "his repugnance to being dictated to." Mack took over from him and altered the curriculum. A month later Adam told a visitor that there had been "interference with his running of the schools, in consequence of which he had withdrawn from it, and it was put under the care of another member, far less competent for the situation."[79] This dismissal of Mack's ability is the most direct evidence of antipathy between the two men. Late in 1843, Adam, perhaps hoping to turn the school back to a more congenial path, sponsored the application of a New Hampshire teacher for admission as a member. On behalf of the executive council, Mack wrote to decline: they could not "avail ourselves of a man of his qualifications," until they were "able to make complete arrangements for a classical education." Adam, resenting the implication that his tuition of pupils was not a "classical education," held the letter up and insisted that the matter be discussed at a full community meeting. But the community endorsed the executive's decision.[80] Weeks later Adam withdrew. He had not been without allies. Some parents were critical of the school's combination of learning with work and the pedagogy that emphasized pupils' exploring for themselves. Martha Turner Hudson, plagued by the unruliness of her two younger sons, regarded the school as lax and unable to instruct children in self-discipline. She considered sending one of the boys to Hopedale, where "they have a small school and well regulated[;] the children are not left to themselves one hour a day." Her views of the Northampton community school contributed to her wish to leave.[81]

In April 1843, Adam had resigned not only as director of education but also as secretary of the community. Mack succeeded to this office too. Alongside the two men's educational disputes were their differences over how the community itself should be run. In 1842, as we saw, Adam joined Benson in a defense of the rights of stockholders. Though Benson and others acquiesced in the 1843 changes, Adam unsuccessfully opposed the erosion of the power of the stockholders, and criticized "the new bad and imperfect regulations" approved by the first annual meeting. His resignation came as these were being completed, and his last act as secretary was to write a long letter to an applicant stressing his objections to the changes. In August he tried to reverse them in a document "setting forth the principles on which changes in our business arrangements should be predicated after the close of the current year," but the new constitution ignored most of his proposals for restoring stockholder control. After his withdrawal during the winter, Adam made a final effort, claiming the right to vote at a community meeting on the strength of his stockholding. The meeting resolved that he had the same right to participate as any other visitor, but firmly rejected his claim to vote as a stockholder. The community's rules precluded voting by nonmembers, and Adam's request contravened the anticapitalist spirit that Mack and the majority of members had instilled in it.[82]

Individuals and Community

By the time the 1843 constitution was adopted, Erasmus Darwin Hudson had left too, disillusioned by the tensions in the community. He and his family formally withdrew in September 1843 and left Northampton early the following summer. His writings during 1843 suggest that Hudson had two tests of a just society: did it allow for spiritual and intellectual individuality? and—a view drawn from the 1830s labor movement—did it accord workers the full product of their labor? Hudson's argument that the community should operate as a family was based on the assertion that families both sheltered their members from the marketplace and permitted them individual freedom. Like many reformers of the 1840s, Hudson was searching for a way of reconciling collective and individual interests.

For a moment, he thought that the Northampton community might have found it. He and Martha had rejoined the group in January 1843 as it shifted toward communalism, but he quickly found it hard to reconcile the practicalities of community life with his ideal expectations. By late summer he had reached the conclusion that communities made too many impositions on their members and that individuality could not be adequately sustained. His criticism of Northampton was not of the institution as such, but of the moral failing of its members in not living together harmoniously as he imagined a family should. According to an increasingly convoluted logic, under these circumstances Northampton's system of equal compensation for labor was unjust. It would have been better to pay wages after all.[83] Hudson drew a conclusion that was being reached by sections of the labor movement. Only individual family farming on freehold property sufficient for subsistence, he argued, could guarantee the shelter and equitable return that justice demanded. In 1844 he moved his family to a small farm in West Springfield. He would probably have agreed with George W. Stacy, who left the Hopedale community in 1845 and concluded that "the practical operation in all the communities of which I have any knowledge,...confirm...that they do abridge *individual freedom*, and put at variance that which ought to be harmonious." This was a path that many former communitarians would take, either into the land reform, free soil, and homestead movements or, in the case of Josiah Warren and Stephen Pearl Andrews' Modern Times, formed on Long Island in 1851, into a community based on the concept of "individual sovereignty."[84]

Yet the communitarian moment of the early 1840s was built on reformers' confidence that community and individuality were not opposites, but could best reinforce one another. Many of the men and women who remained at the Northampton community as Hudson and Adam withdrew continued to hold this view. Advocates of moral suasion, they believed that community provided a framework in which individuals would be best able to reform their own attitudes and behavior and act according to their consciences. Sojourner Truth, an individualist unafraid to express her own views, came to trust a place "where all was characterized by an equality of feeling, a liberty of thought and speech, and a largeness of soul, she could not have before met with, to the same extent, in any of her wanderings." David Mack sustained his hopes for the community throughout the changes of 1843 that he helped to bring about. In the midst of the changes "one of the influential members" told a visitor "that they were fast coming to the conviction of the inutility of any Community," but most members survived the tensions and withdrawals of that year and the next. Until the breakup in November 1846 members sustained the system of equal subsistence and a communal form of organization that might provide a stable basis for their own lives and work. It was a means by which all people, regardless of race, class, or gender might exercise their spiritual individuality and the right to speak freely against evil and injustice. In 1844 the former slave Stephen C. Rush wrote that in the search for a better future "we must turn. . .to the common pepoles," who "will come to the help of the lord against the mighty." For many, community life was an effort to put this into practice.[85]

CHAPTER FIVE

The Business of Utopia:
Output, Silk and Debt

S table and workable as the community was as a social system, it
also had to function as a business. The Northampton Association's founders, in buying the property they did and entering the
business that they did, exposed themselves to the vagaries and
hostility of the world they were seeking to reform. The silk industry and
its connections, and the terms on which they sought to enter it, posed a
considerable challenge to the community and its ideals. The economic
side of the community's story is a long tale of this battle with adversity.
The surprising thing about the struggle is not that the members finally
lost it, but that they waged it for over four years.

The Problem of Debt

The misadventures of the Northampton Silk Company had not arisen
purely from Samuel Whitmarsh's charm and plausibility, and the willingness of others to be taken in by him. Trouble also stemmed from the
difficulties of maintaining and coordinating a business of any size in the
circumstances of the late 1830s. These general difficulties were com-
pounded by the particular conditions of the infant silk industry, which
Whitmarsh had systematically persuaded himself and his partners to overlook. In order to succeed, the Northampton Association would have to
overcome both sets of problems. They needed to be free from debt, and

135

they needed a smoothly running operation to turn silkworms and their mulberry leaves into large quantities of salable silk.

As the Northampton community's founders drew up their plans in the winter of 1841–42, they were conscious of the need for sufficient operating capital to sustain a business on the scale of the Northampton Silk Company, whose property they were buying entire. They originally proposed that the association's capital should reach as high as $50,000 and that they should not commence business until $30,000 had been paid in. They also agreed, and the Preliminary Circular of February 1842 formally laid down, that they would deal only in cash, not credit. After the upheavals of the previous four years, the silk company's own difficulties, and the founders' own experiences, these precautions were understandable and prudent. Since $30,000 was the approximate cost of the property, the mill was a going concern, and the community's occupation of the land would occur as farming and lumbering began in the spring of 1842, the plan also seemed realistic: the property would be free and clear of debt, and sources of income and subsistence would quickly materialize as silk, lumber, and farm production were put in hand.[1]

Unfortunately, the $30,000 did not appear. By the time of the inaugural meeting on April 8, 1842, only about half this sum had been subscribed. There is no direct evidence of the source of these funds, but it is likely that Benson, Hill, and various others contributed the proceeds of the property sales they had made as they left their previous homes to come to Northampton. We do not know how much Joseph Conant subscribed to the stock, but the association represented his only chance of maintaining his position as superintendent of the silk mill. William Adam subscribed $2,000 or more. Other subscriptions were small. Hall Judd apparently put his $600 savings into the association. After it was established, Hiram Wells, Erasmus Darwin Hudson, and others contributed tools, implements, furniture, and other property in kind whose value they negotiated as additions to the capital stock. But none of this came anywhere close to making up the shortfall. The 1842 constitution took account of the situation and modified the proposals of the Preliminary Circular by prohibiting trade on credit only after $30,200 had been paid in.[2] The restriction would never come into force.

By the spring of 1842 the founders were in a fix. They had moved to Northampton and bought the property there, but were unable to raise the sum they had stipulated to start the community on a proper footing. Though there is no evidence of a point at which a decision was made, necessity must have led them to choose to go through with their plan despite the shortage of capital. So even at the moment the community started it was in debt to the tune of $15,487.94. Some of this was attributable to loans given by members against notes issued by the association: Benson provided $2,000, Earl Dwight Swift, Joseph Conant's son-in-law, a further $550.50. But the bulk of the debt was to the Silk Company's largest creditor, Charles N. Talbot, who was owed $9,500, and to other local company creditors such as the Whig politician Lewis Strong, owed just over $3,000. From the start, therefore, the community was unable to fulfill its founders' financial ideals.[3]

This was not all bad news. The depression had, doubtless, made the recruitment of members with substantial capital difficult, but it had also reduced property prices; for some years visitors were impressed with the information that the association had paid $30,000 for an estate and buildings in which the Northampton Silk Company had invested at least three times (some stories said four times) that sum. Very likely, this helped the founders' decision to proceed with their plans. It almost certainly helped keep the community afloat for over four years. Property perceived as undervalued was good security for loans. Perhaps, if silk and other production were to go ahead anyway, the $15,000 shortfall in capital would not much matter. Income from sales would repay the debt; meanwhile operating capital would be available on credit against the expected value of the community's lands.[4]

Again, experience seemed to suggest that these perceptions were realistic. Other communities also started in debt and, as far as anyone could yet tell, would probably survive. Brook Farm, with a smaller initial membership than Northampton, and without Northampton's prospect of earnings from manufacturing, had borrowed $11,000 on mortgages against its land after its founding in 1841, and its debt would rise to over $17,000 by 1847.[5] But the existence of a substantial debt inevitably affected any community's ability to succeed. As one sympathetic account of a visit to Northampton noted in the summer of 1843, the community's debt was preventing the building of additional accommodation. This restrained the admission of new members. The resultant shortage of farm labor, in particular, was preventing the improvement of the community's land, which was "as yet in a very poor state of cultivation."[6] Above all the conditions of the silk industry and the demands that it would make on the Northampton community's resources would make any complacent calculations irrelevant. In fact the association was embarked upon a long struggle for survival. Debt, another writer observed in an article about Northampton in 1845, was "a phantom-guest which has been present at the feasts of all advocates of community reform."[7] To help understand why early hopes were not fulfilled, it is necessary to look more closely, first at the community's general economic activities, then at the process of silk making and the circumstances of the New England silk industry in the early 1840s.

Market and Autarchy

Like the rural households and localities from which many members came, the Northampton community sought from the start to achieve a balance between reliance on outside purchases and sales of goods in the marketplace and its ability to raise and manufacture certain necessities for members' own use. Practical circumstances and ideals both led to this effort at balance. There was insufficient cultivated land for members to expect to raise their own subsistence, and the silk mill seemed to provide a promise of substantial earnings from manufacturing. At the same time, there was a growing community of men and women whose different skills could be put to productive use, and excessive reliance on the outside market, with its price fluctuations and middlemen, might be curbed. A community based on mixed activities could prove an effective model for a society based on justice and equality.

As the founders were preparing to set up the community early in 1842, they arranged with a small Northampton grocery and drygoods dealer that they would "barter with each other," swapping community products for needed articles. In practice, commercial links were much more widespread than this local arrangement envisaged. Abolitionist connections, in particular, helped provide supplies of oil, candles, and other goods from Nantucket, wheat and flour from New York State, and other imported products from friendly merchants in eastern Massachusetts and Rhode Island. Soon after the founding, a community store with Hall Judd in charge was established to distribute groceries and other goods to members. Since neighbors also started to use the store, it was rapidly announced that members would receive a ten-percent discount on the price of store goods. As numbers expanded, of course, subsistence needs grew. The community tried whenever possible to exchange boards, wood, farm produce, and sewing silk in exchange for its store supplies, and so conserve cash; but by June 1843, when there were over one hundred residents and the season's crops were yet to be harvested, it was reported that one hundred dollars a week in cash was being expended to feed and clothe them. Work was directed toward earning or reducing this sum.[8]

The varied and generally low level of working capital meant that success in doing so was slow to come. Much of the first summer was devoted to preparing for different kinds of production. The silk mill, already in working order, with six or so hired women workers to operate it and Earl Dwight Swift in charge, resumed production in May 1842. Members probably assumed that it would be a significant and stable source of income. For reasons shortly to be examined more fully, and because Swift, Conant and Orwell S. Chaffee withdrew from the association after the end of its first summer, these early hopes proved overoptimistic. For the time being other activities had to bear much of the burden of earning income for the community's needs.

The first and most important activity, apart from silk, was lumbering. The community owned a sawmill and shingle mill, as well as a substantial amount of woodland, some of which needed to be cleared for farming. Large areas of woodland in the Northampton region were stripped of their lumber in the early to mid 1840s as local demand for firewood and building materials expanded. The Northampton Association shared in this bonanza. By early 1843, lumber was its main source of income, and during the next few years a new sawmill and machinery were installed to maintain and diversify its production. As a strategy for earning income, however, this could only at best have served for a few years because the community's own woodlands, and those of local customers at the sawmill, were soon depleted.[9]

Already in 1842 efforts were in hand to diversify community production further. Hiram Wells, the blacksmith, with Samuel L. Hill and others to help him, brought a small machine shop and foundry into operation by the autumn and prepared to manufacture cutlery, in addition to metal goods needed in the community. That November Wells was authorized to purchase iron and other materials for this purpose, but shortage of capital meant that he was at first restricted to spending only $125. The following summer approval was given for production of sixty dozen knives. Again, this earned needed income, but the level of output was always constrained, on one hand by the community's inability to purchase larger quantities of raw material, and on the other by calls on the blacksmiths' time to repair machinery and other equipment around the site.[10]

After the first few weeks, decisions about diversification were shaped by an effort to limit the community's need to make outside purchases. A community bakery was started, though efforts to induce the hired baker to become a community member, and so save a regular outlay on wages, were at first unsuccessful. After the first baker left, his successor did accept the offer to "live as a member," but proved unable to bake good bread and was eventually asked to leave. Boot and shoe making was also established. The domestic department organized sewing and other activities essential for making and mending clothes. In 1843 a tannery was proposed, to supply three types of material that would otherwise have to be purchased: shoeleather, harnesses, and drive belts for the factory and sawmill. Carpenters and other skilled workers were sought as members, all to reduce the need to pay for work from outside the community. Above all, farming was begun in the spring of 1842 under the direction of Theodore Scarborough, with cattle and sheep to provide milk and wool, and pigs for the community's meat eaters. Horticulture was encouraged, and periodic inquiries made about types of vegetable and fruit to be raised, though it is probable that most gardening was done by individual families to supplement their community-provided rations.[11]

Its range of activities undoubtedly helped the community achieve a degree of self-sufficiency. Lumber products, carpentry, shoes, farm and garden produce, metalwork, and machinery were available from within, and these could be also be traded locally for other goods. But they were insufficient to obviate the need for cash to buy grain, groceries, and other provisions. Income to pay for these depended to a large extent on the success of the community's plans for silk production.

Silk and Utopia

Silk had a peculiar affinity with utopian visions in the United States. It had a fascination in the eighteenth and nineteenth centuries that is now often forgotten and that is not readily explained. An ancient product of Asia, long associated with exotic trade routes and luxury consumption, silk had been established for some centuries in southern Europe—particularly Italy—and became an industrial product of parts of France, the

Low Countries, England, and Germany between the seventeenth and nineteenth centuries. Its resonance for republican America derived partly from these associations, reinforced by the late-eighteenth-century expansion in Boston and New York trade with Asia, which brought silk goods and imports of raw silk directly to U.S. ports. Schemes for colonies devoted to silk raising had been common in the eighteenth century, and the tradition continued far into the nineteenth. Members of George Rapp's Harmony Society produced silk, and groups such as the Oneida community and land-settlement schemes on the Kansas prairie maintained some silk production after the Civil War. The large-scale factory-based silk industry that grew up in Paterson, New Jersey, South Manchester, Connecticut and other centers (including Northampton) from the late 1840s on relied almost entirely on imported raw silk. But this industry had roots in earlier efforts to combine local silk raising (the feeding of silkworms and production of raw silk from their cocoons) and silk manufacture (the twisting, spinning or weaving of thread and other products). Hopes for an independent domestic silk industry reached a climax in the economic crisis of the late 1830s and were steeped in wider assumptions about work, childhood, gender and society.[12]

Compared with its status among urban elites, silk's associations in rural New England were less exotic, even a little mundane. Though its luxurious character had caused the use of silk to be discouraged during the Revolutionary war, the notion of promoting home-produced silk fitted well with patriotic visions of a thriving domestic industry. Ezra Stiles (1727–95), president of Yale, was said to have sent samples of mulberry seed to the minister of each town in Connecticut to encourage the cultivation of mulberry trees to feed silkworms. Within fifteen years, Stiles claimed, America might have a silk culture worth one million dollars a year, "without interfering with the other Labors of agriculture." Visions such as Stiles's not only helped establish silk production in a few localities, particularly in and around the town of Mansfield, Connecticut, but marked out its cultural and social significance. Until the community was set up, developments in silk raising around Northampton mainly followed Congregational and evangelical channels. In the 1830s and 1840s the local physician Daniel Stebbins corresponded about silk with missionaries to China and the Near East, and solicited small consignments of Asian mulberry seed for trials.[13]

Views about silk production were influenced by perceptions of silkworms themselves, which like some other animals, furnished an array of analogies for ideas about politics and society. For instance, Ann Fairfax Withington has shown how American republican writers and illustrators selectively employed images of bees and beehives, turning an eighteenth-century English focus on the beehive as a symbol of social hierarchy and order into a nineteenth-century republican emphasis on bees as industrious workers and citizens. Silkworms never appeared as frequently as bees in speech or iconography, and were at best ambiguous characters. Compared with upright, active, hard-working bees, that performed necessary services for fellow creatures, silkworms appeared to wallow in idleness and moral degradation. Once they had hatched from their eggs they just lay around waiting to be fed. Their appetites were gargantuan and they rapidly grew fat, symbolizing the ills of excessive consumption. They also stank. Applied to humans, the term "silkworm" implied reliance on unearned wealth and the moral decadence of idle luxury. Nevertheless, silkworms had redeeming qualities. Though they seemed fat and lazy, reflection showed that they in fact worked hard to produce the thousands of feet of filament in which they cocooned themselves, silk filament that human labor and ingenuity could turn into useful products.[14]

Most important for many nineteenth-century New Englanders, the uses of manufactured silk were potentially as varied as the exotic goods that came from Asia. There was significant demand for the silk thread, ribbons, tassels, and other accessories that became common staples of peddlers' packs, general stores, and drygoods dealers across America. The most common rural product was the most basic, sewing silk, and it was to expand the output of sewing silk that most of the schemes with which we shall be concerned were initially devoted. In the New England context the silkworm's association with sluggish consumption was transformed into an opportunity for useful production; Asian exoticism became republican simplicity. American-produced sewing silk would promote the domestic virtues, easing the production and maintenance of clothing, and reducing dependence on foreign imports.

Visions of an American silk industry were heavily loaded with assumptions about family, gender, and domestic authority. Across New England silk raising was presented as an activity that would fit in with and help sustain the system of household production that still predominated in the countryside but was undergoing important changes. At the peak of enthusiasm for silk in the 1830s its promoters, who were invariably men, tempted farmers with a patriarchal vision of its place on their farms, in their families' work, and in their plans for the future. Mulberries could be planted on little-used land, laid out in pleasant avenues or glades for aesthetic effect and by raising the value of land provide, according to one manual, "a rich legacy for your children." Most of the work of collecting mulberry leaves, chopping them, and feeding them to silkworms could be done by women and children. Reeling silk, a promoter wrote, was "a fireside occupation." Money earned from raw silk could pay for a child's education. A silk manufacturer later recalled of this period that "the labor required was light, as the processes were simple and invariably successful, and women and children performed all the work, except during the sixth or last week of the life of the worms, when the men usually gave assistance." In this male-centered view, silk production could improve the farm's appearance and keep women and children usefully occupied without much interfering with men's activities.[15]

Obviously, the hopes of the founders of the Northampton community for silk raising and manufacture were rooted in practical considerations: several of them were experienced silk manufacturers, and they had bought a functioning silk factory, with acres of mulberries for feeding worms. But wider ideological assumptions about silk also suited the community's circumstances. Its group of families, with men, women, and children cooperating at work, could reproduce on a larger scale the household labor system typical of silk raising in Mansfield and other towns, integrate it with the factory production of silk goods, and so avoid the social divisions that were growing up between farms and factories in New England. To abolitionists, silk had a further virtue. Though not a substitute for textiles made from slave-grown cotton, it was a "free" product, made without reliance on slavery, comparable with David Lee Child's attempts to promote sugar beet cultivation, or the hope that land reform in British India would lead to a new source of raw cotton to undercut the South. The most optimistic projectors of the silk industry could envisage its future role in a Northern industrial economy freed from dependence on the products of slavery. Moreover, a cocoonery full of silkworms would provide an "object lesson" of the exact points the Northampton Association was trying to make to society at large: as they spun their cocoons, the worms worked hard to produce something useful, and—unlike the worker bees, who served other bees who did nothing—silkworms were equal and classless. They demonstrated, in other words, that a community of equals could be industrious and productive.

The Stages of Silk Production

In theory the steps involved in producing silk were fairly straightforward, a point publicists insinuated to their male readers when they observed that much of the work could be left to women and children. Silkworm eggs were first set out in a frame, to hatch a week or ten days after being laid. The hatched worms were then moved to feeding trays in a cocoonery. Here, regularly fed with mulberry leaf, they grew for about four to six weeks. There followed a three-day period in which the worms retired to spin their cocoons, each of which consisted of a silk filament between 1,500 and 3,000 feet long. At this point a portion was retained for breeding, and their cocoons were suspended in a dry place for seven to ten days until they hatched as moths. Males and females were placed together for several hours to mate, the females were then left to lay their eggs, and the cycle began again. The majority of cocoons, meanwhile, were sent for reeling, either by the silk-raiser or at a specialist manufacturer. After immersion in boiling water, the thread from each cocoon was drawn out and wound onto a reel, either by hand- or machine-power. Subsequently, in a process known as throwing (conducted by a throwster), the individual filaments of reeled silk were twisted together to form raw silk. Raw silk, often shipped in bales of up to 150 pounds, formed the material for the final stages of manufacture. Thrown again, doubled, twisted, and dyed to different specifications, the raw silk could be turned into sewing silk, thread, floss, tassels or other ornamental material, or prepared as warp and filling (woof) for weaving into ribbon, tape, or silk cloth. As with other textiles, a specialist vocabulary had evolved in the silk industry to denote different kinds and qualities of finished and part-finished goods. "Sewings " were sewing silk; "tram" was coarse silk yarn spun for use as filling (woof) in woven fabrics; "organzine," the finer-spun yarn produced for use as warp.[16]

A brief outline scarcely begins, however, to convey the scale or character of the processes involved. As American interest in silk grew after the mid-1820s, enthusiasts for silk raising generated a vast literature on the subject, which provided calculations about the quantities of mulberry trees, leaves, and silkworms required for a given output of raw silk. As a guide to the realities of silk raising and manufacture, however, this material must be used with extreme caution. Estimates of yields and output varied considerably, and were frequently contradictory, not least because they were usually deployed to promote the sale of mulberry seed, plantings, silkworms, or cocoons to potential producers. A historical survey of the silk industry prepared for the federal manufacturing census of 1880 commented of this literature that "its errors lie all in a single direction. The silk production in past years is often overstated; the probable yield from trees, eggs, and cocoons is often underestimated; plentiful profits are calculated; but the mistake of understating is nowhere made."[17]

There is no reason to assume that unpublished accounts were any more reliable, but a letter from Daniel Stebbins to a missionary leaving for Asia Minor in 1842 does at least provide an insight into the experience of a Northampton silk grower at the time of the community's founding. Stebbins, who had twelve acres planted with trees, was one of the largest growers of mulberry in town, after the Northampton Silk Company estate itself. He stated that the leaves from his trees could feed worms sufficient for a "large bale" of raw silk; at 150 pounds per bale, that would suggest an output of 12.5 pounds of silk per acre of mulberry. At once we get a sense of the scale of the operation. Mulberry trees occupying an acre, a substantial parcel of land, were required to produce a quantity of raw silk light enough to be lifted by a child. Stebbins's calculations concerning the steps that lay between preparing the land and dispatching the silk further indicate the nature of the process. Even taking the lowest bound of each of his statistics, the numbers are mind-boggling. Each acre, he wrote, was planted with five to ten thousand mulberry plants. At a minimum of half a pound of foliage per tree, and at one ounce of leaf fed to each worm, this implied that each acre's trees would feed 40,000 or more worms. Allowing for mortality among the worms, this would provide about thirteen bushels of cocoons, at 3,000 cocoons to the bushel. Each bushel, which Stebbins estimated weighed ten pounds, would produce about 4.5 million feet of silk filament, sufficient to produce just one pound of raw silk.[18]

It only takes a moment's reflection on these brief summaries of the scale of silk raising and the steps it entailed to see that it was a complex and delicate process. That alone would begin to shed a cooler light on the optimistic fantasies that its promoters held about silk production. Even Stebbins's granddaughter remarked that "my grandfather did not seem as anxious to keep records of the failure of the silk culture as of the first successes." Closer examination of the actual practices of silk raising reveals that it was even more risky, sensitive, and demanding of careful organization and effort than an outline summary can suggest. The substantial periodical and pamphlet literature of the 1830s grew up not just

because promoters were seeking to push farmers and others into silk production, but because the different steps in the process were subject to so
much variability that there was ample scope for contradictory advice about
how to succeed. Different promoters advocated different methods.
Though their advice was often couched in systematic terms, and was
sometimes supported by sets of solid-looking statistics, it is evident that
the process was so delicate that everyone was really in a fog about how
to conduct it. The fact that raw silk was produced in any quantity at all
can be attributed to stubbornness, effort, and a considerable amount of
luck.

The producers with the greatest experience were those from the Mansfield area of Connecticut, where silk raising was well established and
conducted largely on a household basis. Data collected for a report to the
state of Connecticut in 1827 suggest that production in Mansfield was
widespread, but quantities varied considerably from household to household. Some families only grew mulberries, supplying leaves to neighbors
who fed silkworms. A still-smaller number reeled silk, from cocoons
raised by themselves and their neighbors. Factory production of reeled
silk was merely an extension of the household system. The average output
of raw silk from Mansfield producers was just over ten pounds; the range
was from two pounds by household producers up to 176 pounds by one
of the town's small silk mills. A multitude of factors determined this
variability in output: the place of silk raising in a household's pattern of
work; soil and weather; the type of mulberry tree; the type of silkworm;
the construction and location of the cocoonery; the care with which feeding was conducted; the death rate among silkworms; and the skill and
equipment used for reeling and throwing filament into raw silk. There
seem to have been as many opinions as to how best to go about the process
as there were people involved in it. A Connecticut manufacturer recalled
of this period that "ignorance of the business . . . frequently made them
the dupes of unwise experiment."[19] Responses to a questionnaire distributed in 1842–43 by the American Silk Institute suggest that even producers with extensive factory experience worked mainly from habit,
personal preference, and guesswork. Joseph Conant, after more than a
dozen years' silk making in Mansfield and Northampton, reported that
he found certain mulberries, certain silkworms, and certain methods to
be best, but since he kept no statistics on the process, could neither prove
nor explain why this should be so. Of the Northampton responses to
the questionnaire the most systematic-seeming was that of William

Adam, on behalf of the Northampton community—but he was the man with the least experience of all.[20]

Few if any nineteenth-century industrial processes relied as much as silk raising on so many poorly understood and unpredictable natural conditions. There were endless debates about the relative merits and suitability of different species of mulberry, debates often more informed by interest in bidding up the price of plants than by observation of their characteristics. Until the 1830s much New England silk raising had used the leaves of a native variety, the white mulberry (*morus alba*). During this decade, excitement and financial speculation focused on new species, particularly the so-called Chinese mulberry (*morus multicaulis*), mentioned by pioneer writers on silk raising such as Jonathan H. Cobb of Dedham, whose manual on mulberries was printed by order of the Massachusetts legislature in 1831. *Morus multicaulis* attracted attention because its leaves grew quickly and, it was claimed by some, could provide two crops of leaf a year. It was widely planted and boosted; one of its foremost promoters was Samuel Whitmarsh of the Northampton Silk Company. Some experienced silk raisers, however, remained skeptical; one writer recalled it as an inferior variety, "absurdly over-rated," that "brought loss and disgrace on the entire silk industry."[21] At times in the late 1830s speculation in *morus multicaulis* reached such a pitch that seeds, plants, and trees changed hands without reference to the needs of silk production at all; in many cases manufacturers in areas well-planted with mulberry were unable to obtain sufficient leaves to feed silkworms because the trees were being raised for seed. Success at hatching and feeding worms depended on the type of worm (again a subject of protracted debate); the moistness, airiness, and shadiness of the cocoonery; the size, freshness, and moistness of the leaves; the degree to which the leaves had been chopped preparatory to feeding; the timing of feeding in relation to the worms' life cycle; and the skill of the feeders at keeping worms clean and regularly provided for. Since these conditions partly depended on the weather, and partly on the spread of or resistance to disease among the worms, and since the weather affected both the growth and quality of leaves and the behavior of the worms, silk raisers were faced with an imponderable collection of variables, whose connections they could not divine and over which they had virtually no control. Accordingly, further debate focused on the suitability of New England for silk raising in the first place. Critics suggested that soil and climate were unfavorable to the cultivation of the most suitable mulberry leaves, and that the climate made hatching and feeding worms too uncertain. That much was clear, but there was little agreement whether this was because the climate was too hot, too cold, too dry, or too wet.

Silk raisers faced considerable practical difficulties as they sought to hatch the eggs, feed the worms, and reel silk from cocoons. Sometimes the eggs did not hatch at all, or did so only in small numbers. Once worms were hatched and laid out on shelves for feeding, they needed careful tending. Overfeeding could lead to accumulated dirt, smothering, or disease; underfeeding would arrest growth or cause starvation. The worms' growing cycle varied from species to species. One type that required feeding for thirty days, for example, shed their skins four times during the period, usually on the fourth, seventh, twelfth, and seventeenth days after hatching, but these intervals could vary and needed to be watched for, because feeding had to cease during molting. After each molt, the husks of the old skins had to be cleared away. As worms grew, their need for food grew as well, and sharply. The worms also needed more space as they grew, so they periodically had to be spread out on their shelves. In even a small cocoonery all this had to be done for tens of thousands of worms. Death rates among worms seem to have been high. Stebbins claimed in 1842 that only 2 to 5 percent of New England worms died during feeding, compared with 33 percent in Europe, but this was almost certainly a large underestimate. In China and Japan, where silk had been raised for many centuries, households devoted intense care and attention to raising and feeding silkworms during the six-week progression from egg to cocoon; loud and profane talk was prohibited, and silkworm gods worshiped to aid the delicate process. American promoters by no means ignored the complexities of the process but some, not least Whitmarsh, asserted that enterprising Americans could afford to cut out fancy "foreign" elaborations. The result was a certain amount of confusion; Whitmarsh wrote, for instance, that feeding worms was simple and could largely be left to children. At critical stages, though, regular feeding was required day and night. He never explained how children could be expected to accomplish this.[22]

The need for care and skill was, if anything, even greater after worms had been fed, spun their cocoons, and were ready for the reeler. Care had to be taken to check each one, to see that there were no signs of damage or disease that could affect the eventual quality of the raw silk. This, in turn, also depended on the skill and equipment used in reeling. Some European producers reeled silk several times; Cobb argued that it could be done by one person. The ideal was a reeled filament of consistent quality, and this was hard to achieve. Most silk manufacturers came to the conclusion that household-reeled silk was rarely of a quality suitable for further processing by machinery. At the manufacturing stage, too, much depended on the skill used in doubling and throwing, particularly in the throwster's ability to obtain a consistent thickness and strength of thread.[23]

Silk Raising and Manufacture at the Community

The point of all this is that the confidence of the Northampton community that it could support itself from silk production was not founded on certainty. That silk raising was successfully carried out in New England, and would be at the community, was not because of the ease of the process, as promoters tended to imply, but in spite of considerable difficulties. The ability of the community to pay its way would depend on success at four different stages of the production and sale of finished silk products: raising or purchasing cocoons; producing or purchasing raw silk; dyeing and manufacturing sewing silk—the main product; and selling it in a competitive market.

The first stage found the community relatively well prepared. The existing mulberry trees, the experience of the Conant group and the labor of the children of community members all contributed to early success at raising cocoons. The existing equipment, the availability of a number of women workers who had been employed by the old silk company as reelers and spinners, and the experience of Conant and his sons-in-law contributed to the production of raw silk. Between them, Conant, Chaffee, and Swift also had sufficient skill at throwing and dyeing to produce good-quality sewing silk. From its inception, the community drew attention for the fineness of its products; it won several prizes at local agricultural fairs, and honorable mentions in national competitions for silk goods. The potential ability to operate successfully and profitably was not in doubt. Early results seemed encouraging. There was considerable production in 1842 and it was later claimed that this first season's work "cleared sixty percent" of the capital invested in silk operations, though this sum included state bounties collected on cocoons and raw silk.[24]

Still, circumstances made the realization of this potential more difficult than it might have been. Only about five of the community's thirty acres

THE SILK WORM.

A SYNOPTICAL TABLE, *Showing the rapid rearing according to the method of* M. Camille Beauvais, *and the process of Ventilation of* M. Darcet.
BY M. BRUNET DE LAGRANGE, PUPIL OF M. BEAUVAIS.

Day of Rearing	Age of the Worms	Progress of the Worms	Thermometer Fahrenheit	Hygrometer Saussure	Number of Feedings	Weight of leaves consumed in 24 hours (Pounds)	Space occupied by the worms (Sq. ft.)	No. of persons employed	Daily Attentions
1st,	1st day, 1st age		86	From 70 to 85	24	(a) 1	2	1	The worms are taken from the hatching room to the Cocoonery.
2d,	2d.........do.		84	do.	24	(b) 2	2	1	Cleaning and separating by means of nets with meshes, 1 of an inch square. (c)
3d,	3d.........do.		82	do.	24	(b) 4	2	1	
4th,	4th.........do.		79	do.	24	(d) 1	10	1	
5th,	1st day, 2d age		77	do.	18	(e) 8	10	1	Cleaning.
6th,	2d.........do.		77	do.	18	11	10	1	Cleaning.
7th,	3d.........do.		77	do.	18	1	20	1	Cleaning.
8th,	1st day, 3d age		77	do.	12	7	20	1	Cleaning and separating.
9th,	2d.........do.		77	do.	12	15	20	1	Cleaning and separating.
10th,	3d.........do.		77	do.	12	40	20	1	Cleaning.
11th,	4th.........do.		77	do.	12	30	20	1	Cleaning.
12th,	5th.........do.		77	do.	12	3	50	1	Cleaning.
13 th	1st day, 4th age		77	do.	12	(f) 40	50	1	Cleaning.
14 th	2d.........do		77	do.	12	65	50	1	Cleaning.
15 th	3d.........do		77	do.	12	100	50	1	Cleaning and separating.
16 th	4th.........do		77	do.	12	67	50	1	Cleaning and separating.
17 th	5th.........do		77	do.	12	5	120	1	Cleaning and separating.
18 th	1st d., 5th age		77	do.	8	(g) 70	120	2	Cleaning.
19 th	2d.........do		77	do.	8	130	120	2	Cleaning.
20 th	3d.........do		77	do.	8	200	120	2	Cleaning and separating.
21st	4th.........do		77	do.	8	340	120	2	Cleaning.

Stages in the growth of the silkworm. From *The Silk Culture in the United States* (New York: Greeley and McElrath, 1844). Courtesy, American Antiquarian Society.

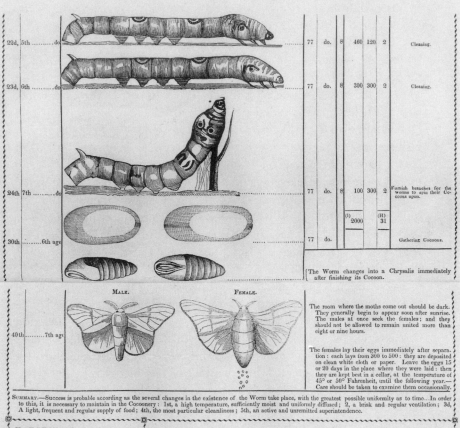

22d, 5th ....do		77	do.	8	460	120	2	Cleaning.
23d, 6th ....do		77	do.	8	300	300	2	Cleaning.
24th 7th ....do		77	do.	8	100	300	2	Furnish branches for the worms to spin their Cocoons upon.
					(1) 2000	(H) 31	
30th ....6th age		77	do.					Gathering Cocoons.

The Worm changes into a Chrysalis immediately after finishing its Cocoon.

MALE.   FEMALE.

40th ....7th age

The room where the moths come out should be dark. They generally begin to appear soon after sunrise. The males at once seek the females; and they should not be allowed to remain united more than eight or nine hours.

The females lay their eggs immediately after separation: each lays from 300 to 500: they are deposited on clean white cloth or paper. Leave the eggs 15 or 20 days in the place where they were laid: then they are kept best in a cellar, at the temperature of 45° or 50° Fahrenheit, until the following year.—Care should be taken to examine them occasionally.

SUMMARY.—Success is probable according as the several changes in the existence of the Worm take place, with the greatest possible uniformity as to time...In order to this, it is necessary to maintain in the Cocoonery: 1st, a high temperature, sufficiently moist and uniformly diffused; 2, a brisk and regular ventilation; 3d, A light, frequent and regular supply of food; 4th, the most particular cleanliness; 5th, an active and unremitted superintendence.

HATCHING...In a heated room or stove.

First Day............70 to 72° F...

Second Day ....75°...

Third Day...................77°...

Fourth Day ....79°...

Fifth Day ....82°...

Sixth Day....................84°...

Seventh Day...HATCHED..86°...

OBSERVATIONS.

(a) During the first three ages the leaves should be cut very fine; and much time would be saved, and the distribution be more equal, by using, instead of the hand, wire sieves, with meshes about three-quarters of an inch square.

(b) Between the Moultings there is always an increased appetite, called during the first four ages Little Confidence, in the fifth age Great Confidence.

(c) The Cleaning consists in removing the litter from under the Worms, and spreading them so as to leave a space between them equal to their own size. During the last ages the worms on one hurdle are put on two.

(d) At the approach of each change or moulting, the worms raise and toss about their heads, and their appetite diminishes: it is not necessary to supply leaves except to those which are not quiet; and when all are at rest the supply may cease entirely.

(e) After moulting or the change, increase gradually the quantity of nourishment in proportion to the appetite of the worms.

(f) During the fourth age the leaves are to be cut, but less fine than before.

(g) At the fifth age cease cutting the leaves.

(H) The number of days' work does not augment in proportion to the number of ounces of eggs; because for ½ oz. 200 days are sufficient, and 1100 days for 100 oz.

(1) In 1837, M. Beauvais obtained 125 lbs. of Cocoons from 2000 lbs. of leaves, (1800 kil) not assorted.

The worms are known to be preparing to spin their Cocoons by the following signs: 1st. They discharge all the excrementitious matter contained in them... 2d. Their skins, and especially their feet, become transparent, and of the color of the Cocoon they are to spin... 3d. They wander about on the leaves without eating, and try to climb upon every thing they meet with, dragging after them slimy threads of Silk.

Each worm requires but three days to wind its Cocoon; but it is not well to remove them until six or eight days, so that the worms which mount latest may have 72 hours, at least, to wind. The best formed Cocoons should be chosen to produce eggs—(one pound of Cocoons will produce an ounce of eggs)—the rest place on hurdles until the suffocation of the Chrysalis, which should take place as soon as possible.

of mulberries were brought under cultivation at first. The departure of Whitmarsh from the Northampton Silk Company had deprived it of the use of a large cocoonery, and the community did not complete a new one, one hundred feet long by twenty five wide, until the spring of 1843. Worse, the withdrawal of the Conant group in the autumn of 1842 to set up their own smaller silk factory nearby deprived the community of some of its most experienced workers. Other leaders of the community had much less, if any, experience of silk production before coming to Northampton: Hiram Wells may have had some knowledge of it, but Hill had been in cotton, and Benson's direct experience was limited to having had mulberry trees on his Brooklyn farm. Adam, Mack, Judd, and most of the others had no relevant background. Almost certainly the departure of the Conant group forced the remaining community members to learn for themselves skills that they had not previously needed.

When the printer James D. Atkins arrived from Cambridge to join the community in late September 1842, he was persuaded to take instruction in silk-dyeing from a skilled dyer hired locally for the purpose, and seems to have learned his new trade successfully. During the first half of 1843, five community members and six hired women handled sewing-silk production, with occasional help from other members. But their direction was assumed by Enos L. Preston, a machinist from Brooklyn, Connecticut, whose skill did not match that of his predecessors. Manufacture, for instance, inevitably entailed some wastage of raw material. In 1842, this amounted to 0.8 percent of the raw silk used. Under Preston the proportion was 6.7 percent. After an inquiry in June 1843, Preston resigned his post, and the next month he and his family withdrew from the community altogether. Such difficulties hindered production and the earnings the community needed. Profits from silk manufacture in the first half of 1843 were found to be little more than one hundred dollars, less than one quarter of the interest accrued on the community's debt in the same period. That the community claimed returns on silk equivalent to 37 percent of capital invested "over the first two seasons" may also reflect the decline in its success in 1843 compared with the previous year."[25]

Added to this problem with manufacturing was another difficulty. Even if fully exploited, the community's own thirty acres of mulberry trees could only feed worms enough for about two and a half bales of silk. Annual output needed to be at least double that to make most efficient use of the factory and to earn sufficient income to pay off debts. One solution would have been to buy mulberry leaves from local farmers, and this may have happened, but it is doubtful whether these were available in sufficient quantity to cover the gap. Indeed, even if they had been, the community's cocoonery was probably not large enough to feed the required number of worms. Like the Northampton Silk Company before it, the community had to rely on buying cocoons or raw silk from other suppliers.

Buying cocoons might have posed few problems, but the end of mulberry speculation and the plowing-up of many mulberry trees almost certainly made local and regional supplies less certain than they had been in the 1830s. It was necessary to buy raw silk to make up the quantity, and here difficulty did arise. Raw silk for processing by machine needed to be uniform. Household-produced raw silk came in small quantities, packed in various ways, and was of uneven and uncertain quality. Whereas Mansfield, Connecticut, manufacturers had access to dozens of local household suppliers, those in the Northampton area were scarcer, geographically scattered, and less experienced. Community correspondence was punctuated by complaints to small suppliers about the unsuitability of their silk for the factory's machines. Community mechanics, led by Oliver D. Paine, worked constantly to modify or develop reeling and doubling equipment to handle different qualities of silk, and the variability also caused difficulties in dyeing and finishing. As early as 1842, in response to the American Silk Institute's questionnaire, William Adam wrote an impassioned critique of the practice of reeling silk in families and sought to insist that the community only buy cocoons, not raw silk, from local suppliers. This never proved possible. Cocoons from the community's own supply or other local suppliers were never plentiful enough to permit the community to stop purchasing raw silk; consequently the factory had to be prepared to handle material of varying quality.[26]

There was also difficulty finding markets for sewing silk and other products. An agent working on commission was appointed in the summer of 1842, but the objections of the members to paying commissions soon ended this arrangement. Considerable reliance was placed on local sales and on the abolitionist network to find customers. The *Liberator* and the local papers carried notices of the community's silk, and commended its high quality. The Northampton merchant Elijah Powers took silk in part-payment for goods he supplied to the community store. During the fall of 1842, Benson's Brooklyn neighbor James A. Stetson was paid a small wage and expenses to peddle community silk in northern New England, and the following year quantities were supplied to a Boston abolitionist. When Benson, Hudson, and others set out on abolitionist business or lecture tours, they carried community silk with them to sell, though with only modest success. David Mack, traveling in eastern Massachusetts in the summer of 1842, sold sixty dollars' worth of silk in ten days, but found "business very dull and the season between hay and grass for selling silk." A year later in New Hampshire Hudson noted that peddlers working for other silk manufacturers were active and there had not been much interest in his goods. When the Conant group brought its own mill into production in 1843, there was also local competition for the community's silk in these regional markets. Contacts with Garrisonian abolitionists in New York State and Ohio led to efforts to sell consignments of silk there; on at least one occasion cocoons were sent from Ohio in exchange. But such contacts could only provide intermittent and uncertain outlets. Above all, it was hard to gauge at such distance exactly what was in demand and to produce goods that satisfied the customers' wants.[27]

The nature of silk dyeing and throwing made it preferable to produce standard articles in a small range of standard colors. To ensure quantity sales, it was plain that access to a larger market was desirable. Already in 1842 efforts were made to sell silk through the community's connection with its mortgage-holder Charles N. Talbot in New York, but Talbot's firm was primarily a silk importer and may not have been the best channel for selling domestically produced goods. Connections with other New York commission houses were sought in 1843, but the decision was then made to focus on Boston as a market. James A. Stetson, who had moved with his family to the community early in 1843, was persuaded to go to Boston to set up the community's own agency there to sell silk. This strategy remained in place for nearly three years and appears to have been at least moderately successful.[28]

The task of producing marketable sewing silk in quantity from diverse and intermittent supplies of raw material was a daunting challenge to the community's silk manufacturing department, which had to be able to prepare goods from both raw silk and cocoons, and so have skills and machinery available for a greater variety of tasks than needed to be done at any one time. Some work was done to develop and acquire new machinery to meet the factory's needs. After the difficulties of early 1843, production increased again. By late that year, there were three men, eight "girls" (three hired, the rest community women), and three youths engaged in processing and dyeing silk, making the community's operation slightly larger than the Conant group's new mill nearby. Manufacture in 1844 and 1845 appears to have been conducted relatively smoothly in light of the inherent difficulties it entailed; however, this demanded further investment. As Samuel L. Hill recalled much later, the community's capital requirements, originally projected at $50,000, rose to an estimated $75,000 or even $100,000. The inability to raise this, and the need to pay off what were in any case rising debts from operating expenses, inhibited the factory's development and made it unlikely that it would fulfill its potential as an income-earner for the community.[29]

A Crisis, and a Shift in Strategy

By early 1844, after its second annual meeting had announced that the association had made only modest gains for a second year, these circumstances helped bring on a serious crisis. Talbot and other backers gave notice that they would not accept the renewal of notes due to them in the first half of 1844, and so withdrew their loans as they fell due for repayment. Injury to the community's credit was impossible to prevent. A local reporter for Lewis Tappan's New York credit-reporting organization, The Mercantile Agency, wrote a damning account at the end of February 1844, which did not miss the chance to drag in the community's religious unorthodoxy to cast doubt on its financial credibility: "The most responsible men are withdrawing and [I] should think it is going down fast—the morals of the people are very bad—[I] should think the responsibility of the Association decidedly bad."[30]

Benson led a frantic effort to find new backers. He, David Mack, and James Boyle had already begun a subscription drive to raise $25,000 through abolitionist contacts, lecture tours, and participation in conventions with the other Massachusetts communities, several of which took place between December 1843 and August 1844. Some new subscriptions for stock were made by arriving members. Talbot's mortgages were reassigned, after negotiations, to Brown University and Amherst College, the former arrangement probably made through Benson's connections in Providence, the latter probably assisted by the presence of David Mack's father on the college's board of trustees. A few abolitionist supporters, including the merchant Abner Sanger of Danvers, Massachusetts, gave support by loan or by arranging accommodations on the repayment of debts to Boston and New York merchants. The spring of 1844 also marked the arrival at the community of William Bassett, the former manufacturer from Lynn, and his assumption of some responsibility for run-

ning its business affairs. Although Bassett himself was to withdraw again
after about six months, changes of direction brought about during his stay
helped set policy for more than another year, and at first gave the community cause to hope that they might yet achieve financial stability.[31]

The biggest change was to the conduct of the silk business, which from
this point on became heavily dependent on imported raw silk. Two things
combined to bring this change about. The first was the effect of the winter
of 1843–44 on mulberries; across much of New England large numbers
of trees were destroyed by harsh weather. Since the speculative boom in
them was long over and most farmers had lost any enthusiasm for dealing
with them again, they were not replaced. Some mulberry production and
feeding of silkworms continued, including on the community's property,
but local sources of leaf, cocoons, and raw silk were probably reduced after
that winter. The community, along with other local silk mills, was forced
to find new sources of supply. It continued to advertise for cocoons and
offered for sale a new silk reel manufactured by Oliver D. Paine, that
"prepares the silk directly for the doubling frame, with little waste," in a
persistent attempt to secure more reliably prepared local raw silk.[32] But
the need for large, consistent supplies of a quality suited to the factory's
needs so that it could concentrate on production rather than constantly
adjust its work to process small quantities of indifferent raw material,
inevitably led to the purchase of imported raw silk. Whether Bassett insisted on this, or it had already been in hand, the spring of his arrival
coincided with the community's decision to seek significant supplies of
raw silk, mainly Chinese, from merchants in New York and elsewhere.
Though the community had obtained some in 1842 and 1843, imports
were now to provide the bulk of its supply.[33]

Apart from the productive advantages to this, renewed contact with
New York supplemented Stetson's Boston outlets for the community's
goods and helped ensure that there would be a market for an increased
output. But it also, of course, tied the community ever closer to the types
of market transactions it had partly been formed to avoid. Probably it was
an unavoidable strategy for any concern wanting to stay in the silk business. The imbalance between the factory's capacity and the community's
inability to supply its own needs for silk, the technical difficulties associated with local, domestically produced raw silk, and the fall-off in local
supplies all led to a reliance on imports, for which payment would be
required in cash or goods. The shift finally cemented the community's
fortunes to its members' ability to work their way out of debt.

Letterbook entries for 1844 and 1845 reflect the increased pace of work and outside contacts that this effort entailed. Some silk was purchased from importers in Boston and Hartford, but the main sources were New York firms, including Talbot's, through an agent employed in the city to track down and relay information about supplies. Inevitably, there were teething problems with the new strategy. Connecticut manufacturers had, around 1840, sent to China samples of local raw silk prepared to the specifications they required for machine production, and had some success in obtaining Chinese silk suited to American needs. But quality still varied. The community's first shipment from Talbot, Olyphant and Company in New York, for example, contained silk "not . . . equal to sample"; the next consignment, wrongly judged by the community's agent, was "beautiful, but too fine for our machinery." Gradually, these difficulties were ironed out. By late 1844 purchases of locally reeled raw silk seem to have ceased, though the community did continue efforts to obtain cocoons from which to prepare its own silk. For 1844 as a whole, the community's gross earnings—to which silk production was the largest contributor—exceeded $7,300, nearly enough to cover its expenses and interest payments, and the trustees claimed that $5,000 of this amount had been earned in the second half of the year. They implied that the effort to get out of debt might, at last, be succeeding.[34]

The struggle, however, proved an unequal one. By the spring and summer of 1845 it was evidently being lost. William Bassett's verdict after he left Northampton pointed to the classic dilemma the community faced. "Embarrassed by a heavy debt" and "exceedingly deficient in productive power," it needed more capital and a larger membership to increase output, but with its credit already stretched to the limit was unable to obtain the one or house the other. Earnings from the silk that was produced were insufficient to do more than keep creditors at bay. By 1845, as suppliers realized this, they increased the pressure further. Some declined further dealings with the community; others sought additional security for the credit they extended; still others began once again to ship inferior silk, which further compromised the community's output. Though manufacture using imported silk continued, mid-1845 marked the point at which it became clear that this policy could not solve the financial problems. The community was locked in a descending spiral from which it could not escape.[35]

Correspondence of all kinds reflected the pressure. The officers sent departed members statements of account and sought repayment of bal-

ances owed to the community. They also wrote to stockholders who had
requested repayment of their stock, seeking forbearance. Inevitably these
exchanges led to recrimination. Hill and Judd swapped bitter letters with
Hudson in particular. As they sought to resist his demands to have stock
repaid, he disputed their statement of his account with them, and each
side implied that the other was guilty of unchristian, unbrotherly behavior. There was an unedifying effort, extending over two years, to collect
a legacy promised by a former supporter of the community, whose family
predictably enough refused, after she died, to recognize the bequest. Since
the community's articles of association prohibited formal resort to the
courts, and the woman seems not to have put her wishes in writing, there
was little to be done except send letters full of moral indignation.[36]

By the summer of 1845 several factors had come together to provoke
a further change in the association's arrangements. David Mack, for instance, had abandoned hope for the community as a vehicle of social
reform and was also faced with the severe pressure that community life
was imposing on his wife. Benson, likewise, was probably disillusioned
with his inability to restore the community to some semblance of its
original organizational form and had given up any notion of reforming
it. During the first half of the year, they had attempted various expedients
to solve its financial problems. On the strength of an inquiry she had
made a year earlier about joining the community, which had been turned
down, Mack approached the Lowell millworkers' leader Sarah Bagley
with an offer by the community to form a partnership with "the Lowell
mill-girls," to operate the Northampton factory in circumstances that, he
presumably felt, would be superior to their present oppressed condition.[37]
In April 1845 there were rumors that offers had been made to buy or
lease the community's mill. By August two things had happened. Mack
and his family withdrew from the community, and Benson had followed
a strategy that would also bring his formal connection with the community to an end, while providing it with some means of scaling down
its debts.

Reorganization

He and the community agreed to divide up the association's property.
Benson would receive ninety acres and the four-story mill. The community would continue on its remaining 380 or so acres, without the mill,

but with an old boardinghouse, a number of dwellings, workshops, and the cocoonery. In many ways this meant that Benson would effectively switch sides in the community's struggle to realize an abolitionist view of the ideal society. He had arranged backing from local evangelicals and political abolitionists, including J. P. Williston, his brother the East-hampton manufacturer Samuel Williston, and the Williamsburg manu-facturer and Liberty Party man Joel Hayden, to refit the silk factory as a cotton mill, and would no doubt use slave-grown cotton in the bargain. The community would maintain silk production on a modest scale, in a new building to be erected for the purpose, and it would also seek to earn more income from local sources by relying on milling, sash-and-blind making, and metalworking.

After Benson's withdrawal and the division of the property, the re-maining members settled down to what turned out to be the final year of community life. Once further withdrawals had occurred during the winter of 1845–46, the membership stabilized at about forty-six for the remain-der of the community's existence. In his memoirs, the principal remaining leader Samuel L. Hill suggested that this was also a stable period for those still in the group; departures had removed many of the sources of disharmony that had marred previous years, and life continued in relative peace. But it was a life of considerable hardship. Annual allowances for subsistence and clothing were cut back to barely half their 1843 level. The division of the property had reduced but not removed the burden of debt, and unremitting work was needed to continue the process of meeting its demands. Hill wrote in December 1845 that members were committed to what would, in ordinary circumstances, be "a dog's life," and that they could expect to be "under the harrow . . . for several months yet."[38]

Reorganization placed greater emphasis than ever on the other activities from which income could be earned. The saw- and shingle mill, machine shop, blacksmith's forge, and farm were all potential sources either of revenue or of substitutes for outside purchases that cost the community cash or exchange goods. Improvements to machinery and equipment made by Hiram Wells and others contributed to this. New saws and a planing machine helped the community participate in the local lumber boom of the mid-1840s. Community woodworkers made and assembled sash windows and doors for local builders, filling orders from Haydenville, Northampton, and as far away as Charlemont. During 1845, the com-munity offered to supply lumber to the Springfield and Northampton Railroad, then under construction. New grindstones permitted more output of cutlery and tools; the forge supplied nuts and ratchets to hardware dealers in Boston and elsewhere, and manufactured lengths of chain of various sizes to machine builders in Westfield, Cabotville, and other regional centers. The farm continued to provide milk, grain, and other crops, which helped eke out the increasingly meager subsistence allowances, though efforts to improve it were largely abandoned for lack of labor by 1845, and it never played the role in the community's output that the founders had envisaged.[39]

Such activities undoubtedly enabled the reorganized community to keep going, particularly as it tried to restore silk production to a remunerative level in the new building erected at the end of 1845. But they seem unlikely to have been sufficient to stave off financial collapse for very long. Without extra members to run them and extra capital to help build them up, they all had to be conducted on a relatively small scale and in some cases, as Hill later put it, were "more expensive than profitable." After Oliver D. Paine withdrew in June 1845, and the manufacture of silk machinery ceased, there was little the community produced that was not also made by other small manufacturers in the region. This, in turn, placed a premium on an ability to turn out custom work, which is what the community mainly specialized in, but that too created difficulties when orders were received for small quantities of items, or with specifications that were difficult or costly to meet. Orders were turned down because demand was insufficient to justify the effort. Though the community had a shoemaking department, certain types of shoes were purchased in town for members, because it was too expensive to make them in small quantities and there were too few shoemakers to obtain an outside contract to make larger batches.[40] In an economy where larger scale and batch production for long-distance markets were becoming the principal means of earning significant revenues, the small-scale, custom-work output of the community's diversified activities were insufficient to remove its burden of debt, and under this burden, the community could not attract enough capital or credit to reverse its fortunes.

The Utopia of Business

The story of the Northampton community's commercial misfortunes reminds us of one of the paradoxes of antebellum American history. In the 1840s reformers, pioneers, and adventurers were trying out new practices and institutions of all kinds. The conventional wisdom usually places communitarian groups among the "failures" of these attempts and regards their efforts to find new ways of organizing society and human relations as "impractical," either in the short or the long term. In fact, however, very large numbers of conventional businesses also failed in this period. According to one estimate, published in 1848, over nine out of ten traders could expect to have debts in excess of their capital after twenty-five years in business. In the Northampton area about half of all businesses failed or were forced to reorganize over the twenty-year period from 1841 to 1860. Its burden of debt and its inability to shake it off only made the community more typical, not less.[41]

The Northampton community's difficulties stemmed from its business efforts, not its social organization. The arrangements evolved in 1842 and 1843, in which work was conducted cooperatively and members' subsistence and other essential needs provided for collectively, remained a stable basis for community life until late 1846. The unrealizable, "utopian" aspects of the community were its efforts to establish a silk-manufacturing business substantial enough to repay its debts. Indeed, the community's social system probably permitted it to continue these efforts longer than a conventional capitalist firm might have survived under similar circumstances.

The long struggle to make community organization a source of financial success had not been insignificant, however. Like other aspects of its ideology, the Northampton community's productive efforts embodied a moment of vision in U.S. history when new paths to social organization seemed possible. That this search for social harmony was linked to the production of silk was, in various senses, more than just fortuitous. Optimism about social reform and optimism that new business schemes could succeed went hand-in-hand at the beginning of the 1840s and helped shape the Northampton community at its outset. There was confidence that new forms of social organization and productive relations in industry could overcome the evils of the early factory system. The Northampton community was a testing ground for this vision. It had a local impact. In 1845, for instance, not only the community mill, but the Conant mill and another small silk mill nearby were all working a ten-hour day when working hours in factories were generally longer.[42] The difficulties of silk production, and the hope that a new kind of society could solve them, symbolized the wish of community reformers not only to find a moral way to run an economy, but to build a world whose material circumstances reflected that new, cooperative, moral approach. Silk, with its demands for skill and cooperation across age and gender barriers, seemed an example of a new product for a new world.

The vision proved illusionary, but in a more prosaic sense the Northampton community's ventures in silk production did have a part to play in the significant transformation of the U.S. silk industry that occurred during the early 1840s. Up to that time silk production had mainly been a cottage industry. The Northampton Association's efforts were among several in the 1840s to transform this household-based domestic industry into a mechanized, large-scale producer of finished silk goods. Undisciplined speculation, the harsh New England climate, and the inherent complexity of silk production doomed these efforts, but they did prove to be the starting point for a new, mechanized silk industry based largely on imported raw silk. The Northampton Association was one of a handful of New England institutions that bridged the gap between the old and the new silk industries during the depression of the early 1840s. It parallelled the early growth of large-scale silk production in centers such as Paterson, New Jersey, and the roots of what would become Connecticut's largest silk firm, Cheney Brothers of South Manchester. It gave shelter, temporarily, to two figures, Joseph Conant and Orwell S. Chaffee, who would help build the "new" silk industry in Northampton and Mansfield from the mid-1840s onward. It also formed the nucleus of the firm established by Samuel L. Hill, which was to grow into Massachusetts's largest single producer of silk goods.[43]

These firms would all be run on industrial capitalist lines, however. With its commercial failure the community's attempt to establish more cooperative working and social arrangements was also ultimately reversed, to further the wage system and market competition many of its members had abhorred. We shall trace how this happened in Chapter 7 but to understand why it happened, we need first to examine the tensions that continued to underlie community life over the last two years or more of its existence. Though its social organization successfully sustained it through a difficult period, Samuel L. Hill and some others would draw conclusions that encouraged them not to repeat the experience.

CHAPTER SIX

"Too Despotic Power":
Members and Leaders

I f utopian communities inspired nothing else, it was exaggerated rumors of their own demise. Reports of failure were legion. Enemies and skeptics were prepared to interpret even a minor reorganization as a collapse. As early as October 1842, after the Conant group had withdrawn, William Adam's Boston acquaintance Epes Sargent Dixwell wrote that the "community scheme . . . at Northampton, owing to disorder in the camp & want of finances, is likely to fall through." Four years later, this would have been a sound prediction. In fact it was only another eighteen months before Dixwell reported "that the community had failed!"[1] More or less throughout its existence, debt and its consequences pressed the community to tighten its affairs or abandon its efforts. It took a certain resilience to keep going.

Community life under these pressures was often harsh, and its tensions added to the discomfort of members. Many did start to leave. Between the summer of 1844, when the community was at its peak, and March 1846, when membership stabilized again, the number of residents fell by five-eighths. Among the first to join the exodus were the family of William Bassett, who returned to Lynn in the autumn of 1844 after only six months at Northampton. When Bassett arrived, he had been optimistic about the community's prospects and imagined that he was making a permanent move. Disillusionment arose not only from the religious disputes, which Bassett could not abide, and the heavy burden of work assumed by his wife and daughters, but from the difficulty he faced

authority, but by relying on the voluntary efforts of the community to do what had to be done.

In these circumstances leadership acquired a complex character. On one hand, a succession of figures, including William Adam, David Mack, Hall Judd, James Boyle, William Bassett, and Joseph C. Martin, by virtue of their personal character or offices they held, attempted to steer members toward decisions on day-to-day issues or important matters, and often obtained some influence over them. On the other, because they were among the original founders and had substantial stockholdings in the association, George W. Benson and Samuel L. Hill each had a prominence enjoyed by no one else. But neither were in a position to dictate to the membership.

Hill served as treasurer throughout the community's existence and controlled its finances, but before the winter of 1844–45 does not figure very prominently in the records. He was not a loquacious man and may have exercised more influence in private than in the long lectures or debates at general community meetings. Keeping in the background, he was rarely mentioned by visitors. But in time he quietly emerged as the community's last main leader and principal arbiter of its fortunes. His influence grew not because he was a charismatic leader but because he stayed with the community longer than most of the other founders. Benson's character and role were different. From early on he acted as a sort of roving financial ambassador, traveling to raise funds and conduct business for the community. This continued after he was elected its president in late 1842. Benson was seen by many members as a key figure. When she arrived in May 1843 Sophia Foord noted his influence and what she saw as a tendency to await his decisions on important matters. There were occasions where what Benson said counted, but he by no means always got his way. He had lost the wages debate of 1842. In 1844 he failed in a bid to buy the community out to reduce its debts and was unable to secure the appointment of Samuel J. May as director of education. Neither Benson, Hill, nor the other officers who provided collective leadership could act far beyond the bounds that members wished to place on them. Even the community's spatial arrangements reflected, and helped reinforce, the sometimes distanced relationships between leaders and members. Whereas the majority of members, families and single people, crowded into the factory boardinghouse, or the six or seven smaller houses nearby, some of which held several families, Benson and Hill lived in their own houses, in less crowded conditions, a short distance from the others. If the two leaders held themselves aloof from full participation in community life, many members were determined to ensure that neither they nor other officers would decide how their lives should be run.

Members against Leaders

The Northampton Association's democratic structure ensured that struggles between leaders and members did much to shape its development. Even the community's original constitution gave the membership considerable potential influence. The 1842 debates over wages, the 1843 subsistence provisions, and the revised constitution of that year all reflected the willingness of the members to use their power and to curb that of their leaders. When the English Owenite John Finch visited in May 1843, he noted that because it was "conducted upon democratic principles, there is a great jealousy about governors, and all the members seem to do pretty much what appears right in their own eyes." Finch had been hosted by William Adam, who had recently resigned his offices, and his conclusion that the community could do no better than place itself immediately under Adam's guidance and authority doubtless reflected Adam's own wishful thinking on the matter.[6] Of course, the community did nothing of the sort. Adam's departure early in 1844 marked the end of the broad dispute over the constitution, the rights of stockholders, and the abolition of wages, but it did not end dissatisfaction among some leaders with the 1843 changes and the lack of order they created.

Indeed, soon after the changes had been completed, and the community reached its peak size, four of the six remaining founders considered bringing it to a close. At a private meeting in April 1844, Samuel Hill indicated that he was prepared to end the community and declare its failure. The only surviving account of the meeting does not state his reasons, but they almost certainly concerned debt. Hill was supported by David Mack, who believed that more effort should have been made to make the group genuinely communal, and by Hall Judd, who had probably come to feel that further communal experiment was futile. Hiram Wells, too, was said to be likely to follow Hill, his ally. The leaders decided to carry on only because George W. Benson returned from a trip to announce that he had received pledges of new financial support and that seventeen families, including William Bassett's, were ready to arrive within the next few weeks.[7] But it is significant that the discussions remained private and were not referred to in the association's records. There was no general debate about the proposal to close the community and good grounds for thinking that the members would have rejected the suggestion if there had been. Continued financial difficulty induced Benson himself to offer in June to buy the association out, and this time a formal community meeting did take place in his absence to discuss it. The result was a resounding defeat for the idea and a strong endorsement of continuing as before. Five members, Hall Judd, the Haywards and the Scarboroughs, voted to continue discussion, but twenty-six—including Hill, Mack, James Boyle, Sojourner Truth, and Frances Judd—rejected it. Though the vote induced a few people, including the Scarboroughs and the Haywards, to withdraw anyway, it marked a determination by the majority to carry on.[8]

Yet throughout the period from 1843 to 1846 mounting pressures put community institutions and practices under steady strain and created undercurrents of discontent among members. These pressures could be traced most clearly in the community's education department and to its ambitions for a system of schooling that would combine manual work and intellectual development.

The school should have achieved a degree of stability in 1843, when the rivalry between William Adam and David Mack was resolved in Mack's favor, and he took charge of education. In fact, though Mack was a more popular teacher than Adam, and his ideas more congruent with community opinion, he faced challenges posed by tight material circumstances. First the increasing numbers of residents, then shortages of resources, and finally financial pressures coupled with a steady decline in the number of members, pushed the department away from formal schooling and toward the use of child labor for the community's work. Members debated the periodic shifts in the conduct of the school, and some, especially parents and older scholars, tried to resist the direction it was taking.

As the community grew, pressure on accommodation became acute, and by 1843 applicants for membership were regularly being turned down on the grounds that there was nowhere to house them. Growth doubly affected schooling. The number of children and youths to be taught rose. In June 1842 there were twenty-eight boys and girls under eighteen, including fourteen under eight; a year later those numbers had risen to fifty and twenty-seven, and a year after that to fifty-five and twenty-nine. The rise in the overall number of residents from 1842 to 1844 meant that living and working took up space that might otherwise have been used for teaching. The school rapidly overflowed Adam's house, where classes had first been conducted, but removal to the factory boardinghouse made for new difficulties because it now shared a building with the silk factory, a machine shop, and living quarters for more than half the members. By June 1843, after she had endured less than two months in these conditions, Sophia Foord had had enough and resigned her post as teacher, citing the completely inadequate accommodation. She retracted her resignation only after a community meeting had agreed to assign a different room for her classes and instructed Mack to seek out a permanent solution to the school's severe overcrowding. During the winter of 1843–44 there was talk of building a large community house, and it was expected that proper space for schoolrooms would be provided there, but as the hope of erecting this building faded, Mack was asked to see to the conversion of an old barn on community's land for fitting up as a school building. This was, at length, accomplished, but by the time it was ready for use the number of children needing it had started to fall. Between June 1844 and December 1845, the number of residents under eighteen fell from fifty-five to thirty-three.[9]

As membership peaked in 1844, renewed efforts were made to recruit outside pupils of suitable moral character to study and labor alongside members' children for an annual fee of one hundred dollars. Advertisements for boarding scholars appeared in the *Liberator* and other abolitionist publications, and when James Stetson attended a convention at Hopedale as Northampton's representative, he was reminded to let it be known that there was room for eight or ten of them. Publicity generated inquiries, and a few pupils arrived from abolitionist families in New England and New York. Indeed, opening the school may have brought some financial benefits. But the main advantage was that it brought in some income in the form of cash, much needed for other purposes. The fees collected were never sufficient to make a contribution to reducing the community's debts or paying for better accommodation for the school.[10]

Acting apparently in secret in an effort to promote the school to outsiders, George Benson attempted late in 1844 to persuade his old neighbor Samuel J. May to come to Northampton as director of education in place of David Mack. May, who had just resigned as head of the Massachusetts state normal school at Lexington would undoubtedly have drawn pupils to the community, but he declined Benson's proposal, taking up an appointment to a Unitarian pulpit in Syracuse instead.[11] As the community discussed steps toward reorganization in the spring of 1845 and decided to concentrate on manufacturing, it abruptly announced that the boarding school would close to nonmembers and that pupils due to arrive should not come.[12] Most of the experienced teachers—Adam and his daughter, Emily Farwell, Sophia Foord, the Macks, and others—had left, or were soon to do so. Unlike Brook Farm, whose school helped sustain it up to its conversion to Fourierism in 1844, and again after the March 1846 fire that destroyed its phalanstery building, the Northampton community never had the means to make its school widely attractive or its educational ambitions a source of dynamic expansion from within.

Instead, the school was subordinated to the need for labor. Over time the participation of its children in the work of the community became increasingly crucial. In theory the curriculum, by combining formal teaching, work, recreation, and spiritual instruction, achieved the balanced education envisaged in the Preliminary Circular and constitution of 1842. In practice, steps to emphasize work over formal schooling were being taken as early as 1843 and were a factor in the conflict between David Mack and William Adam. In the spring, at roughly the time Mack succeeded Adam as director of education, the hours for work and study had been changed: instead of morning study and afternoon work, the pattern was reversed. Mack was soon confronted by a petition from the young abolitionist Thomas Hill, who asked the community to abandon the changes and revert to the original policy of having study in the morning and putting pupils to work after the noon dinner break. Hill argued that the new practice of working first, then studying, exhausted scholars like himself and hindered their academic preparation. But Hill's opinion did not meet with general approval at the community's discussion of his complaint. The view that work for the benefit of the community should (literally and symbolically) come first carried the day, and the new schedule remained in effect.[13]

The effect of this pressure to work was evident in the terms offered to prospective pupils from outside the community. In February 1843, before the schedule change, Adam informed a young student that he would be expected to study between 7 A.M. and noon, and to devote the afternoon, from 1 P.M. to sunset, to manual work. In spring and summer such a regime would involve six to seven hours' labor a day, in winter four or five. By August, Mack was offering to receive a young woman as a boarding pupil on the understanding that she would study from three to five hours a day, and devote five more hours to "industrial pursuits" *in addition* to domestic work and looking after her child. In December Mack was accepting three girls—aged seventeen, fourteen, and twelve—for an annual fee of fifty dollars, on condition that they each spend ten hours a day at silk manufacture, sewing, or kitchen work; only their evenings could be devoted to "studies, recitations, lectures, etc."[14] Though terms varied from pupil to pupil, the community's need to secure either cash or the promise of work from outside scholars ensured that the manual-labor aspect of its "training" was outweighing all others. Financial shortages and demographic change merely heightened this emphasis. By mid-1844 the community's descriptions of its schooling sought to make a virtue out of necessity by arguing that pupils learned from working, but this was a thin disguise for the increasing use of child labor. When Mack wrote to Sarah Bagley in March 1845 to propose leasing the community's factory to Lowell mill women, he dropped any pretense about the matter. Twenty or thirty children, he told her, would be available to work in the mill. This would have included every boy and girl over the age of about six.[15]

By this stage the steady drop in membership also forced the community to rely more and more on young people's labor. As families were recruited and babies born to existing members, the proportion of children in the community had risen as its overall population grew between 1842 and mid-1844. But during the decline in membership that followed, the number of adults fell faster than the number of children and youths. The proportion aged under eighteen rose from 41 percent of residents at the end of 1842 to 50.8 percent three years later. Throughout the last eighteen months of the community's existence, adults represented only half of all residents, a lower proportion than at any previous time. The labor of the young was never more important to its day-to-day activities. In the financial straits that the community was in after 1844 its educational ambitions degenerated into a system of child labor, with few features other than a relentless struggle over work.

Eventually, members began to object on behalf of their children. In January 1845 two parents, James Kerr and Louisa Ann Haven, who had each brought children to the community to be educated, complained at a meeting that the conflict between work and schooling was spoiling their children's opportunities to learn and that excessive work was leaving them too exhausted to study. In discussion Mack, Benson, and other leaders spoke up to defend the system. That winter a broader consideration of educational arrangements left the existing regime undisturbed, and though the Haven family remained in the community, the Kerrs withdrew in March 1845. With the closure of the school to outsiders, and the withdrawal later that year of the Macks and the Bensons, little was done to maintain more than a minimum of formal instruction. In consequence further families, notably the Stetsons in March 1846, withdrew, and other parents shielded their children from what they saw as excessive demands for work. When the remaining members of the community assembled that September, decided soon to bring it to a close, and discussed how they had come to reach this point, some blamed others for being unwilling to let their children work sufficiently.[16]

Under the pressure of debt it became inevitable that the issue of authority would arise, above all, in questions relating to the control of work. But if members—young and old—worked harder over time, it was by their own volition and in spite of various efforts to increase the demands made on them. As membership and the range of activities grew, leaders called for more systematic means of organizing and accounting for production. The issue first arose in 1842. Though the fixing of a wage rate was postponed that June, it was agreed that departmental directors should compile weekly reports of the work done by each individual. By July, Benson and Adam, concerned that these reports were being kept irregularly, proposed that wages be withheld from members who did not report what work they had done. In voting to reject this, members initiated a pattern that they would hold to consistently over the next four years: they would approve methods for keeping track of departments' work and expenses, but resist any attempt to impose sanctions for failing to adhere to them. The principle of moral suasion permitted no coercion. The members, in pursuit of their vision of a morally guided society, resisted all efforts to impose authority or rules that would reduce the scope for exercising personal, individual responsibility. This vision contradicted leaders' perception of a need to organize and monitor production.[17]

This conflict was not diminished by the introduction of equal subsistence allowances in 1843. Even David Mack, who had helped achieve the abolition of wages, found himself opposed when, as the association's secretary, he attempted to tighten its procedures. In July 1843 Mack proposed that William Larned, a Boston merchant who had lived in the community for nine months and worked as its accountant, be accepted as a full member. The membership rejected Larned and even disputed whether to pay him anything for the work he had already done.[18] The following year, when William Bassett took over the directorship of the silk factory, he had a marked effect on the promptness and character of the association's dealings with other businesses and also obtained better internal reporting on and accounting for work done. In July 1844, he wrote, "a more thorough system of labor went into operation." But within months, the disputes that this caused helped send Bassett and his family on their way back home to Lynn. In the absence of other effective authority to ensure that members performed the hours of labor that were agreed on, Bassett and some other leaders advocated the reintroduction of wages, as a means to compensate labor actually performed. Members upheld the principle of equal compensation.[19]

Interest in Fourierism

From late 1843 on, the struggle over authority began to shape the interest of some leaders in the growing Fourierist movement. While the Northampton community was developing, reformers in the North were becoming increasingly attached to Fourier and the American interpreters of "Associationism," as it became known. The movement's most notable achievement in New England was to persuade the leaders of Brook Farm to convert to Fourierism early in 1844. Between December 1843 and August 1844, at a series of community conventions, representatives from the three Massachusetts communities, Brook Farm, Hopedale, and Northampton, gathered with others to discuss the progress of communitarian efforts and attempt greater coordination between them. Northampton leaders, particularly George Benson, David Mack, and James Boyle, became involved in this convention movement as part of their strategy to drum up financial support. Benson signed the call to the first meeting in Worcester in December 1843, and he and Mack also signed the call for a meeting in Boston that followed it, of which Benson was a vice-president. Through these meetings and their contacts with the wider community movement the three men evinced a growing interest in Fourierism. Their reasons varied, but linking them was a perception that Fourierism might offer the chance to reimpose a degree of structure and organization on a community whose members had taken effective control out of the hands of its leaders.[20]

Adopting Fourierism at Northampton would have meant reversing the changes of 1843. A form of wage payment would have replaced guaranteed subsistence; the division of profits would have given greater weight to capital; and there would probably have been a more formal division of labor and rotation of tasks, in accordance with the theory of "attractive industry." Underlying Northampton's instinctive suspicion of Fourierism was the perception, derived from its Christian, abolitionist, and nonresistant roots, that Fourier's "social science" was rooted in material, not moral precepts, that its scheme for changing society was mechanistic and did not rely on individuals to do what was right, and that it was not truly egalitarian. To differing degrees, Benson, Mack, and Boyle sought to reconcile their curiosity about Fourierism with these objections, but they could not overcome the skepticism of their fellow members.

The Worcester and Boston meetings resulted in a small influx of new residents at Northampton who were interested in the community as a Fourierist prospect. After the Worcester convention a reformer named Luther Brigham joined for a while with his children. In particular, the presence at Northampton in January 1844 of the prominent Fourierist lecturer John Allen and his wife signaled the leadership's interest in the movement. We can only surmise what discussions took place. Allen removed to Brook Farm within a few weeks, when it converted to Fourierism; it is probable that Northampton members indicated their reluctance to convert also. Mack, Boyle, and Benson, however, continued to attend conventions and gave other signs of interest in Fourierist ideas.[21]

There was discussion, for instance, of a new building program to create a communal building along the lines of a Fourierist "phalanstery." In April 1844, it was arranged for a fresh member to join the community, the New Hampshire abolitionist and master builder Elisha Hammond, who was said to be arriving with designs for a new communal dwelling. David Mack even took to calling the existing factory boarding house "the phalanstery," as if the community had already converted to Fourierism. Mack's interest in its doctrines was probably in pursuit of his wish to further the group's communal development; to him they provided, with their prescriptions for social and spatial arrangements, a guide for constructing "true association." Mack may have hoped that this would turn Northampton in the direction he had long been seeking for it. During 1844 he kept up contacts in other communities—with Hopedale as well as Fourierist groups—and attended conventions, in an effort to revitalize the Northampton community.[22]

James Boyle also took part in the effort to adapt Fourierist ideas. During the winter of 1843 and spring of 1844 he was hard at work on a book, published under the title *Social Reform*, that outlined a model communitarian society heavily influenced by Fourierism. In accordance with his perfectionist views, however, Boyle's central purpose was spiritual rather than material. The aim of his work was to bridge the gap between abolitionist-nonresistant moral reform and what he saw as the excessive materialism of Fourier's American followers. Merging Fourierist and nonresistant language, he advocated "Association" as the form of come-outerism that would alter social arrangements to conform with "the discovery of the Divine Order of society." His views were given some notice in the abolitionist and Fourierist press, but they seem not to have gained a wider following. Nonetheless, they conformed with the hope he expressed as long as he remained at Northampton, that this community could be reshaped to become a suitable moral vehicle for its associationist ideals. He signaled his concern for social order by citing the work of the authoritarian reformer Clinton Roosevelt, whose *Science of Human Government*, published in 1841, put forward a vision of a tightly structured and disciplined network of communities as a new basis for society.[23]

George W. Benson, whose interests in Fourierism lasted longest, may also have perceived its tighter, more systematic organization as a means to restore at Northampton the kind of balance between owners and members that the changes of 1843 had upset. Fourierist divisions into groups and series for work took further the departmental divisions already existing at Northampton, but articulated clearer patterns of work discipline. Fourierist arrangements for the remuneration of capital, labor, and skill also took further than Northampton's original assumptions its early leaders' notions of reconciling the conflicting interests of labor and capital. Had they been implemented, they would have given stockholders a return on investment that the current arrangements could not ensure. Fourierism, from Benson's point of view as a community leader, was therefore a potential opportunity to set the clock back and to regain what he and his early colleagues had lost at the hands of the membership in 1843.

Throughout the summer of 1844, as there was talk of a new community building at Northampton, as Boyle's book appeared and as Benson continued to do the rounds of associationist conventions, New England's Fourierists expressed optimism that the community would come over to their camp, joining Brook Farm and a growing network of phalanxes. It never happened. Benson at length stopped going to associationist meetings. By September 1845 the Fourierist journal the *Harbinger* was taking care to deny that the Northampton Association was part of the movement and to assert that it would be better off if it were; "They have trusted more to spontaneous good-feeling than to scientific organization, and if they had availed themselves more freely of methods indicated by Fourier we have no doubt that it would have greatly conduced to their prosperity."[24]

Benson, Mack, and Boyle never succeeded in bringing the Northampton community to a serious consideration of Fourierist ideas. This was, in part, because they approached Fourierism from different angles and were not united among themselves. With other leaders, such as Samuel Hill, showing little obvious interest, the enthusiasm for Fourierism at Northampton faded. Above all, though, Northampton's general indifference to it reflected the membership's commitment to existing policies, and the relative weakness of the leadership in the face of this. The struggle between members and leaders continued.

The Logic of Moral Suasion

Tension over work and authority came to a head at the third annual meeting in January and February 1845. While the meeting was going on, David Mack wrote confidently to a prospective member that it would pass "a few by-laws calculated to produce a more systematic cooperation to our business."[25] He was proved wrong. During the meeting a succession of members complained about the attempts by officers or directors to dominate the work process. Gorton G. Loomis and Jason Sulloway said that George W. Benson had interfered in the running of the farm "so as greatly to impair the independence of the director, and derange the operations of the department." The mechanical department had suffered disputes between members and the director, Elisha Hammond, partly over the keeping of accounts. But the most revealing complaint came from women in the sewing department, including Susan Parker and Mary Sulloway, who argued that a requirement that accounts be kept was "vexatious and impossible" and implied "distrust of the industry of the women." The director Louisa Rosbrooks said that even though she had "asked to be spared the hearing," she had been "most unpleasantly assailed with complaints against the rendering such accounts and against the Executive." Opposition to the leadership had come into the open.

David Mack and James Boyle defended the need for accounts. Mack sought to smooth things over with the practical argument that only proper records would permit accurate calculation of members' allowances for the year, and hence the equal subsistence they wanted. Boyle, with his usual lack of tact, cast aspersions on the women's diligence: since they were so sensitive on the issue, perhaps that suggested the need for accounts to be kept? Members once more rejected an attempt to penalize failure to submit regular accounts. Mack also proposed that the directors and executive council should be able "to make deduction from the support of such children or adults as in their opinion have been delinquent in industry," but members voted this down too, "as investing the Directors and Council with too despotic power."

The meeting did make one concession to the leadership. It agreed to appoint an "Intendant of Order," who would keep an eye on the community's activities and "suggest to every one . . . the proper care and arrangement of any property or business . . . and to persevere in such suggestions until they were attended to." At once, though, any influence that the new officer might have had was curbed by a rider, that "it was expressly understood that the [Intendant] had no power *authoritatively* to interfere in the business of any department." No evidence concerning the activities of the Intendant, or even of the office's continued existence, has come to light, and it is most likely that it rapidly fell into disuse.[26]

It would be tempting to view the resistance to control of work in the community as evidence of the materialism and individualism of the members. Perhaps, as James Boyle implied, they were out to get something for nothing, to satisfy their desires rather than their obligations to community. The evidence from the 1845 annual meeting, however, tends to refute such an interpretation. The issue was management, not reward. Had members been feathering their own nests they would not have remained in the community for long. Subsistence allowances were meager, and the work was hard. At this and other meetings, members made decisions about the scale and distribution of subsistence allowances with little of the intense debate that met proposals to tighten procedural controls. No one, for instance, proposed an increase in allowances; any discussion usually focused on how to ensure that what there was was shared equally.[27]

Members, by staying in the community at all, demonstrated their willingness to make sacrifices to uphold certain principles, above all that they were morally autonomous individuals living and working together willingly, not at anyone else's direction. This was better promoted, in their view, by a system of equal subsistence than by wage payments or other unequal compensation. They fully accepted the obligations to community that this entailed, but insisted that they did so voluntarily, not on compulsion. Resistance to efforts to impose authority followed logically from this. Measures to enforce accounting controls, in particular, implied that the leaders did not trust the members to regulate their own work habits and behavior, and members resisted the implication.

But it is also significant that the 1845 dispute over control arose most sharply in connection with metalworking, farming, and domestic work— activities that in the wider society of the 1840s were not subject to close formal supervision or financial control. Most machinists and blacksmiths worked in small shops, where accounting was informal and skilled workers retained considerable autonomy; the disputes in the mechanical department reflected the unwillingness of the members to accept within the community controls that were still rare outside.[28] Formal processes of supervision or reporting were, of course, even rarer in farming or sewing. Among the households and small farms from which many community members came, the notion of writing down how much work each individual did would have seemed absurd as well as irksome. Ironically, the community's desire to measure and equalize work clashed with the values of its own members. At Brook Farm during its Fourierist phase, similar accounting requirements apparently generated less resistance than at Northampton. Elizabeth Curson, who kept accounts for Brook Farm's domestic and sewing group in 1845 and 1846 certainly found the work tiresome, but she recorded no unpleasantness about it. Still, most members of this group were single women, and the organization of Brook Farm allowed them more time to concentrate on their work. The main objectors to keeping accounts in Northampton's sewing department were married women, already experienced in running households and burdened with other responsibilities, for whom the demand to produce written reports of their activities seemed both intrusive and insulting.[29]

So the Northampton community faced a fundamental conflict between its leaders' desire to tighten management procedures in an effort to boost production and reduce the community's debt and its members' loyalty to the principles of moral suasion and autonomy. The members preferred to trust in their collective individual responsibility, to run the community as a "moral economy" in which their commitment to community would itself be a sufficient guarantee of effectiveness. At one level all involved in the community were aware of this. Leaders such as Mack repeatedly told prospective applicants that they should not expect generous material rewards, that they should be prepared for sacrifices in the common cause, and that the community was seeking only those who were prepared to accept that its benefits lay in the moral, rather than the material sphere. On a day-to-day level, however, officers and directors pressed by harsh financial conditions sought solutions that conflicted with their own ideal. Members of the Northampton community faced a choice between a moral economy upheld by collective personal autonomy and a system of hierarchical authority designed to pursue material gain. Most opted for the former.

Leaders Withdraw

The 1845 annual meeting demonstrated that attempts to systematize the community's operations were incompatible with the democratic power of the membership. In the light of it Boyle, Mack, and Benson, the three men most influenced by Fourierism, all began to make preparations to leave. Indeed James Boyle's interventions at the annual meeting marked his last appearance in the community's records, and he and Laura Boyle probably withdrew shortly afterward. He next cropped up, according to a garbled newspaper report in May, working as a clerk in a drugstore in Newark, New Jersey.[30] Demonstrating that its debates concerned principles, not persons, the meeting overwhelmingly reelected Benson as president and Mack as secretary, but Mack at first refused to serve and only withdrew his objection after a few days' consideration. Over the next few months both men decided to withdraw, and they both resigned their offices on May 31, 1845. Mack soon left with his family for Wesselhoeft's water cure in Brattleboro, Vermont. Benson set about making his plans for taking over the silk factory building and part of the community's property and for starting cotton production at the mill.[31]

After Benson and his family formally withdrew from the association at the beginning of October, Samuel L. Hill, Hall Judd, and Hiram Wells were the only men left from among the original founders. All would play a role in the community's aftermath. All had largely avoided the debates on work and authority whose outcome had helped persuade the others to leave. Wells, indeed, seems to have taken little part in community discussions for several years. A skilled mechanic who kept his opinions to himself, he lived quite privately, concentrating on his work in the forge and machine shop, suffering the death of his wife in 1843 and marrying again in 1845. He remained attached to, and in the shadow of, his friend Hill. Hall Judd also became quite detached from the community for a period between 1843 and 1845, because of illness and because he did not fully share his wife Frances's enthusiasm for community life. On Mack's resignation, however, Judd was elected secretary, joining Hill and Joseph C. Martin, Benson's replacement as president, to form the community's last executive council.

It was Hill who did most to hold this group, and the financial arrangements of the community, together for most of its final year and a half of existence. The lack of many private papers makes his role difficult to interpret fully. Though rarely an active participant in debate, community records show him as an increasingly frequent writer of business correspondence, ordering goods, contacting customers and suppliers, explaining circumstances to creditors, and holding off the pressing demands of lenders and former members seeking repayment of their stock. A substantial stockholder without much other property of his own, Hill could ill afford the loss or long-term tying-up of his investment in the community. He decided to remain where his money was and take steps to look after it.

Hill's actions from 1844 to 1846 suggest that he was playing a long game that could bring about the repayment of the community's debts, rescue his own investment, and give him control of a significant part of the community's assets. It was a game that he would eventually win, in a way that he could not have foreseen, but which in the space of several years he came close to losing more than once. The fact that he contemplated the end of the community in 1844 suggests that its long-term survival was not his uppermost concern. If he had a plan, it certainly involved bringing the community to a close at some point. But his and Judd's doubts about its existing arrangements did not extend to a wish to disperse the families and individuals who belonged to it. At their meeting in April 1844, they held the first recorded discussion of a proposal to form a "neighborhood community," based on individual family holdings, and this was almost certainly Hill's long-term aim.[32] But the immediate strategy between 1844 and 1846 was to keep the association going as long as possible.

Ironically, this was because of the level of its debts. As treasurer Hill must have acquiesced in the attempts during 1844 to expand silk production and increase earnings. He probably approved a decision taken in January 1845 to abandon investment in farming activities, including silk raising, and concentrate instead on improving the community's facilities as a waterpower site. This could permit more manufacturing and would also raise the value of the property. These decisions, of course, required investment either in fixed or in working capital, and they help explain why the community's debt rose from about $30,000 in April 1844 to $40,000 nine or ten months later. The failure of the 1844 campaign for more stock subscriptions meant, however, that an increasing proportion of the community's liabilities were for mortgages and notes held at short term; too little of the investment was represented by stock that could not be withdrawn for four years. During 1845 and into 1846, therefore, Hill came to see the struggle to maintain the community not just as an end in itself, but as an essential means of preventing a total financial collapse.[33]

In 1846, as members who had first acquired stock four years before served notice of their wish for repayment, Hill not only admonished them for pressing their demands but told them that the end of the community would bring about the loss of all their investments. Meanwhile, however, he was making arrangements to sell parts of the property to meet immediate calls for interest and loan payments. The 1845 division of the property between the community and Benson, finally completed the following summer, removed some of the debt burden. Hill made arrangements with his brother-in-law Edwin Eaton, a prosperous landowner from Chaplin, Connecticut, for the development of community and adjacent land into house lots, both to raise cash and put in train the provision of housing for community members who planned to stay in the neighborhood once the association was disbanded. By the autumn of 1846 enough had been done to permit the community to end without a complete financial collapse. That September members concluded that the community was no longer feasible and that they should continue individually. With little disagreement, they voted on November 7 to cease subsistence allowances from the beginning of that month. Title to the remaining property, and the obligation to settle the community's outstanding debts, would in due course be transferred to Samuel L. Hill.[34] Hill would now embark on another four-year effort to repay the remaining liabilities, an effort that would nearly bring him to ruin.

Though he had ridden out the community's debates on authority, and not, like most of his fellow founders, withdrawn in frustration at the membership's exercise of its moral autonomy, Hill would make sure not to run his businesses along the same lines in the future. The notion of "community" might continue to inform his concepts of neighborhood, reform, and spiritual life, but he would keep it separate from his property and manufacturing interests. In those spheres authority would belong to him or to his carefully chosen partners. With the end of the Northampton Association, the vision of a harmonious community embracing all fields of human activity faded.

From Community to Factory Village

I n November 1845 Erasmus Darwin Hudson, passing through Milford, Massachusetts, on a lecture tour for the American Anti-Slavery Society, visited the Hopedale community. There he met and talked to the famous British reformer Robert Owen, who at the age of seventy-four was on his last visit to the United States. Hudson was evidently intrigued and quite impressed by Owen; he hoped the great man would visit Springfield so they could have another conversation. He remained true to his New England, abolitionist, and nonresistant roots, though, by rejecting Owen's environmentalist philosophy. Their conversation turned to communities, a subject they had in common. Owen mentioned his latest scheme for an American community (it envisaged a one-million-dollar investment and was never attempted) and talked about the past. Instead of referring—as we might expect—to his community at New Harmony, Indiana, of the 1820s or to the one at Queenwood in England that he had just abandoned, Owen dwelt on his earlier experiment at New Lanark in Scotland, where as owner of a textile mill he had created a pioneer "model" industrial village. As the communitarian enthusiasm of the early 1840s began to die away, what seemed left was a pattern, not for rebuilding the world into a harmonious New Jerusalem, but for reforming it into controlled communities where capital and labor were bound again under patriarchal authority. The dream of a great community faded into the more prosaic picture of a factory village. Unconsciously, Hudson's account of his conversation with the reformer touched this point: as if symbolically, Owen's imagination had returned to fasten on his older paternalist venture, not on his efforts at communitarian equality.[1]

Though he had formally left the Northampton community two years before, Hudson's feelings about it were still ambivalent. At Hopedale he heard several rumors that the Northampton Association had folded, that Samuel L. Hill had withdrawn, and that the members had dispersed. Hudson did not quite credit these stories, even though one of his informants was another former Northampton community member Charles May, who had married fellow resident Caroline Gove in 1845 and moved to Hopedale. Hudson's skepticism was partly based on sentiment. "I find after all when I hear others telling of their downfall a strong disposition to controvert them"; he had "a lingering attachment" to the people of the Northampton community and wished that "they might prosper in the right." He was correct to be skeptical of May's story. The Northampton community had not folded; the rumors were probably a garbled version of reports about the division of its property two months before, in which the departure of George W. Benson somehow became reported as the departure of Samuel L. Hill. But like Owen's harking back to New Lanark the premature announcement of the Northampton community's death contained a measure of significance. The August 1845 division at Northampton would come to seem, in retrospect, the beginning of the end. The conversion of the silk mill into Benson's cotton mill, and the final fifteen months in which members remained in the Northampton Association marked an important stage in its transition from community to factory village.

The Decline of Communitarianism

The retreat from the optimism of the early 1840s and the enthusiasm for communities, which many reformers had then displayed, was long and complex. A recent list of American communal and utopian societies counted forty-seven founded in the years 1841 to 1845, only thirteen between 1846 and 1850, and another fourteen over the next five years. For some people disillusionment came quickly, as they visited or arrived to look at new communities that turned out to be tiny, hideously impoverished, chaotic, or riven by dissension. At the other end of the spectrum a small number of reformers retained their faith in the principles of cooperation and association even though this involved them in a perpetual search for communities that could both accommodate them and meet their ideals. Stephen Young, for instance, the unsuccessful applicant to the Northampton community who eventually settled at Brook Farm for some time, did not relinquish his commitment to the cause. In the late 1850s he tried to join the Fourierist Réunion colony in Texas, then lived at a vegetarian community in Kansas and at the Hygeiana community near Chillicothe, Ohio, before helping in the 1880s, over forty years after the start of his quest, to establish the Topolobampo colony in Mexico.[2]

Some of the communities founded in the 1840s lasted less than a season; the average survival time was under two years. This suggests that an element in the decline of the communal movement was that it could not provide in a timely manner the sort of material or spiritual benefits that popular promoters such as Albert Brisbane promised. In addition, as Carl Guarneri has pointed out in his study of American Fourierism, the energy and resources of supporters of the movement were dispersed across a large number of small groups. Perhaps if they had been more concentrated, the resultant larger communities would have survived longer. In both respects the communal movement faced a classic dilemma. It successfully attracted supporters by conjuring up an ideal social vision, but needed members who were prepared to stick out the long years of sacrifice and hard work that actually realizing this vision would entail. The dispersal of small communities across the northern states helped make the movement accessible to people in many localities, but arguably split scarce resources so much that many ventures were doomed to failure. Inadequate time and resources ended many of the movement's hopes. As Samuel L. Hill concluded, looking back on the Northampton community, "We had . . . an idea that the Associative movement would generally obtain and would ultimately revolutionize the old system, but we were shortsighted. It takes much longer to bring about such results than we anticipated. The millennium we thought so near seems a good way off now."[3]

The four main Massachusetts communities each illustrated different aspects of this general process of communitarian retreat during the second half of the 1840s and into the 1850s. Fruitlands—by far the smallest—collapsed rapidly, under the impossible burdens that Alcott and Lane's domestic and dietary ideals imposed, particularly on Alcott's family. Brook Farm was fatally crippled by the fire that destroyed its nearly completed phalanstery building in 1846; though it struggled on for another eighteen months or so, its members ultimately dispersed, some of them to other communal groups such as the North American Phalanx. Hope-dale lasted longer than the others, underwent successive organizational changes in the late 1840s and early 1850s, but was brought to an end as a community venture after 1856 when its wealthiest members, the Draper brothers, bought up a majority of the shares and converted the community into the nucleus of their own factory village and large manufacturing business.[4]

The decline of the Northampton community had parallels with those of both Brook Farm and Hopedale. Many former members dispersed, but a significant number remained to take part in the conversion from community to factory village. The financial arrangements at the com-munity's end were more complex, protracted, and uncertain than those at Hopedale, and there was no sudden takeover comparable to that achieved by the Drapers. Still, Samuel L. Hill did in time make the community's property the basis of industrial ventures in which he was prominent. Above all the process reflected significant ideological shifts of various kinds among rank-and-file abolitionists and social reformers, which a more detailed examination of the Northampton community's aftermath will allow us to trace.

A "Neighborhood Community"

Even during the community's tranquil final period, Hill and others were taking steps that would mark out a future for certain members of the group. For well over two years before the dissolution, some members were thinking about new kinds of social arrangement that would alter the community's balance between individual and group interests without breaking it up altogether. Labor reformers such as Lewis Masquerier had long been calling for individuals to buy land and live as neighbors, as a step toward more complete association. At the private meeting of early April 1844, Hall Judd, Samuel L. Hill, and Hiram Wells contemplated something similar as a feasible step back from communalism. It was said that Judd wished to "form a neighborhood community—and so would Samuel."[5] Hill had already been living for a year in his house off the community's land, and he remained there even as his influence over the association increased. When dissolution did occur in 1846, leaving Hill in effective control of the community's assets and debts, his leadership, business connections, financial means, and credit helped to bring a version of the "neighborhood community" vision into being.

Several things fostered the belief that the community could usefully be dissolved into a collection of individual family houses and properties whose proximity to one another would retain some of the community's spirit while rejecting its economic foundations. Two types of consideration are suggested by the evidence that an original proponent of the "neighborhood community" idea was Judd, supported by Hill. Hall Judd's extreme asceticism and religious individualism quickly set him apart from most other members of the community, and his continued membership did not prevent him from becoming quite detached by 1844. Individual houses and property close to those of other members may well have seemed an ideal that reflected the reality of his own position. Hill's motives for supporting the suggestion are less easy to document. It is possible that he perceived the practical benefits of a "neighborhood community" scheme in reducing the association's debts, and that it could be a springboard for personal ambition without interfering with the spiritual or reform benefits of community life.

The basis for a "neighborhood community" had been developing for some while by the time the association dissolved in November 1846. By the mid-1840s, the settlement at Broughton's Meadow, once a remote, sparsely inhabited part of Northampton, had started to grow. This was partly a result of the sequence of withdrawals and reorganizations that the community had endured since 1842. Conant, Chaffee, and Swift's small silk mill had started operation in 1843, and subsequently another silk mill without direct connections to the community had been established nearby. These factories, the availability of relatively cheap accessible land, the community's store, and its reputation as a center of abolitionism and religious toleration all attracted new settlers of various kinds. They included skilled craftsmen; former slaves such as Basil Dorsey; and the abolitionist Olive Gilbert, the Bensons' friend from Brooklyn, Connecticut, who would work with Sojourner Truth on her autobiography during the late 1840s. Benson's separation from the community and the establishment of his cotton mill brought in more factory workers. New houses were built. In 1845–46 the community store kept accounts with 138 individuals other than community members, many of them workers or farmers in the locality. There was at least one marriage of a community member to a local resident in this period.[6]

As this suggests, even before November 1846 the association was becoming indistinguishable from the neighborhood. This could cause embarrassment. The locality was known as "The Community," and events there could easily be attributed to the association by mistake. When a man called Barron almost beat his wife to death with a hammer in May 1846 and then hanged himself in Northampton jail, he was described as "living at the Community," even though he was not connected with the association.[7] Still, population growth and interaction between community members and their neighbors created new opportunities for earning livelihoods and eased the transition from community to neighborhood.

Families and individuals from the association continued to live on or near the site after it broke up. At least sixty-seven men, women, and children from the community lived in the locality for some period after 1846; some remained for decades and never moved on. Kinship, neighborhood, and religious fellowship continued to bind members well after the association had formally disbanded. For the Atkins, Bensons, Hills, Judds, Hammonds, Havens, Sulloways, Wellses, and others, "neighborhood community" would enable them to continue cooperating together. The new arrangements, based on individual property, also provided part of the financial means to pay off the Northampton Association's debt.

The division of the property with Benson in 1845 had reduced community debt somewhat, but additional expense was incurred replacing buildings that had been sold; by the time the association was dissolved the debts amounted to an estimated $40,000. Before and after the breakup, the sale and mortgaging of community property reduced this amount. Land was set aside at one end of the estate and sold on a mortgage to David Ruggles for a water-cure establishment. Austin Ross purchased the fifty-acre farm nearby that Samuel L. Hill had originally moved to Northampton to occupy, and set up a dairy farming business. Above all, Hill's arrangement with Edwin Eaton to divide parts of the community property into lots for sale enabled Eaton to purchase land and resell it to members and other individuals. One estimate suggests that he bought 35 acres for $1,000 and quickly sold four acres as house lots for more than $500. Plans were drawn up for laying out what was called "Eaton's village lots," consisting of three streets and about two dozen house lots. Hall Judd bought his lot only days after the community dissolved. The Havens, the Hammonds, and Sojourner Truth also subsequently acquired land in the development, and other families remained close by.[8] The sale of land to newcomers provided one means by which Hill could start repaying the community debts that he had assumed and helped subsidize the provision of property to the members who remained in the area. As the Judds and others erected small houses on their new lots, they began to transform utopia into a kind of suburbia.

An institutional approach to utopian communities would probably end the analysis at this point, concluding that the Northampton community had "failed" and its story was over. Certainly contemporaries, both hostile and friendly, drew this conclusion. Fourierists, conscious that Northampton was sometimes mistaken as one of their ventures, took pains to point out that its failure was no reflection on their own doctrines. John Humphrey Noyes, writing a quarter of a century later, added the Northampton community to the long list of groups that, unlike his own, still-thriving Oneida community, had proved unequal to the challenges of communal existence.[9]

But the story of the community was also the story of the lives of its members. By following the men and women who left the Northampton community or who stayed until its end, we can trace some of the influences of community life on later patterns of reform, economic activity, and social organization. We can also trace more precisely the fading of the "communitarian moment" from the mid-1840s on, as ideological issues that the community and its members attempted to test while they were at Northampton also changed in character.

Community, Reform, and the Retreat from Radicalism

Northampton had throughout its existence shared in the wider world of communitarian reform of which it was a part; like other groups it attracted men and women who had already had, or would go on to seek, community experience elsewhere. David Mack and William Adam had contemplated joining Brook Farm before they opted to come to Northampton, and William Bassett's daughter Susanna had lived there for a period before she joined her family at Northampton in 1844.[10] Visitors such as Stephen Young and A. L. Smith were among many inquirers who saw Northampton as just one among many opportunities to participate in a community. Individuals and families also went from Northampton to other communities. Most of the Brooks family, who left in 1842, went to join the Shaker community at Enfield, Connecticut, and a few remained there for eight years or more. John Allen, who was briefly at Northampton, moved on to Brook Farm, which better suited his Fourierist ideals. At least three members went to the Hopedale community. Cyrus Bradbury, who was at Northampton for eight months in 1844, remained at Hopedale until after its formal dissolution as a community in 1856, and at the start of the Civil War still sustained, with Adin Ballou and a few others, the nonresistance principles that had drawn him to Northampton nearly two decades earlier. It may be significant that Bradbury withdrew from Northampton in December 1844, the same month that Charles May also left after two years there, and gravitated to Hopedale. With May went another Northampton member, the widow Caroline Gove, whom he married in February 1845. Both stayed at Hopedale until at least the early 1850s. No doubt in different ways and for different reasons, the Brooks, Mays, and Bradburys withdrew not from community life as such, but to find a better community in which to participate.[11]

Other former residents still kept up their interest in the community movement. Eldad Stebbins, having retired to a rented house in Hatfield, Massachusetts, to live out his old age, corresponded with members of the Northampton community and Brook Farm, obtained prospectuses for Fourierist phalanxes, and followed the movement in the *Phalanx* and the New York *Tribune*. William Adam's son Gordon still had "crude notions about communities and such like nonsense" when he went to work as a clerk in Boston in 1846. Sidney Southworth and John Allen were both members of the Fourierist American Union of Associationists and of the Boston Religious Union of Associationists after they left community life. George W. Benson still had contact with Fourierists in 1849, and David Mack was invited to functions in Boston Fourierist circles in the 1850s. Sojourner Truth became associated with the spiritualist Harmonia community after she moved to Michigan in the 1850s—her third communitarian connection in as many decades. She also maintained contact with friends from Northampton. In 1851 she called on the Bensons in New York and saw James and Laura Boyle as well; later that year she stayed in Cleveland with William and Susan Parker. One of the two speakers at her funeral in 1883 was Giles B. Stebbins, whom she had known for almost forty years, since he was a student at the community.[12]

Withdrawal from the community movement did not signal withdrawal from all efforts to change things. In the lives of women such as Roxcy Brown Nickerson there was no inherent contradiction between leaving the community to marry and establish a more conventional family life and continuing to support reform causes such as abolition, nonresistance, and religious radicalism. Few if any of the known abolitionist members who withdrew from the Northampton community seem to have done so because they were abandoning their involvement in the causes that had led them to join it. Most continued to work in reform movements, and accordingly came to see their period in the community as merely one part of a longer commitment. But their involvement was not necessarily the same after they left the Northampton community as it had been before. Tracing patterns in the later lives of members allows us to follow some significant ideological shifts of the mid- to late 1840s.

On one hand, on the question of abolitionism itself there was a split between those who retained their loyalty to Garrison and continued to make this the center of their activity, and those who shifted to less radical ground. On the other, there was a more general sense in which most members, Garrisonians and others, having once experienced community life, now started to draw back from the radicalism they had once embraced. Where once they had seen moral reform, social change, and economic critiques as wrapped up together in a collective effort to transform American life, they increasingly came to separate these elements and distinguish between them. The passing of the "communitarian moment" did not just entail the "failure" of communities; it marked the end of optimism about the possibility of a complete social transformation.

Most former members who remained abolitionists maintained connections with the Garrisonian wing of the movement. This was particularly so of the men and women who stayed in the Northampton area after 1846. The Haven family, Elisha and Eliza Hammond, and Hall and Frances Judd continued to support radical abolitionist positions, as did William and Susan Parker, who remained in the village until 1851 while William worked as a carpenter. Sojourner Truth, who lived first in the Benson household and then in her own house, maintained close links with the Garrisonians as she developed her own career in the abolition movement. Elisha Hammond remained active in abolitionism and temperance. He, David Ruggles, and Samuel L. Hill helped sustain the area's links in the underground railroad. By the early 1850s, the group of abolitionist neighbors was starting to dwindle: the Bensons had left; Ruggles and Hall Judd had died; Sojourner Truth shifted her focus to a national field and would soon leave for Michigan. But its remaining members played an important role in sustaining a Garrisonian vision in the area right up to the Civil War. In 1857 for instance, the Massachusetts Anti-Slavery Society organized a National Disunion Convention to press for the separation of North and South that had been Garrisonian policy since 1844. Abolitionists in a large number of Massachusetts towns collected signatures on a petition for the dissolution of the Union. In Northampton, over eighty men signed the petition, a higher proportion of the adult male population than for any other large town in the state. All the male former members of the community who remained signed their names; their presence and their influence, together with a willingness to work with other sympathetic abolitionists, helped to bring this about. After the Civil War Frances Judd would follow other abolitionists into the campaign for women's suffrage.[13]

Members who moved away from the area after leaving the community also retained their abolitionist or nonresistance ties. We have noted Cyrus Bradbury's move to Hopedale and his continued commitment to nonresistance. Abner S. Meade returned from Northampton to Danvers, continued to work as a shoecutter, and was active in the Danvers Anti-Slavery Society. The Haywards returned to abolitionism in Salem, and later joined the Salem Freeman's Aid Society; when he died in 1874, Josiah Hayward was remembered particularly as a forthright abolitionist, who never hesitated to give his views.[14]

Erasmus Darwin Hudson continued his periodic lecture tours for the American Anti-Slavery Society, losing none of his tough resilience in the cause. His and Martha's continued advocacy of abolitionism finally brought them into conflict with their church, the Congregational society in Torringford, Connecticut, and they were effectively excommunicated from it in 1848. In 1845 and 1846 Erasmus Darwin Hudson was also embroiled in legal proceedings arising out of an incident at a Northampton hotel in which he had attempted to assist a slave, Catherine Linda, to escape from her master, who had brought her with him as his servant on a visit from the South. Hudson had been arrested on the complaint of the slaveholder for interfering with Linda, who denied that she had sought to escape. The resulting criminal case, which dragged on over several court terms, became something of a cause célèbre in Garrisonian circles. Hudson, who received legal assistance from Wendell Phillips, was twice in the Springfield jail, first after being arrested and then after refusing to pay a thirty-dollar fine on conviction. The case brought him contact with old Northampton friends and adversaries; among the witnesses who testified in his behalf was David Ruggles, but he was also helped by Moses Breck and the evangelical abolitionist J. P. Williston. To Hudson, the Garrisonian abolitionists were still the central focus of his life. In a letter to Phillips written during the Linda case, he wrote that "I feel a stronger attachment to them than any other portion of [the] community—yea even more so than to blood relatives."[15]

Though his abolitionism held firm, Hudson joined others who drew back from communitarian solutions to social problems. He became an advocate of land reform, his removal to a small farm in West Springfield both providing the independent family life that Martha had wished for during her two years with the community and signaling a preference for a society of individual homesteads. Robert Adams, after he left Northampton, worked to forge links between abolitionism and the labor movement, attending at least one convention of the New England Working-Men's Association in 1845, as it turned to the ten-hour movement, land reform, and cooperative dealing as steps toward a more general reform. James Boyle was also sufficiently interested in links with the labor movement and its increasing concern with land reform to attend the first Industrial Congress in New York in October 1845.[16]

Others, though, broke away from the Garrisonian "community." As they abandoned their old confidence in communitarian solutions, William Adam and William Bassett also retreated from radical abolitionism. Adam's retreat was in some ways the more predictable because he had maintained throughout 1843 the "conservative" position within the community that its organizational changes that year violated the principles on which the association had been founded. As a stockholder and advocate of the joint-stock principle, his objections to the consolidation of members' interests, the abolition of wages, and the reduction of returns to capital were not surprising. The moves toward greater communalism would also have conflicted with the free trade principles he had expressed in the late 1830s and early 1840s before he came to Northampton. Soon after withdrawing from the community, he reacted to the decision of the May 1844 annual meeting of the American Anti-Slavery Society to adopt the principle of disunionism. Writing to Maria Weston Chapman, Adam rejected the new policy and asked to be dropped from the published list of managers of the society. In part his objection to disunion was personal and practical. He was an alien in the United States, he wrote, and could not consistently accept the protection of the state while at the same time advocating the overthrow of its government. (Though he did not mention it to Chapman, Adam was also seeking naturalization as a United States citizen, and presumably could not be publicly associated with disunionism if he wished his petition to succeed.) At a deeper level, however, Adam also rejected much of the basis upon which nonresistance and the Northampton community had rested. It was wrong, he argued, to "come out" from states or from churches. If he were an American citizen he would defend the Union as the only ground on which the North could seek the extinction of slavery. Reform, he implied, could only be brought about from within existing institutions, not by rejecting them.[17]

As he put ground between himself and the Garrisonians on disunion, Adam also retreated from the Northampton community's nonsectarianism. During an unsuccessful attempt to teach English literature to "young ladies" in Boston, Adam reforged his links with the Unitarian church and was appointed missionary to establish a congregation in Toronto. He signed a petition of Unitarian clergy against slavery in 1845. Subsequently Adam moved, with his family, to Chicago to accept appointment as the first pastor of the town's new Unitarian church. When he withdrew from the Northampton community, in other words, Adam also set out on a path that took him away from its effort to replace existing "corrupt" organizations in society.[18]

But this path did nothing to reverse a lifetime of distinguished and conscientious lack of success. The stint as Chicago's first Unitarian minister did not last long. Within a year or two his name disappeared from the city directories. His marriage, stressed by long separations and life on three continents, finally broke up. Phebe and two of her daughters returned to Boston, settled in Jamaica Plain, and worked as teachers; they received occasional visitors from India into the late 1880s.[19] By 1851 William was trying to reestablish his links with Harvard. In a series of letters that were politely received but firmly rebuffed, he sought to persuade the college to purchase his collection of oriental books and provide him with a room. After that he returned to London. He lived until 1881, his eighty-fifth year; late in life he abandoned orthodox Christianity for Vedantism. He would be remembered chiefly in India, where his association with Ram Mohun Roy and his work on education made him of interest to students of moderate reform. His last recorded work was a long defense of religion against Comte's positivist philosophy. Modest to a fault, he published it anonymously in 1862, a 441-page tome already made marginal by the midcentury secularization of intellectual inquiry. Copies remain in a few libraries, but there is reason to think that Adam's last great work was largely ignored. The British Museum's copy had, until 1992, been opened only as far as page 316. From there to the end, its pages were uncut.[20]

For William Bassett, also, membership of the Northampton community was the high point of his radicalism. While there he had written his most damning condemnation of capitalism and the wage system, but within months, as he withdrew from the community and returned with his family to Lynn, Bassett started along a path that would take him back toward acceptance of capitalism, free labor, and the political wing of abolitionism. In Lynn, probably with help from family or friends, he set up first as a small-scale drygoods dealer; later he built a business as an auctioneer, real estate broker, surveyor, and insurance agent. He was also taking steps that would mark his departure from the Garrisonian, non-resistance principles he had once so strongly espoused. Rejecting the radicals' critique of "secret" organizations—to say nothing of his own original support of Antimasonry—Bassett joined a new Odd-Fellows' lodge that had been established in Lynn. He drifted closer to political abolitionism, leaving the Massachusetts Anti-Slavery Society around 1846 and becoming editor in 1848 of a campaign paper, the Lynn *Sizzler,* that urged Liberty Party supporters to vote for a free-soil alliance in the autumn elections. Bassett then became involved in the formalization of this alliance in the Free-Soil Party, and as one of its first leaders in Lynn was rewarded with election to the post of clerk to the new city council that was established in 1849. Subsequently, he became an officer of one of Lynn's leading banks and remained in this position for the rest of his life. So although he was never again directly involved in manufacturing, Bassett in his politics and in his mercantile and banking career returned to the position of supporting the capitalist wage system that he had for a period so vigorously repudiated. He died in 1871 with considerable property in Lynn and other assets; by the time his son had distributed his estate a decade later, over $90,000 had been made in payments from it, and this sum probably did not include the bulk of Bassett's real estate.[21]

Bassett's shift to political abolitionism and free soil, like Adam's rejection of come-outerism and support of reform from within the system, reflected disillusionment with the radical rejection of existing social institutions that the Northampton community had stood for; with Hudson and the land-reformers they sought more limited change. A handful of others, however, claimed that they had withdrawn from community because it was not radical enough, and that other reforms would be more far-reaching or fundamental. They adopted ideas relating to hygiene and medical treatment especially focused on methods of water-cure therapy, or "hydropathy." In fact, though, by uncoupling their moral critique of social evils from a critique of society itself and focusing it on the moral imperative that individuals reform their own bodies, the hydropathists contributed to the retreat from radicalism.

Hydropathy

Several among those who left the community had come to the view that reform would follow not from the reorganization of society as a whole, or even from the spiritual regeneration of its members, but from the physical and moral regeneration of the human body itself. Nonresistant theories of the late 1830s and early 1840s had provided some of the roots of this view. Joseph S. Wall, who joined the Northampton community in 1842 after publishing many of William Bassett's attacks on the Society of Friends, had also written articles on health. The human body, he wrote in 1841, combined elements of "heaven" and "hell," and individuals could either elevate themselves to salvation or plunge themselves to destruction according to their capacity for self-control.[22] Most obviously, this entailed curtailing the corrupting wish to consume harmful substances, particularly alcohol, as part of a wider effort to achieve a simple life. Hydropathy grew up alongside temperance and other reforms as a technique for achieving the moral conquest of human passions.

Interest in the therapeutic effects of diet, regimen, or treatment had taken several forms at the Northampton community. Some members were vegetarian. The community invited lectures from Sylvester Graham, the dietary reformer who lived in Northampton center, and usually stocked quantities of "Graham flour" for members' use.[23] James Boyle, after leaving Northampton, became a patent-medicine salesman and eventually returned to his native Canada to practice as a physician. Erasmus Darwin Hudson continued to practice medicine and later became an orthopedic surgeon. Perhaps ironically for a nonresistant, the Civil War gave him international recognition as an inventor of artificial limbs for the wounded.

But the community's most distinctive contribution was to the growing popular interest in hydropathy.[24] Water cure had a few American practitioners in the early 1840s, but interest in it expanded rapidly after articles appeared in reform newspapers devoted to the development by a Silesian farmer, Vincent Priessnitz, of therapies based on a variety of applications of cold or lukewarm water to the body. Hydropathy's sudden impact on the American scene was in many respects comparable with the contemporary explosion of interest in other novelties—including communities and silk production. Like them, it was explicable in a variety of terms; like them, too, it took many forms. Word about hydropathy was spread by German practitioners who traveled to promote its techniques in the United States. There was plenty of room for a new kind of cure that promised to improve upon the failed remedies of existing medical practice. Priessnitz's humble origins appealed to American republican ideals, and to patients seeking therapies that could be readily comprehended, not hidden behind the veils of learning and formal medical training.[25] Treatment with water also appealed to reformers at the peak of a popular temperance movement that emphasized the purity of cold water as a beverage. Nonresistants welcomed methods, like homeopathy and hydropathy, that avoided the heroic and violent practices of allopaths and surgeons. Above all, hydropathy was an exercise in the moral reform, as well as physical cure, of its patients; treatment demanded the exercise of self-control, and this in turn was seen as contributing to its effectiveness. It involved showers and baths of various types and temperatures, the application of wet sheets, towels, and bandages, and the intake of large quantities of cold water. Treatment was supervised by "physicians" whose prescribed regimes tended to grow rapidly in variety and elaborateness as the practice of hydropathy expanded in the 1840s. Practitioners tended to claim that like any self-respecting medical practice or patent medicine of the period, it could cure virtually any condition one cared to imagine.[26]

Interest in hydropathy took root in several of the early 1840s communities.[27] At Northampton it had various origins. An article about it by David Lee Child in the *National Anti-Slavery Standard* in 1842 was one of the first to bring the subject to the attention of abolitionists, and a reference by Lydia Maria Child that year to "cures in Northampton," suggests that treatment was already available in the town. Soon after his arrival in the spring of 1843 James Boyle's horror at seeing men and boys bathing naked in the Mill River prompted him to secure the community's agreement to build a bathhouse. At roughly the same time David Ruggles, who had arrived late the previous year invalided by blindness and other ailments, came across hydropathy as he searched for the cure that other treatments had failed to give him. Ruggles began treating himself by a sort of correspondence course, receiving guidance by letter from Robert Wesselhoeft, a German hydropathic physician in Boston who had made influential contacts in abolitionist circles.[28]

Other members also tried hydropathy. To Hall Judd, already chronically ill, it must have appealed not just as a cure, but as something particularly well-suited to his rigid asceticism. He undertook treatment during the winter of 1844–45. According to his mother, that January (when temperatures will have averaged about 23°F) he "bathes drinks five or six quarts of cold water in a day wears wet clothes walks saws wood and is in the open air most of the time." (Judd died in 1850.) Erasmus Darwin Hudson also had sufficient interest in the new therapy to consider an offer to help run a hydropathic institution in New York, but he turned it down and seems never to have become a practitioner in his own right.[29]

To two members in particular, however, hydropathy became a preoccupation as they left the community and continued their careers in the "world." Ruggles's course of treatment had involved the construction, not only of the bathhouse, but of other plunges and showers along the riverbank or fed by springs on and around the community's land. His correspondence with Wesselhoeft extended from his own treatment to hydropathic methods in general, and as Ruggles began to develop his own concepts of diagnosis and treatment, he was convinced to set up in practice for himself. There is evidence that by late 1845, if not earlier, Ruggles had other community members "under his care" for courses of hydropathic treatment, and townspeople in Northampton were also seeking his advice and direction. Contributions from abolitionists, originally sent for Ruggles's support and treatment, were now solicited for the building of facilities, and by April 1846 he was on the point of starting his own water-cure establishment on land adjacent to the community. That August he received a $2,000 subscription from townspeople to enable him to expand it and by late in the year, according to a local newspaper, he had room to accommodate thirty or forty patients in a building fifty feet long by thirty-six wide, to which a large ell had been added with the subscription money. In this building, which he ran until his death in 1849, Ruggles continued to refine his distinctive approach to water-cure therapy and laid the basis for what would become a minor local industry during the decade before the Civil War.[30]

Meanwhile, David Mack had also become a proponent of water-cure therapy, though chiefly as a writer rather than as a practitioner. When he left Northampton in the summer of 1845, he moved his family to Brattleboro, Vermont, where he and the exhausted Maria took treatment at the water-cure establishment that Wesselhoeft had recently opened there. Since Maria's treatment took eighteen months, Mack found time and energy to edit and publish a monthly journal, the *Green Mountain Spring*, devoted to publicizing the cause of hydropathy in general and Wesselhoeft's infirmary in particular. He used his editorials to develop his own theories about the place of water cure in the wider pattern of social reform movements.[31]

Ruggles and Mack remained on friendly terms, exchanging correspondence and avoiding the rivalries and disputes that were prone to spring up between different centers of water-cure treatment. Mack supported Ruggles in print when his methods came under attack from other practitioners. In some respects, their approaches had little in common, but there were important senses in which for both of them hydropathy was a further development of their experience of community life. Although water cure, like any other therapy, was in the first instance directed at individuals and their complaints, it also entailed institutional and ideological assumptions that gave it strong parallels to utopian efforts to reform society. In Ruggles's and particularly Mack's view, water cure had wide moral ramifications.

Ruggles's practice started with methods of diagnosis brilliantly adapted to his own circumstances. A highly literate but medically untrained man who had learned his new profession largely by correspondence, he offered to conduct initial consultations with potential patients by letter. This was not particularly unusual. But he was also a man whom blindness had obliged to live by his other senses and who could not see the patients who consulted him in person; accordingly he developed a method of diagnosing with his hands the suitability of his prospective patients for the treatment he could offer. Ruggles evolved a theory, influenced by the language of mesmerism, that the state of disease in an individual was indicated by electrical discharge in the body that could be detected by touch. With his patient's descriptions of their symptoms and his own divination of "that electric symptom of the skin which is to me evidence of the ability of the patient to bear such varied applications of water as will affect a cure," Ruggles accepted or rejected applicants for treatment, and then subjected those he did accept to lengthy, rigorous regimens of wet-sheets, baths, towels, and showers, adapted to each individual's case.[32]

Though Ruggles's diagnostic technique was probably unique, his treatments followed a pattern common to hydropathic institutions. The purpose in each case was to precipitate a "crisis" in the condition of the patient whose outcome would signal either the incurability of the condition or the beginning of the patient's progress toward recovery. Both practitioners and patients referred to the "crisis" almost with reverence, and it is clear that it was invested with considerable moral, as well as material, significance. It was comparable to a religious conversion experience, the climax of a course of treatment that itself took moral courage to endure. Descriptions of hydropathic methods—of cold or lukewarm baths, of showers, bandages, or wrappings in cold wet sheets and their systematic repetition over the days and weeks necessary for a cure—made it clear that patients would need to summon up considerable inner strength and endurance. Successful completion of a course of hydropathic therapy was a mark, not merely of physical, but of moral fitness.

To ensure that the patient's commitment to the demands of water-cure treatment should not flag, hydropathic physicians insisted that this individualized experience should take place within an institutional framework. Water-cure establishments were new versions of utopian communities: one in New York State was actually called "Our Home on the Hillside." Patients were repeatedly warned that they would not be cured if they refused to accept institutionalization and the regimens dictated by the proprietors. Ruggles suggested, for example, that "the greatest impediment to hydropathic cure is to try and get along at home." Once in the establishment, patients should follow the treatment prescribed and endure it for the length of time it would require to take effect; no practitioner would predict a chance of cure for someone who decided to give up and discharge themselves prematurely. Above all, they should act with conviction on what they were told to do, placing their faith in the physician and his methods. "My mode of practice," wrote Ruggles in 1846, "will not admit of an indifferent or evasive course on the part of the patient." We can regard hydropathic establishments as an alternative form of "utopian community" controlled, not by their members, but by their proprietors, who claimed total authority over the daily activities and treatment of their patients.

As Ruggles made the claim, which he shared with other water-cure practitioners, to be allowed practical control of patients, Mack was working out a theoretical moral justification of the grounds for such a claim. To him, leaving the community and becoming editor of a hydropathic newspaper was not a step back from the front line of social reform, but a step toward a higher basis for realizing it. Mack had gone to Northampton with high hopes for such communities. He periodically reminded fellow members that they had not achieved what they were seeking, but were merely trying to build it. His interest in Fourierism was an effort to find a way of pushing the process of community-building onward. But by 1845 he must have become disheartened at the Northampton community's inability to realize the hopes he had placed in it. This had happened, Mack reasoned, because humans were imperfect. How, then, could perfect humans be obtained? Mack deduced that this was because human bodies were themselves as yet imperfect, and he saw water cure as the literal and symbolic means of removing the human impurities that alone stood in the way of radical social change. "A sound mind, in a sound body," Mack wrote to William Lloyd Garrison in 1845, "is a desideratum of culture. But without the sound body, there cannot be a sound mind—so intimately blended are body and mind in human life."[33]

Surveying the reform movements of the day, Mack could see no successes. Abolitionism, temperance, and the community movement had all failed to achieve what they had set out to do. This, Mack argued, was because men and women were not in proper physical condition to accept their arguments and act on them. Efforts like the Northampton community had been premature; only a population of healthy, purified men and women could make them work. Hydropathy was, in this view, much more than a set of techniques for curing disease. It was therapy for all individuals that would, once universally adopted, enable society to be cured as well. It was, Mack wrote, the fundamental "purifying reform" from which all others would flow, "the instrumentality by which a generation may be trained up *capable* of Temperance, Moral Purity, Human Brotherhood." But hydropathy was, he implied, more than just a reform. It was also the most fundamental science. Fourierism was essential for understanding society, he suggested, and phrenology essential for understanding the mind, but hydropathy underpinned them both, because it was the means for training people to break no longer the lower laws of human existence and so become capable of obeying "the higher laws of God." He captured the argument that human perfection lay in the healthiness that water cure could provide with a striking ironic image: "Who can conceive [of] a dyspeptic Angel?"[34]

In practice and theory, Ruggles and Mack took the experience of community and its inadequacies to its logical ends in the search for a scientifically constituted, heavily symbolized therapeutic system that could claim to reform both individuals and, through them, society as a whole. Unlike Fourierism, phrenology, or theories of social reform such as Owenism, hydropathy did not rest on a straightforward progression from material circumstances to moral results. By demanding the active involvement of patients in their treatment, by ensuring that this treatment would be rigorous, and by employing the symbolic connection between water and purification, Ruggles and Mack evolved a system that drew heavily on the tradition of reform through moral suasion. Above all, its practitioners advocated hydropathic treatment not merely as a "cure" for existing ailments but as an aid in preventing disease, effective because it would strengthen the moral, as much as the physical fiber of those who subjected themselves to it. For this reason, particularly in its early years, hydropathy enjoyed considerable popularity with abolitionists and other moral suasionists, with whose philosophic outlook it accorded. It was this ideological predisposition to hydropathy, not merely personal connections or the proprietor's gratitude for his support, that led William Lloyd Garrison himself to travel again to Northampton in the summer of 1848 to accept several weeks' treatment, free of charge, at Ruggles's water cure.[35]

But its focus on the moral purity of individuals, and on the efforts of individuals to achieve this, detached hydropathy from the earlier communitarian focus on social equality, harmony, and justice. Despite Mack's claim that it was "fundamental" to social change, it was in fact another facet of the retreat from the radicalism of the communitarian moment. In 1846 Mack was still being considered by other community reformers as a potential recruit to a new scheme in central Massachusetts that would have served to continue the failed Fruitlands community in a different form, but he did not get involved. Instead he and Maria Mack, once her treatment was over and Mack's engagement to edit the *Green Mountain Spring* had expired, turned their thoughts again to education. They would return to what they knew, running a boarding school for young ladies, but they would include in it the physical, moral, and therapeutic methods they had learned at Northampton and Brattleboro. Mack planned to acquire a large house and grounds for the school, with a plentiful supply of good water that would be used both for "strengthening and invigorating" the pupils and "to cure disease, under Dr Wesselhoeft's advice by letter."[36] The Macks proposed to marry their educational and medical interests in a new kind of school regime, but it was one that turned away from the radical social critique that, in 1842, had so strongly motivated David Mack to give up his previous school in Cambridge and join a community.

In parallel ways, Adam's, Bassett's, the hydropathists', and the Garrisonians' retreats mapped a perspective on the possibilities of community reform that was increasingly common from the mid-1840s on. The "communitarian moment" of the early 1840s had generated ideas and actions that tested ideological assumptions to the limit and revealed the existence of a strongly articulated strand of radical social thought among ordinary supporters of abolitionism and nonresistance. The difficulties of maintaining this community vision under internal and external pressures led to its fragmentation. Adam and Bassett withdrew to more conservative positions; Mack and Ruggles redirected attention from society to the human body itself; other Garrisonians continued their work without the same social vision of community that had brought some of them together at Northampton, Hopedale, and elsewhere, as the new stress on disunion after 1844 redirected their attention to the political arena. The wider cultural and social challenges posed by nonresistance and come-outerism lost much of their significance to the movement.

This, too, was a retreat of sorts, one that left abolitionists less likely to perceive the need for communitarian ventures, less likely to criticize social conventions, and more likely to accept—as Bassett did—the growing consensus that the "free labor" system was the only logical alternative to slavery. The collapse of the communitarian moment, in other words, helped cement the alliance between abolitionism and capitalism that some radical reformers had sought to avert at the beginning of the 1840s.

Economics and Morality

Northampton's change after 1846 from community into factory village was another strand in the shift from social critique to acceptance of industrial capitalism. The end of the association marked the abandonment of its attempts to secure equitable subsistence for its members and operate a productive system without wages. Its two most prominent leaders, George W. Benson and Samuel L. Hill, led efforts to build an industrial community on capitalist lines. As private manufacturers, they could exercise the kind of control over production that community members had denied them in 1843. They could continue to sponsor and support social-reform activities and espouse the principles of human equality without being forced, as they had been in the community, to let equality interfere with their economic authority. Garrisonian abolitionism and religious radicalism would again coexist with the wage system. The tactics of moral suasion were not abandoned but moral concerns would, in time, be limited to issues that did not directly impinge on the economic fortunes of the village's employers.

The separation of capitalism from morality did not take place at once. In fact, reform efforts nearly destroyed Hill's and Benson's attempts to establish themselves as manufacturers in the late 1840s. Benson's activities precipitated the crisis. As we noted, when he separated from the community in 1845, he had to make some compromises with his former principles. He entered a partnership to manufacture cotton, a slave-grown product, with three local capitalists who had remained staunch opponents of Garrisonian abolitionism and the ideals of the community: the brothers Samuel and J. P. Williston, who were Presbyterian supporters of the American and Foreign Anti-Slavery Society, and Joel Hayden, who in 1845 was helping J. P. Williston set up the *Hampshire Herald* as an organ of political abolitionism. These three men provided most of the capital for the factory. Though Benson was an investor and its name—the Bensonville Manufacturing Company—reflected his leading role in it, he was in fact only the others' agent, effectively an employee responsible for managing the firm.[37]

Benson saw no conflict between his role as manufacturer and his commitment to reform. Sojourner Truth was part of his household for a period; he helped maintain the religious practices of the community; and there is evidence that he used the factory to employ black workers from among Northampton's small but growing population of former slaves, some of whom had settled in the area through contacts with evangelical abolitionists like Williston. But by 1848 his reform activities were bringing him into conflict with his employers. A memoir of Benson's family suggests that part of the dispute was over wages. Benson, it was said, had wanted to employ skilled workers at higher wages than his backers would allow. But contemporary sources emphasize a clash over religion. Benson maintained his radical views on churches and sabbath observance. It was claimed that he had mill machinery repaired on Sundays, and when he was nominated president of an anti-sabbath convention held in Boston in 1848 he was obliged to resign as factory agent; as William Lloyd Garrison put it, "the proprietors of the factory here are rigid Presbyterians and this public act of Mr Benson, in connection with . . . his religious freedom and independence on other subjects, was manifestly so distasteful to them, as to make the retaining of his position no longer agreeable to either of the parties."[38]

In search of new employment, he eventually negotiated assistance from Samuel L. Hill and others to set up once more as proprietor of a small silk factory. There were soon signs that this would not be a success. In 1849 a credit reporter noted that Benson was "trading and speculating in many things and borrows a good deal of money, by the aid of friends, but is not remarkably prompt to meet his engagements." By 1850 he was sliding into bankruptcy, and his failure that year nearly bankrupted Hill as well. Benson was sued by at least a dozen creditors and was obliged to flee the state. He moved his family to Williamsburg, New York. His last known appearance in Northampton was late in 1850, when he acted as a witness in another court case under an agreement that protected him from arrest in the debt suits against him, and he ended up leaving Massachusetts in a hurry to evade his creditors. Benson's attempts to reconcile reform principles with business had failed. The credit reporter summed him up: "People speak of him as a good sort of man . . . , but queer in his business notions. In short[,] business *monied* men are shy of him." By early 1851 Benson was reported to have "gone off, leaving debts here to a large amount." For a while he ran a laundry in Williamsburg and then became a merchant in Manhattan in the mid-1850s, but subsequently moved with his family to Kansas and returned to farming.[39]

Samuel L. Hill's policy was to steer clear, if he could, of the reputation for laxity that dogged Benson. How conscious he was at the time of the lessons the Northampton Association had taught him is not certain, but in retrospect he regarded it as subject to two conditions that he would avoid in future: its debt had impeded the raising of sufficient capital for its needs, and the lack of capital had prevented it repaying its debts.[40] His assumption of the remaining property and debts of the Northampton community gave him both the resources to restart in business and, if he succeeded, the basis of a reputation for probity that could secure his credit in the future.

It was a risky strategy. From about the end of 1846 on Hill continued the community silk business in conjunction with two local partners, Macomber and Parsons, who had not been connected with the association. His attempts to retire the community's debts were accompanied by efforts to assist former community members; this led him both to lend money on mortgages for property and to help Benson in his financial difficulties. Benson's misfortunes compromised Hill severely; Hill later recalled that he was left to carry $15,000 of Benson's debts in addition to his own. Macomber and Parsons forced Hill out of their firm, and he came close to failing. Hill was saved, however, by the intervention of a Northampton capitalist, Samuel L. Hinckley, another member of the local elite the Northampton community had so abruptly challenged a decade earlier. Confident in Hill's abilities, and with Hill's property holdings as security, Hinckley agreed to back him as he reestablished a silk business and repaid

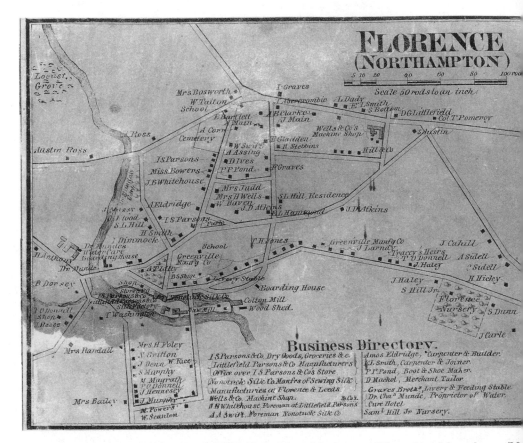

Florence, Massachusetts, from Henry F. Walling, *Map of the County of Hampshire, Massachusetts* (New York, 1860). The former Northampton community silk mill and boarding house is the structure labeled "Cotton Mill" at the eastern end of the power canal. The houses of ex-community members Hill, Hammond, Judd, Wells, Haven, and Atkins are marked on the streets to the north. Courtesy of the Jones Library, Inc., Amherst, Mass.

his debts during the early 1850s. His success at doing so, and Hinckley's continuing support, formed the basis of Hill's subsequent career as the preeminent manufacturer in the growing factory village.[41]

When Hill and others successfully petitioned for a post office in 1852, the village was named "Florence," in token of its small but growing silk mills (though a proposal to rename the Mill River the "Arno" never caught on). The post office was established in the successor to the old community store, now run by Hill in conjunction with a local farmer's son, Isaac S. Parsons. With Hinckley's capital behind him, Hill built up his revived silk mill, first as the firm of Hill and Hinckley, then as the Nonotuck Silk Company, that became Florence's largest employer and was claimed to be the first in the United States to produce silk twist (thread) for use in sewing machines. There were periodic setbacks in the firm's expansion—in the early 1850s and again in the depression of 1857 to 1858—but Hill rapidly diversified his interests across a range of commercial and manufacturing activities. In so doing, he laid the basis for what the historian Agnes Hannay would call the "Florence group" of companies, a network of interlocking partnerships and directorates that would grow during the 1850s and 1860s to dominate the business of the village.[42]

Hill became involved in two substantial firms in addition to the Nonotuck Silk Company. He backed his former community partner Hiram Wells in a foundry and machinery business that evolved into the Florence Sewing Machine Company in 1861, for a while one of the leading U.S. sewing-machine makers. He formed another partnership with Isaac Parsons to make carriages, and then acted as Hinckley's agent in a firm that he and Parsons backed to make buttons and daguerreotype cases, at first run by an English immigrant Alfred P. Critchlow and eventually incorporated as the Florence Manufacturing Company. Though Hill did not permanently retain direct interests in all these businesses, he was influential in bringing into them the overlapping network of men who were to run them in the post–Civil War period. Apart from Hinckley, and Hill's brother-in-law Edwin Eaton, for instance, directors of the Nonotuck Silk Company included Alfred T. Lilly, brought from Mansfield, Connecticut, in 1853 after a long connection with the local silk industry there, and James D. Atkins, the former printer who had been the Northampton community's dyer for several years and was among the members to stay on after its dissolution. Eventually, in 1873, Hill, Lilly, and J. P. Williston's nephew A. Lyman Williston were among the incorporators of the "Workingmen's Savings Bank of Florence," capping their position in local business by forming their own bank.[43]

After his nearly ruinous entanglement in Benson's failure, Hill increasingly divorced his business affairs from his interests in social reform. Some of his land deeds specified that no liquor should be retailed from property that he sold, but otherwise he tended to let prudence, rather than idealism, guide his business decisions. His support for Hiram Wells derived from the two men's long connection, stretching back to their Connecticut days, but it was not based on sentiment: Wells had a reputation as a hard-working, hard-driving employer. Hill felt affinities with the Englishman Alfred P. Critchlow, who had abolitionist sympathies and reputedly left England in part because of his strong objections to monarchy; but Critchlow's firm ran into difficulties in the 1857 depression and the following year Hill and others reorganized it, dropping him as a partner. Above all, Hill's connection with Hinckley reflected a willingness to separate business from reform principles that as a founder of the Northampton community he would once have been unable to accept. Hinckley, apart from being a wealthy man of orthodox religious views, had family connections with the South. Had Hill been able to see the opinions about race and politics expressed in some of the private letters exchanged by Hinckley and his relatives, he might not have been so willing to maintain his partnership with this man.[44]

But the alliance with Hinckley proved the turning point of Hill's fortunes, and between the early 1850s and his death three decades later he oversaw the completion of Florence's transition from community to factory village. As production and employment expanded the population of Florence also grew, from around two hundred when the community dissolved, to 1,654 in 1865 and nearly 3,500 in 1895. Though former community members and their families remained in the village and continued to play a significant role in its public institutions, they also witnessed the rapid growth of a working population whose ethnic and religious diversity and class position contrasted notably with the character of the small community they had originally joined. Hill and others recognized the retreat they were making from the wholesale social transformation the community had intended. Complete change was not possible. Instead, business and philanthropy would be pursued side by side, in an effort to achieve a form of harmony that would not demand social equality.

The expansion of industry and wage-work did not mean a wholesale return to the economic practices of the 1830s against which the community had rebelled. Under Hill and his partners the businesses of mid-century reflected the community's abhorrence of competition. To them concentrations of capital powerful enough to withstand fluctuations and competitive pressure seemed superior to individual proprietorships and informal connections between small manufacturers. The firms Hill and others built in the 1850s and 1860s did, indeed, survive better than many smaller ones in the area. Admission to this group was closely controlled. Hill saw these partnerships as the center of a new form of "ideal" com-

Stockholders of the Nonotuck Silk Company in the late 1860s. Samuel L. Hill is seated second from the left, S. L. Hinckley sits to his left, and former community member James D. Atkins stands in the middle of the back row. Courtesy of Historic Northampton, Northampton, Mass.

munity, run on sound business principles and immune from the influence of men and women with "impractical" notions about how society should be organized. The Northampton community's debates over labor and wages, its financial difficulties, the dependence of its members on patrons of means both during its existence and after its dissolution, all led to a reinforcement of the practices of industrial capitalism and to widespread skepticism that alternative forms of social organization could effectively be pursued.

Nevertheless, the ideals of cooperation that the community promoted also helped shape the industrial firms that emerged in midcentury. Students of capitalism too often stress its individualistic ethos and overlook its heavy reliance on patterns of cooperation. Giles B. Stebbins, after a long career as a Unitarian minister, spiritualist, and lobbyist for protective tariffs, looked back on the community as an effort of "human fraternity to uplift the common lot, and its members carried that aim into the business enterprises in which they were engaged." In Florence, he concluded, "business sagacity and fraternal humanity are combined."[45] The influence of community ideals operated, however, in a new context and with effects different from what had originally been intended.

On one hand, the "Florence group" practiced a form of cooperation in investing and operating businesses, but restricted it to owners and managers. Control of business was not, as it had been in the community, subject to general discussion or interference. Directors of Nonotuck Silk and other companies kept firm control even over information about their affairs. Credit reporters always noted their "closeness" and privacy. One commented in 1873, "Some think they have half a million $ invested in their business ab[ou]t which they are silent in order to avoid taxation." They ran the company in such a way that they did not conform to Massachusetts joint-stock laws, but regarded their stock as "a personal liability." In 1877 a credit reporter wrote that "their stock is so gild edged amongst themselves that none of it is to be had by outsiders, being held by a few friends who control it and will not part with it—they keep their matters very closely." Hill persisted in this policy of privacy to the end of his life, making it a condition of his will that no bond or inventory of his estate be filed with the probate court. His "community" of partners was a private sphere.[46]

On the other hand, industrial work demanded cooperative effort between workers. Yet this effort was very much under the authority of proprietors. If the failure of the Northampton community had convinced its leaders of anything, it was the need for sufficient capital and sufficient capacity for extracting work that the tide of debt could be resisted and turned back. Though they sponsored philanthropic and reform activities, and visitors praised their mills, Hill and his colleagues became indistinguishable from other employers when it came to the control of a labor force. Hiram Wells, formerly the association's machinist, was well established in his own firm in Florence by 1854 when his workmen struck for a ten-hour day. His wife told a friend that the men would not win, because her husband was "as obstinate as an ass and won't be drove into any such thing," and the strike apparently collapsed. Wells's obstinacy would eventually prove fatal. One morning in 1859, he ordered the safety valve on his works' steam engine held down to raise more pressure; the boiler exploded, killing Wells and two workmen.[47] Local silk mills worked a ten-hour day in the mid-1840s, but there is evidence that the working day subsequently lengthened; an 1866 report found ten to twelve hours normal in Northampton mills. The use of child labor remained common, too; ten Northampton factories employed boys or girls under fifteen in 1868, and these included mills in Florence. J. P. Williston, still a proprietor of the Greenville Manufacturing Company that had succeeded Benson's cotton business, argued in 1867 against laws restricting child employment and requiring lengthy periods of schooling: "I believe," he wrote, "that twelve hours' confinement in a factory is less injurious to health than six hours in school."[48] Paternalistic control, of proprietors over their workforce, and of parents over children who worked alongside them in the factories, marked patterns of "cooperation" that were structured by authority, rather than equality. Though it was not his intention, Giles B. Stebbins's comment on the influence of community ideals in Florence subtly reflected this change. The Northampton Association had been "the place of their joint efforts for a better life for all." Florence was now an example of "a town where large industries employ many persons," whose "character . . . is modified by the spirit and methods of the managers and employers."[49] Equality had yielded to philanthropy.

Philanthropy and the Vision of Harmony

Most former members continued to live modestly, as they had before they came to Northampton. The Hammonds and Frances Judd had their small houses and plots of land, but for some years after Hall's death Judd rented her house out and lived in another household, supporting herself on a teacher's small salary. Joseph C. Martin farmed for a while on less than forty acres elsewhere in Northampton, but this was not in a fertile district, and he moved back to Florence; only some of his sons achieved prosperity. Austin and Fidelia Ross, who took over the community's farm and established a dairying business, owned between eighty and ninety acres of fair land, but lived quite simply. Helen Garrison visited them in 1848 and "found them real old fashioned country people living alone in a small house but comfortably furnished." Three years later, Ross was taxed on the house, land, and just $375 worth of personal property.[50]

Florence remained a center of the reform tradition, in a region still often hostile to it. Hill and others merely kept their reform interests distinct from their business concerns. Until the Civil War abolition still set the reformers of Florence apart in the minds of local people. Hill's son Arthur recalled growing up in a neighborhood whose members were "ostracized and maligned by their fellow townsmen, meeting with fictitious stories of themselves when visiting neighboring places and warned against being associated with."[51] Northampton's hotels and water cures, including Ruggles's former establishment, in new hands after his death, continued to attract southern visitors, and there was occasional antagonism between them and residents of this known center of abolitionism. Such antagonism added to the disquiet caused by the passage of the Fugitive Slave Act in 1850 to increase the insecurity of black families and individuals in the area, and there is evidence that some of them moved during the early 1850s to places where they felt less exposed to possible danger.[52]

The former community's religious beliefs and activities also provoked controversy and opposition. Members continued to hold periodic meetings for worship similar to those held at the community, though for nearly twenty years they maintained the principle that these were free religious meetings, not the gatherings of an organized church or sect. Hall Judd's father attended one of them, held under the pine tree near the factory one Sunday in August 1848, and heard addresses by the black minister J. W. C. Pennington, William Lloyd Garrison, "Mr. Sheldon, a raving Millerite," and "Mr. Randolph, a sort of deistical christian." Nonetheless, the growth of Florence's population and its ethnic diversity altered the context in which the group functioned. New adherents to its meetings were attracted, sometimes by marriage or by workplace connections, but it was quickly exceeded in size by other denominations. Catholic, Methodist, and orthodox Congregational societies were all formed in Florence before the Civil War. Former community members seem to have been on best terms with the Methodists, and their gatherings were moved from private houses to the Methodist meetinghouse at some point in the late 1850s. But the new Congregational minister evidently regarded Florence under the community's influence as a foreign territory to be conquered, and decades later still recalled the private disputes he held with Samuel Hill and others on the age of the universe, the evidence of geology, and the importance of scripture. Just as the Northampton community had been a thorn in the side of the Connecticut Valley's religious establishments in the early 1840s, its remaining members held their ground as a pocket of freethought in the 1850s and 1860s.[53]

As their own numbers slowly rose, and as other churches were built up around them, Hill and his fellow freethinkers were obliged to consider placing their own group on a more formal footing. In 1863, at least fourteen former community members helped found the Free Congregational Society, which explicitly declared its toleration of all Christian viewpoints and continued the Northampton Association's tradition of nondenominational worship. Among the society's early "speakers" (as its ministers were called) was a woman. Hill wrote, shortly after its founding, that it was part of the Northampton Association's "legitimate fruit, . . . possessing the same spirit as other kindred institutions established by influences having the same origins." Part of a loose network of such groups affiliated with the Free Religious Association, the Florence society was well regarded in the movement for practices that rejected the trappings of traditional denominations.[54]

Though business was kept separate from reform activities, reform came to depend on business as it became the object of village leaders' philanthropy. Hill never became a plutocrat, but he advanced to quite substantial wealth. By the 1860s, he was rumored to be "worth $100,000" or more and his taxable income in 1865 alone exceeded $12,000. He started making substantial donations to local institutions, and it is likely that Hill's wealth increased in the 1870s as the value of the Nonotuck Silk Company and his other manufacturing interests grew. The Free Congregational Society was only one of a series of organizations that Hill and his associates sponsored during and after the Civil War. Schools, Cosmian Hall—an impressive meetinghouse for the Free Congregational Society for which Hill contributed $40,000—the savings bank, and, eventually, a library were among them. The network of former community members connected with the Free Congregational Society, including Hill's family, Frances Judd, the Havens, and the Martins, were among those asked to help set up or run these organizations. Like other factory villages with idealist or community roots, Florence became an exercise in philanthropic capitalism. This, as much as its broader reform ideals, was a legacy of the Northampton community.[55]

In Florence's industries and institutions we can follow the transfor-

Cosmian Hall, built for the Free Congregational Society of Florence between 1872 and 1874, and demolished in 1948. Courtesy of Historic Northampton, Northampton, Mass.

mation of the community ideals of the 1840s into the more limited, less egalitarian visions of midcentury, which were rooted in industrial capitalism rather than seeking to supplant it. But Florence represented a vision of a particular kind. A brief comparison with Hopedale, the other Massachusetts factory village that grew out of a utopian community, suggests some contrasts that help locate the ideals of Hill and his associates in the wider context of later-nineteenth-century social thought.

Hopedale's demise as a community was rather different from Northampton's. In some ways it was the victim of its financial success. Its valuable properties, including a substantial water-power site, proved too tempting for members of the Draper family who were important stockholders in the Hopedale community by the mid-1850s. In 1856 a temporary financial setback gave the Drapers an excuse to buy out the remainder of the stock, and the property came into their hands. They used it to develop a large and very successful textile-machinery business; the Northrop loom, manufactured by the Draper company in the late-nineteenth and early twentieth centuries was widely used to reequip the U.S. textile industry and made the company's stockholders rich. But the Drapers had effectively ousted Adin Ballou and other Hopedale community leaders, and as Edward K. Spann has shown in his recent study, they and their apologists lost no opportunity to celebrate the superiority of capitalist enterprise over the old "futile communistic experiment." They denounced the community's "dry, barren, prosaic and somewhat repellent character" and condemned Ballou's failure to understand "scientific sociology," that had led him to conduct "a fatuous experiment . . . in pursuit of a chimera." Business methods, a politician claimed in 1887, had rescued Hopedale by bringing the community to an end: "Enlightened and liberal selfishness became, as it usually does, a beneficence to which a weak communism was as the dull and cheerless gleam of a decaying punk to the inspiring blaze of the morning sun." These attacks embodied what we might call the "social Darwinist" version of communitarian history, which dismissed the search for harmony and cooperation as manifestly inferior to "scientifically" sanctioned competition and selfishness. Though Ballou remained in Hopedale for the rest of his life, he still smarted from the shock of the Drapers' move against the community and the shattering of its promise of a better world.[56]

Hill and the others in Florence were in a different position. They had ended their community more or less by agreement, and their prominence in local businesses and organizations gave them much better control over its legacy than Ballou could retain. Instead of rejecting the ideal of social harmony, they sought to engraft it onto capitalism, to build institutions that they hoped could overcome the inherent conflicts within the system, while business itself was left to run without interference. As the Free Congregational Society sustained the tradition of nondenominational worship and religious toleration that the community had initiated, another local institution of the 1870s developed the community's concern

The Florence Kindergarten building, constructed in 1876. The kindergarten, subsequently renamed the Hill Institute, still uses it in the 1990s. From Charles A.
Sheffeld, ed., *History of Florence, Massachusetts.*

with social harmony, and its stress on education as a means of instilling
this.

From the early 1870s onward Hill was the main sponsor of the Florence
Kindergarten, established to provide free nursery education to three- and
four-year-old children in the village. In 1876 he chose a board of trustees
to administer it; former community members and members of the Free
Congregational Society were prominent among them. He also set out in
his will, drawn up in 1881, the conditions on which the kindergarten
could continue to benefit from his substantial bequest. It was to provide
for the "healthy physical, moral and intellectual development of children
. . . unmixed with ecclesiastical or theological exercises or influence," and
should be open to all "residents of the village without distinction of race,
nationality or previous condition."[57] Nonsectarian, nondiscriminatory
ideals infused the kindergarten movement in Florence as they had done
the community three decades before.

The Florence Kindergarten was one of a number set up in the United States in the 1860s and 1870s, based on the work of Elizabeth Palmer Peabody and other interpreters of the methods of the German educationalist Friedrich Froebel.[58] Two aspects of the kindergarten movement stand out, and presumably attracted Hill: the practical terms in which it advocated as essential the early moral education and training of children, and its argument that such training promoted social harmony.

Froebel's methods, as adopted by Peabody and other American practitioners, emphasized the systematic cultivation of children's talents and self-discipline through the use of exercises and routines in an environment where structure and formality were made implicit rather than explicit. They appealed to reformers like Peabody because, unlike conventional methods of instruction, they were designed to inculcate a moral sense, engaging children's curiosity rather than their fear of punishment. Elizabeth Powell Bond, "speaker" of the Free Congregational Society and an educationalist in her own right, described the Florence kindergarten soon after it was opened in Peabody's periodical, the *Kindergarten Messenger*. She contrasted the rigid discipline of contemporary public schools with the "freedom of speech and of movement" that the kindergarten permitted. But she stressed that the "seeming disorder" of a kindergarten classroom was made up of activities carefully designed to stimulate and develop children's capabilities, and that this had a wider social purpose. Though to untutored adults kindergarten exercises appeared to be "play," they were intended to inculcate, early in a child's life, the self-motivated desire to take part in purposeful activity and were, according to Bond, "as real work to these little ones as any they will grow to in the coming years." Such techniques echoed the efforts of the Macks, Sophia Foord, and other teachers at the Northampton community to teach through play and practical exercises as well as formal instruction. The notion that kindergarten was an introduction to work and work-discipline also echoed the place of formal work in the education of children at the community. Other exponents of Froebel's methods stressed their intellectual derivation from a tradition that regarded work, instruction, and play as indivisible aspects of education, and asserted that they would cultivate manual dexterity in early childhood, to prepare children "for all the demands of later life."[59]

Though they developed self-discipline and motivation, kindergartens were intended to promote, not individualism but an ability to live and work together with others. Froebel's methods, it was argued, would work well with children regardless of their class, and Peabody envisaged kindergarten exercises as a means of bringing people of diverse backgrounds together; in the classroom, contrasts and discords between children "shall be resolved into sweet accord, the rich harmony, of an undivided, a perfect life."[60] Kindergartens such as that at Florence not only brought children together, but also organized meetings and training sessions for mothers, events that were seen in terms that explicitly crossed class lines. Though the Florence kindergarten was only one of many in the late-nineteenth-century United States, Hill's bequest allowed it to claim that until the 1890s it was "probably the only endowed kindergarten in the country." As a result, Hill's grandson wrote in the early 1890s, "At a time when in our large cities such an institution existed only for the favored few, the children of wealth, and occasionally in connection with mission work for the very poor, the little village of Florence enjoyed the distinction of having a well equipped kindergarten which was thoroughly democratic, knowing no high and no low, no rich and no poor."[61] Not only on race and religion, but also in class terms, the Florence kindergarten fostered the ideals of harmony that the community had once upheld; it was another institution that could be seen as the community's legacy.

Yet these ideals were adopted in the context of a village that was in fact socially divided, as its working population grew and control of philanthropic organizations remained in the hands of the former members of the community and their associates. Cultural events, as much as anything, measured the distance between sections of the village. In 1874 heavy rain burst a poorly constructed dam (owned by local mills, including the Nonotuck Silk Company) high on a tributary of the Mill River, and the resultant flood killed at least 136 people in the factory villages above Florence. The disaster brought forth relief efforts and contributions from across the nation; citizens of Florence, whose homes and factories largely escaped damage, played a significant part in the work of rescue and reconstruction. The Free Congregational Society organized a concert in aid of the relief fund. Women members performed Handel and other classical works, but found themselves with only a small audience. The local newspaper expressed dismay at the low turnout, blaming it on the "popular preference for minstrel shows, Jim Crow, Old Hundred and familiar entertainments."[62] Even a major disaster failed to bridge the gulf between the members of the Free Congregational Society and the majority that had grown up around them, whose tastes and ideology contrasted with theirs. Nothing could have illustrated more eloquently that these heirs of the Northampton community had become a small elite in their own neighborhood.

By the 1890s Florence's leaders were playing the theme of social harmony against a background of anxiety about the dangers of disorder. Averting conflict between capital and labor had been one of the Northampton Association's ambitions; it remained part of the ideology of Florence's manufacturers even when the social relations of production were different from those of the community. In a speech at the dedication of the village library building in 1890, Samuel Hill's son Arthur cited Edward Bellamy's novel *Looking Backward* as a vision of a future freed from social conflict, and claimed it as congruent with Florence's tradition. Two publications four years later reflected in different ways on Florence's vision of harmony. Charles Sheffeld, Samuel Hill's grandson, collected in his *History of Florence* a series of memoirs and historical accounts testifying to the unity and brotherhood of the village that was heir to an association specifically founded to foster those ideals. Olive Rumsey, in an article about the Northampton community, commended its social and economic arrangements as worthy of study in a period preoccupied with conflict between capital and labor. Both, ironically, were being produced as that conflict spread to Florence itself. In 1894, silk winders at the Nonotuck Silk Company had struck, in what was merely the first of a series of confrontations that occurred in the village's mills and shops over the next three decades.[63]

C H A P T E R   E I G H T

The Communitarian Moment

Florence's capitalist philanthropists of the late nineteenth century were eager enough to seize on the memory of the Northampton community as the backdrop to their own efforts at social improvement. Arthur G. Hill in particular made it a reference point in his efforts to portray Florence as a center of continuing social harmony. As Northampton workers became more militant in the early twentieth century, Hill sought to hold the line for a vision of cooperation between capital and labor that he saw being threatened both by greedy employers and dictatorial labor unions. He buttressed this interpretation with a series of reflections on the community's role in the creation of a progressive twentieth-century society.

Old disputes and suspicions about abolitionism and religion were now things of the past, Hill suggested. Slaves were free; religious intolerance was being forgotten in a more liberal environment. In short, the community's view of the world had gradually come to be the common view. Overlooking the racial repression of the New South and playing down the labor struggles of the new industrial economy, Hill saw the defining moments of American history in what he called "the moral warfare of the central third of the nineteenth century." For Hill, born in the community and raised in its aftermath, the members of the Northampton Association had played an important role in that struggle and helped lay the basis for the better society that had emerged from it. His progressive interpretation incidentally helps to explain why no memorial to the Northampton Association was ever erected. The institutions it helped propagate—the factories, schools, kindergarten, and Free Congregational Society—were memorials enough to a generation still conscious of the influence of community ideas on their own lives. They could use the community to explain their own positions of prominence in a divided factory village.[1]

This view of communities as respectable constituted one strand of the reinterpretation of the movement that took place toward the end of the nineteenth century. In addition to memorialists and historians who had themselves had links with communities, there were those, like Charles Nordhoff, who viewed the communal tradition as essential for calming the strife that threatened to overthrow capitalist society. In his study, *Communistic Societies of the United States*, first published in 1875, Nordhoff advocated communities to capitalists as a means of providing security and hope to the "great mass of our poorer people," who would, without them, "gradually sink into stupidity, and a blind discontent which education would only increase, until they became a danger to the state." Communities would head off the formation of labor unions, Nordhoff argued, and avert the "folly" of asserting "necessary and eternal enmity between capital and labor." For Nordhoff, Arthur Hill, and others—including followers of Marx and Engels's "scientific socialism"—the community legacy was an adjunct to stability in capitalist society.[2]

More commonly, however, communities were ridiculed, or just forgotten. Tracing the effects of participation in the Northampton community on the later lives of individual members is not easy. Even abolitionists and other former enthusiasts played down their involvement in such groups. Though William Lloyd Garrison had found its principles faulty, he was sympathetic to the Northampton community, regarding its successes as a benefit to the cause of reform and its failures as a sign of victory to humanity's opponents. After his death, however, Garrison's sons sought to distance their father's memory from such community schemes, which (with their uncle, George W. Benson, evidently in mind) they saw as drawn up by "the insane, the unbalanced, the blindly enthusiastic." Such rewriting was not unique. Several late-nineteenth-century genealogies and memoirs of former members similarly glossed over or suppressed altogether the involvement of their subjects in the community.[3]

This amnesia did not, however, simply arise from a wish to deny involvement. It also reflects the place that experiments like Northampton had in the development of the social reform movement and the lives and careers of its members. To men and women looking back over long years of commitment to abolition and other causes, the few months or years they belonged to the Northampton Association seemed only a small part of the story. The shifts in abolitionism, the rise of Free Soil, and the intensification of political conflict with the South all distanced community visions from the concerns of those once strongly attracted to them. To the generation of children who lived at or were born in the community, the Civil War came to dominate their lives at the same stage that their parents' had been shaken by the depression, the abolitionist splits, and the communitarian efforts of the early 1840s. Principles, social position, or other circumstances kept many former community children out of military service; however, of those still living in Florence, for instance, two sons of Joseph C. Martin joined the army; elsewhere, Edwin P. Richardson, who had joined the community with his mother, served as an engineer in the U.S. Navy, and William E. Stearns was commissioned a captain in a New Hampshire regiment.[4] But the significance of war, for both parents and children of these abolitionist families, was that it became the instrument of the change they had struggled for. Communitarian ventures that could show little tangible success came to seem unimportant by comparison.

Either by appropriating the communitarian tradition for their own ideological purposes, or by ridiculing and forgetting it, late-nineteenth-century commentators helped distort our ability to view the movements of the 1840s in the perspective of their own moment. I have tried to recover this, and to reinterpret the stories of the Northampton community and its members in light of it. As the community demonstrated, the early 1840s were a period in which, despite enormous impediments, some reformers could envision a radically new future for the United States and had the courage and confidence to set out to try and build it. That future contained racial, gender, and economic equality and religious toleration. Its advocates were willing to speak out against any institutions and habits that stood in the way of its realization. For an active majority in the community, that involved conducting a three-year experiment with a noncapitalist economy, an experiment that collapsed under the weight, not of its own contradictions, but the external pressures ranged against it.

The "communitarian moment" of the 1840s arose at a particular conjuncture of economic, political, and religious change in the United States that linked the moral critique of chattel slavery to a wider critique of society. For the abolitionist nonresistants at Northampton, this conjuncture was particularly potent, but it affected groups and individuals throughout the contemporary communitarian movement. Under the circumstances in which the community was founded, moral-suasionist arguments about sin, power, and the character of social and political action became peculiarly radical instruments, potentially sweeping the whole range of day-to-day experience into the paths of change. To many members of 1840s communities the ideal of "harmony" was more than just an idyllic vision. It was a powerful reproach to the many forms of inequality, competition, and "slavery" in American society.

Here, all too evidently, moral suasion contradicted itself. The need to follow the dictates of conscience and belief sowed dissension, and moral-suasion principles posed in practice an especially difficult challenge for those who sought to establish mechanisms of authority or control. Many individuals and families withdrew from the community, either disgusted at the conflicts that arose, or frustrated by institutional arrangements with which they could not agree. Ironically, though, the contradiction was not fatal. The ideal of harmony was sufficiently powerful for a considerable number of members to want to stay and achieve it, and they sustained a set of economic relationships that they believed could best resolve the contest between unity and individuality.

The "communitarian moment" passed at Northampton for several reasons. Business failure compromised a stable set of social arrangements, just as a broad economic recovery began to make them look less necessary or attractive. New political circumstances altered the direction of abolitionism, leaving behind part of the original rationale for community experiments. Above all, individuals began to apply the lessons of the community experience to their own search for fresh ways of ordering the world about them. Though some communities undoubtedly fell apart because the people who joined them imagined that perfection could be achieved overnight, this was hardly so at Northampton, whose members knew that the ideal society would have to be built. But time and effort took their toll, and the rural New Englanders who for a long time sustained their vision under adverse circumstances were not people to pursue what they came to perceive as impossible.

That, paradoxically, is why their attempt was significant. They sought to realize a vision that, for a while at least, did *not* seem impossible.

NOTES

AAS   American Antiquarian Society, Worcester, Mass.

BPL   Boston Public Library.

CCLMC *The Collected Correspondence of Lydia Maria Child, 1817–1880,* ed. Milton Meltzer and Patricia G. Holland. Millwood, N.Y.: Kraus Microform, 1980.

CSL   Connecticut State Library, Hartford.

CtY   Beinecke Rare Book and Manuscript Library, Yale University, New Haven, Conn.

Deeds   Hampshire County, Register of Deeds, Hall of Records, Northampton, Mass. Cited by volume and page number.

EI   James Duncan Phillips Library, Peabody and Essex Institute, Salem, Mass.

FL   Forbes Library, Northampton, Mass.

HBS   Baker Library, Harvard University Graduate School of Business Administration, Boston.

HCL   Houghton Library, Harvard University, Cambridge, Mass.

HN   Historic Northampton, Inc., Northampton, Mass.

HSP   Historical Society of Pennsylvania, Philadelphia.

HUA   Harvard University Archives, Cambridge, Mass.

MHS   Massachusetts Historical Society, Boston.

NAAS   *National Anti-Slavery Standard* (New York).

NAEI   Northampton Association of Education and Industry.

NEHGS New England Historic Genealogical Society, Boston, Mass.

RIHS   Rhode Island Historical Society, Providence.

SSC   Sophia Smith Collection, Smith College, Northampton, Mass.

UMass   Manuscripts and Archives Department, University of Massachusetts Library, Amherst

WHM   Worcester Historical Museum, Worcester, Mass.

Preface

1. Dale Cockrell, *Excelsior: Journals of the Hutchinson Family Singers, 1842–1846* (Stuyvesant, N. Y., 1989), 102, 104, 264–70, 274.

CHAPTER ONE
"One Common Enterprise"

1. The 1800–59 figure is based on Otohiko Okugawa, "Annotated List of Communal and Utopian Societies, 1787–1919," in *Dictionary of American Communal and Utopian History*, ed. Robert S. Fogarty (Westport, Conn., 1980), 173–233; that for 1860–1914 on Robert S. Fogarty, *All Things New: American Communes and Utopian Movements, 1860–1914* (Chicago, 1990), 227–33. These figures do not include communities for which only plans or prospectuses exist. Neither figure is definitive; scholars continue to find evidence of previously unknown communities; see Philip N. Dare, *American Communes to 1860: A Bibliography* (New York, 1990), and Timothy Miller, *American Communes, 1860–1960* (New York, 1990).
2. *Harbinger* 1, no. 13 (Sept 6, 1845).
3. Okugawa, "Annotated List," 183–95.
4. Financial details may be traced in Deeds, 93: 73, 95: 231, 100:154, 100:355, 105:190, 111:73, 111:307, 114:154, 114:269, 121:143, 121:467, 124:417, and 124: 434. Correspondence in the Charles N. Talbot Papers, folders 3–4, RIHS, provides background information.
5. Recent general studies of American communalism, in addition to those cited in note 1, include Robert S. Fogarty, "Communitarians and Counterculturists," in *Encyclopedia of American Social History*, ed. Mary Kupiec Cayton, Elliott J. Gorn and Peter W. Williams (New York, 1993), 3:2241–50; Brian J. L. Berry, *America's Utopian Experiments: Communal Havens from Long-Wave Swings* (Hanover, N.H., 1992); Edward K. Spann, *Brotherly Tomorrows: Movements for a Cooperative Society in America, 1820–1920* (New York, 1989); and Yaacov Oved, *Two Hundred Years of American Communes* (New Brunswick, N.J., 1988). A major study by Donald E. Pitzer is forthcoming. On Owenism, see J.F.C. Harrison, *Quest for the New Moral World: Robert Owen and the Owenites in Britain and America* (New York, 1969); Anne Taylor, *Visions of Harmony: A Study in Nineteenth-Century Millenarianism* (Oxford, 1987); and Carol F. Kolmerten, *Women in Utopia: The Ideology of Gender in the American Owenite Communities* (Bloomington, Ind., 1990). Outstanding works on Fourierism are Jonathan Beecher, *Charles Fourier: The Visionary and His World* (Berkeley, Calif., 1986), and, for the American movement, Carl J. Guarneri, *The Utopian Alternative: Fourierism in Nineteenth-Century America* (Ithaca, N.Y., 1991). Rosabeth Moss Kanter, *Commitment and Community: Communes and Utopias in Sociological Perspective* (Cambridge,

lores Hayden, *Seven American Utopias: The Architecture of Communitarian Socialism, 1790–1975* (Cambridge, Mass., 1976), are also important.

6. Brook Farm's connections with Boston's social and literary elite gave it a prominent place in late-nineteenth-century histories and memoirs; significant works include Octavius Brooks Frothingham, *George Ripley* (Boston, 1882); John T. Codman, *Brook Farm: Historic and Personal Memoirs* (Boston, 1894); and Lindsay Swift, *Brook Farm: Its Members, Scholars, and Visitors* (New York, 1900). Fruitlands benefited from restoration and publicity in the early twentieth century; see Clara Endicott Sears, comp., *Bronson Alcott's Fruitlands* (Boston, 1915). Recent works include Guarneri, *Utopian Alternative*, esp. part 3 which deals with Brook Farm's Fourierist phase and its wider role in the movement; Anne C. Rose, *Transcendentalism as a Social Movement, 1830–1850* (New Haven, Conn. 1981), which discusses both Brook Farm and Fruitlands in chaps. 4 and 5; and Joel Myerson, ed., *The Brook Farm Book: A Collection of First-Hand Accounts of the Community* (New York, 1987).

7. For long the best accessible accounts were Adin Ballou, *Autobiography of Adin Ballou*, ed. William S. Heywood (Lowell, Mass., 1896), and Adin Ballou, *History of the Hopedale Community, from Its Inception to Its Virtual Submergence in the Hopedale Parish*, ed. William S. Heywood (Lowell, Mass., 1897). The standard work is now Edward K. Spann, *Hopedale: From Commune to Company Town, 1840–1920* (Columbus, Ohio, 1992). Discussions of Hopedale by John L. Thomas, "Antislavery and Utopia," in *The Antislavery Vanguard: New Essays on the Abolitionists*, ed. Martin Duberman (Princeton, 1965), 240–69, and especially Lewis Perry, *Radical Abolitionism: Anarchy and the Government of God in Antislavery Thought* (Ithaca, N.Y., 1973), chap. 5, are still useful.

8. John Humphrey Noyes, *History of American Socialisms* (1870; rpt. ed., New York, 1966), 154–60; Charles A. Sheffeld, ed., *The History of Florence, Massachusetts, Including a Complete Account of the Northampton Association of Education and Industry* (Florence, Mass., 1895); Olive Rumsey, "The Northampton Association of Education and Industry," *New England Magazine* 12 (Mar. 1895): 22–32; referring, on page 24, to the association's initial "peculiar union and at the same time separation of capital and labor," Rumsey judged it "worthy of serious attention." See also [Edward P. Pressey?], "Northampton Community I," and "Northampton Community II: Comment on Its Failure," *Country Time and Tide* 5 (Dec. 1903–Jan. 1904): 37–43, 63–67. The best scholarly discussions of the community: Arthur E. Bestor, "Fourierism at Northampton: A Critical Note," *New England Quarterly* 13 (Mar. 1940): 110–22, and Alice Eaton McBee, "From Utopia to Florence: The Story of a Transcendentalist Community in Northampton, Massachusetts, 1830–1852," *Smith College Studies in History* 32 (1947), had to rely on Sheffeld's incomplete transcriptions of the records. Thomas, "Antislavery and Utopia," 260–62, based his discussion of Northampton largely on Noyes. Quotations from Hope Hale Davis, "The Northampton Association of Education and Industry," in *The Northampton Book: Chapters from 300 Years in the Life of a New England Town, 1654–1954* (Northampton, Mass., 1954), are on 110 and 112.

9. Northampton Association of Education and Industry Records, 1836–1853, hereafter cited as follows, using the volume numbers under which items are cataloged: Membership Register, "NAEI, vol. 1"; Record of Proceedings, 1842–1848, "NAEI,

vol. 2"; Northampton Silk Company, Account book, "NAEI, vol. 3"; Letterbook, 1843–1847, "NAEI, vol. 4"; Daybook 1842–44, "NAEI, vol. 5"; Daybook no. 2, "NAEI, vol. 6"; Daybook no. 4, "NAEI, vol. 7"; Silk Manufacturing Department Account book, "NAEI, vol. 8". In quotations from manuscripts throughout this book, I retain original spelling and punctuation as far as possible, consistent with clarity.

10. *Liberator* (Boston), Sept. 8, 1843.

11. Fogarty, *All Things New*, 16. Sydney E. Ahlstrom, *A Religious History of the American People* (New Haven, Conn., 1972), 491, emphasizes charismatic leadership in religious communities. Interest in charismatic authority and the organization of sects derives from Max Weber; see H. H. Gerth and C. Wright Mills, eds., *From Max Weber: Essays in Sociology* (London, 1948), 51–55, 267–359.

12. Judith Wellman, "Women and Radical Reform in Antebellum Upstate New York: A Profile of Grassroots Female Abolitionists," in *Clio Was a Woman: Studies in the History of American Women*, ed. Mabel E. Deutrich and Virginia C. Purdy (Washington, D.C., 1980), 118; Nancy Hewitt, "The Reform Tradition in New York State: A Comparison of Benevolent Women and Woman's Rights Advocates in Antebellum Rochester" (paper presented to the Seneca Falls Women's History Conference, June 1979), 9, and idem, *Women's Activism and Social Change: Rochester, New York, 1822–1872* (Ithaca, N.Y., 1984); Lawrence J. Friedman, *Gregarious Saints: Self and Community in American Abolitionism, 1830–1870* (Cambridge, 1982), 6; Richard Ellis and Aaron Wildavsky, "A Cultural Analysis of the Role of Abolitionists in the Coming of the Civil War," *Comparative Studies in Society and History* 32 (Jan. 1990): 89–116. Other useful studies include Jean Fagan Yellin, *Women and Sisters: The Antislavery Feminists in American Culture* (New Haven, Conn., 1989); Debra Gold Hansen, *Strained Sisterhood: Gender and Class in the Boston Female Anti-Slavery Society* (Amherst, Mass., 1993); and Jean Fagan Yellin and John C. Van Horne, eds., *The Abolitionist Sisterhood: Women's Political Culture in Antebellum America* (Ithaca, N.Y., 1994).

13. Frederick Engels, *Socialism: Utopian and Scientific*, trans. Edward Aveling (1892; rpt. ed., New York, 1975); the quotation is from Karl Marx and Frederick Engels, *Manifesto of the Communist Party* (1848; rpt. ed., Moscow, 1969), 92.

14. For a recent view of these issues, see Charles Sellers, *The Market Revolution: Jacksonian America, 1815–1846* (New York, 1991).

15. Gertrude K. Burleigh to Abby Kelley, Philadelphia, Dec. 28, 1843, Abigail Kelley Foster Papers, WHM. For a different view of the 1840 election, see Daniel Walker Howe, *The Political Culture of the American Whigs* (Chicago, 1979), 7–8.

16. Sellers, *Market Revolution*; Bruce Laurie, *Artisans into Workers: Labor in Nineteenth-Century America* (New York, 1989); Thomas Dublin, *Transforming Women's Work: New England Lives in the Industrial Revolution* (Ithaca, N.Y., 1994), includes a good bibliography. I have discussed these issues with particular respect to the Connecticut Valley in Massachusetts, in Christopher Clark, *The Roots of Rural Capitalism: Western Massachusetts, 1780–1860* (Ithaca, N.Y., 1990).

17. Quoted in Carleton Mabee, *Black Freedom: The Nonviolent Abolitionists from 1830 through the Civil War* (New York, 1970), 72.

18. In *Liberator*, Jan. 5, 1844, Garrison argued that "an internal regeneration must precede the external salvation of man from sin and misery." Whitney's recollection

was in *Old Anti-Slavery Days: Proceedings of the Commemorative Meeting, Held by the Danvers Historical Society at the Town Hall, Danvers, April 26, 1893* (Danvers, Mass., 1893), 58. See also Louis S. Gerteis, *Morality and Utility in American Antislavery Reform* (Chapel Hill, N.C., 1987).

19. For a critique of historians' rigid distinction between "social" and "moral suasion" see Guarneri, *Utopian Alternative*, 77–78.

20. Samuel Myers to Erasmus Darwin Hudson, New Lisbon, Ohio, Apr. 27, 1843, Hudson Family Papers, Box 1, folder 20, UMass.

21. Perry, *Radical Abolitionism*, 63–70.

22. Millenarian influences on one Northampton community member are noted in [James Boyle], *Social Reform, Or an Appeal in Behalf of Association, Based upon the Principles of a Pure Christianity* (Northampton, Mass., 1844), 37. On millenarianism and its variants, see J.F.C. Harrison, *The Second Coming: Popular Millenarianism, 1750–1850* (New Brunswick, N.J., 1979).

23. Lydia Maria Child to Abby Kelley, Northampton, Oct. 1, 1838, Abigail Kelly Foster Papers, Box 1, folder 2, AAS.

24. *Sixth Annual Report of the Board of Managers of the Massachusetts Anti-Slavery Society* (Boston, 1838), 23. A parallel argument, concerning the adaptation of joint-stock forms for reform purposes, was made by Fourierists; see "False Association, Established by the Capitalists, Contrasted with True Association," *Harbinger* 3 (Nov. 14, 1846): 365–68.

25. See the essays collected in Thomas Bender, ed., *The Antislavery Debate: Capitalism and Abolitionism as a Problem in Historical Interpretation* (Berkeley, Calif., 1992). The quotation is from NAEI, Preamble and Articles of Association, Jan. 18, 1843, A. J. Macdonald Collection, p. 72, CtY.

CHAPTER TWO
Founders, Origins, and Contexts

1. Minutes of the meeting are in NAEI, no. 2, pp. 3–5.

2. Information on the Benson family in the preceding paragraphs is drawn from [Wendell Phillips Garrison], *The Benson Family of Newport, Rhode Island, together with an Appendix concerning the Benson Families in America of English Descent* (New York, 1872), 38–44, 51–54. Samuel J. May, *Some Recollections of our Antislavery Conflict* (Boston, 1869), 42–43, 53–56, describes Benson's role in the Prudence Crandall affair; Crandall's epithet for the Benson house was reported by Helen E. Benson to William Lloyd Garrison, Providence, Feb. 11, 1834, HCL bMS Am 1906(13); Benson's abolitionist activities are recorded in Windham County A[nti]-S[lavery] Society, Record, 1837–47, CSL, and George W. Benson to Samuel J. May, Boston, Dec. 30, 1837, BPL MS A.1.1.2.74; his plan to move from Brooklyn, in Benson to May, Brooklyn, Conn., Feb. 8, 1841, BPL MS A.1.2.11.59. See also Brooklyn Female Anti-Slavery Society, Records, 1834–40, CSL.

3. Biographical material on Hill is in *Hampshire Gazette* (Northampton, Mass.), Apr. 21, 1866, Apr. 2, 1867, Dec. 19, 1882; Charles A. Sheffeld, ed., *The History of Florence, Massachusetts, Including a Complete Account of the Northampton Association of*

Education and Industry (Florence, Mass., 1895), 205–11; and William Sanford Hills, comp., *The Hills Family in America*, ed. Thomas Hills (New York, 1906), 331, 398. Evidence of his role in Willimantic abolitionism is in Samuel L. Hill to Amos A. Phelps, Willimantic, Jan. 13, 1836, BPL MS A.21.6(4), and Feb. 24, 1836, BPL MS A.21.6(17).

4. Information on Conant, Swift, and Chaffee is in William H. Chaffee, *The Chaffee Genealogy* (New York, 1909), 412; *Commemorative Biographical Record of Tolland and Windham Counties, Connecticut* (Chicago, 1903), 595; L. P. Brockett, *The Silk Industry in America: A History Prepared for the Centennial Exposition* ([New York], 1876), 57–58; Ruth V. Munsell, "Early Years of the Silk Industry in Mansfield" (Mansfield Historical Society, Mansfield, Conn.), and other notes collected by Mrs. Munsell that she kindly allowed me to see; and J. R. Cole, *History of Tolland County, Connecticut* (New York, 1888), 259–64 (which contains many inaccuracies). Accounts of Joseph Conant, Earl Dwight Swift, and Olive Conant Swift with the Northampton Silk Co. are in NAEI, vol. 3. On Conant's reform sympathies, see Wilbur H. Siebert, *The Underground Railroad from Slavery to Freedom* (1898; rpt. ed., New York, 1968), 403, and Frances P. Judd, memoir dated 1853, in A. J. Macdonald Collection, pp. 67–70, CtY (misattributed by Macdonald to "Mrs. Judson").

5. Samuel Brooks's property transactions are recorded in Deeds, 90:320 and 96:30. U.S. Seventh Census, Population Schedules, Connecticut, 1850, National Archives, Washington, D.C. (microfilm 432, reel 39, pp. 41–42), lists three of his children, Joshua, Lorenzo, and Lucinda Brooks, among the Church Family of Shakers at Enfield.

6. On Hall Judd's father and his views, see Christopher Clark, *The Roots of Rural Capitalism: Western Massachusetts, 1780–1860* (Ithaca, N.Y., 1990), 3–7. Sylvester Judd Jr.'s best-known work was the novel *Margaret: A Tale of the Real and Ideal, Blight and Bloom, Including Sketches of a Place Not Before Described, Called Mons Christi* (Boston, 1845); the biography of him by Richard J. Hathaway, *Sylvester Judd's New England* (University Park, Pa., 1981), also contains material about the Judd family.

7. Quotations are from Hophni Judd to Chauncey Parkman Judd, Windsor, Oct. 19, 1841 (emphasis in original), and Apphia Judd to Arethusa Hall, Northampton, May 1, 1842, both in Judd Papers, *55M-1 Box 2, HCL.

8. Nathaniel Hawthorne to David Mack, Boston, July 18, 1841, MS Am 1067(4), and May 25, 1842, MS Am 1067(5), both in BPL. Biographical information on Mack is in *Obituary Record of Graduates of Yale College deceased during the Academical Year ending in June 1879* (n.p., n.d.), 337, and Isabella Mack Hinckley, "Recollections of Some Interesting People I Have Known and Met" (typescript, n.d.), 18–20, Belmont Historical Society Collection, Belmont Memorial Library, Belmont, Mass.; these memoirs of Mack's daughter stress that it was her father who was eager to move to a community. There is an advertisement for the Macks' school in Cambridge in *Liberator*, Dec. 25, 1840.

9. Hudson's biography is outlined in Samuel Orcutt, *History of Torrington, Connecticut, from its First Settlement in 1737, with Biographies and Genealogies* (Albany, N.Y., 1878), 146, 177, 209, 218, 463, 498–512; see also *Charter Oak* (Hartford, Conn.), Mar. 1838–Apr. 1840. His assessments of the others were in his copy of

T. H. Gallaudet, *The Philanthropist's Remembrancer* (Hartford, Conn., 1835), in Hudson Family Papers, Box 1, folder 9, UMass.

10. William Adam, "Reminiscences," *The Liberty Bell: By Friends of Freedom*, [ed. Maria Weston Chapman] (Boston, 1844), 74–88, was his own account of his early career. Other details are from *Second Memoir Respecting the Unitarian Mission in Bengal* (Calcutta, 1828); Sophia Dobson Collet, *Life and Letters of Raja Rammohun Roy*, ed. Hem Chandra Sarkar ([Calcutta, 1913]), 65–74, 117–28; William Adam, *A Lecture on the Life and Labours of Rammohun Roy*, ed. Rakhal-Das Haldar (1879; rpt. ed., rev. Dilip Kumar Biswas, Calcutta, 1977), esp. 23–25; S. C. Sanial, "The Rev. William Adam," *Bengal Past and Present* 8 (1914): 251–72; see also William Adam, *Third Report on Vernacular Education in Bengal* (Calcutta, 1838). Other background is from Joseph Di Bona, ed., *One Teacher, One School: The Adam Reports on Indigenous Education in Nineteenth Century India* (New Delhi, 1983); Kenneth W. Jones, *The New Cambridge History of India*, vol. 3, part 1, *Socio-Religious Reform Movements in Modern India* (Cambridge, 1989), 30–39; David Kopf, *The Brahmo Samaj and the Shaping of the Modern Indian Mind* (Princeton, 1979); and Spencer Lavan, *Unitarians and India: A Study in Encounter and Response* ([Boston], 1977). The Brahmo Sabha was the forerunner of the better-known Brahmo Samaj.

11. Phebe Adam's arrival in Boston and her contacts there are noted in Epes Sargent Dixwell, Diary Extracts, Wigglesworth Family Papers, Box 17, MHS. William Adam's academic appointment is detailed in Harvard University, Overseers' Records, vol. 8, pp. 322 and 325, and Corporation Records, vol. 8, pp. 87 and 122, both in HUA; and his antislavery activity in *Proceedings of the General Anti-Slavery Convention, Called by the Committee of the British and Foreign Anti-Slavery Society and Held in London, from Friday, June 12th, to Tuesday, June 23rd, 1840* (London, 1840), esp. 573–84; see also William Adam, *The Law and Practice of Slavery in British India, in a Series of Letters to Thomas Fowell Buxton, Esq.* (London, 1840).

12. *British Indian Advocate* (London), 1841–42. In William Adam to Wendell Phillips, London, June 29, 1841, HCL bMS Am 1953(187), Adam asked for information about settlements and praised the *Dial*'s "pure generous and free spirit which I love and admire"; William Coe's transfer to Adam of his interest in the former Northampton Silk Co. property is in Deeds, 95:16; William Lloyd Garrison to George W. Benson, Boston, Mar. 3, 1843, in *The Letters of William Lloyd Garrison*, ed. Walter M. Merrill and Louis Ruchames (Cambridge, Mass., 1971–81), 3:137, praised Adam as "a man who would be constantly rising in my estimation, if that were possible; for I have long regarded him as one of the noblest specimens of manhood to be found among our race."

13. Anne Talbot to Charlotte Richmond Talbot, Northampton, Mar. 16, 1837, Charles N. Talbot Papers, folder 3, RIHS. On the depression in western Massachusetts, see Clark, *Roots of Rural Capitalism*, 201–3, 243–46. S. N. Richmond to Charles N. Talbot, Providence, Apr. 17, 1837, Charles N. Talbot Papers, folder 3, RHS, reported the failure of a partner of Crawford Allen, a Rhode Island manufacturer who had employed Hill in Willimantic.

14. Hill recalled his plans to farm in *Hampshire Gazette*, Apr. 2, 1867; Adam's plans were mentioned in Esther Dixwell to George B. Dixwell, Boston, Oct. 30, 1841, Wigglesworth Family Papers, Box 3, MHS, and Hall Judd's in Hophni Judd

to C. Parkman Judd, Oct. 19, 1841. On Ripley's preparations for Brook Farm, see Anne C. Rose, *Transcendentalism as a Social Movement, 1830–1850* (New Haven, Conn., 1981), 104–6; his intention to farm instead is mentioned in Sophia Ripley to Anna Alvord, Boston, Oct. 30 [1840], Society for the Preservation of New England Antiquities, (microfilm).

15. Brooklyn, Assessment List Abstracts, 1837–1841, Town Clerk's Office, Brooklyn, Conn.

16. A certificate in Deeds, 84:221, shows that the Northampton Silk Company had paid-up capital of $94,450 by March 1839.

17. Samuel L. Hill, undated memoir, quoted in William A. Hinds, *American Communities and Cooperative Colonies*, 3d ed. (Chicago, 1908), 279.

18. The story of the Northampton Silk Company is outlined in Alice Eaton McBee, "From Utopia to Florence: The Story of a Transcendentalist Community in Northampton, Massachusetts, 1830–1852," *Smith College Studies in History* 32 (1947): chap. 1. *Hampshire Gazette,* Jun. 8, 1836, advertised the company and listed its officers. The Talbots' difficulties with the company and with Whitmarsh are noted in G. W. Talbot to Charles N. Talbot, Northampton, July 26 and Sept. 21, 1837, Charles N. Talbot Papers, folder 3, RIHS, and John Taylor to Charles N. Talbot, Northampton, Jan. 1[6?] and May 5, 1838, Charles N. Talbot Papers, folder 4 RIHS. Lawsuits against Whitmarsh are noted in Charles E. Forbes Papers, folder 24, FL. Accounts of the Jamaican silk scheme are in *NASS*, Mar. 11, 1841, and Levi Pratt to Thomas Pratt, Ocha Rios, Jam., Mar. 12, 1841, HN A.L.18.97b.3a.

19. G. W. Talbot to Charles N. Talbot, Sept. 21, 1837.

20. The preceding paragraphs are based on *The Letters of William Lloyd Garrison*, vols. 2 and 3; Aileen S. Kraditor, *Means and Ends in American Abolitionism: Garrison and His Critics on Strategy and Tactics, 1834–1850* (New York, 1967), chaps. 3–7; Bertram Wyatt-Brown, *Lewis Tappan and the Evangelical War against Slavery* (New York, 1969), chap. 10; James Brewer Stewart, *Holy Warriors: The Abolitionists and American Slavery* (New York, 1976), 88–116; Ronald G. Walters, *The Antislavery Appeal: American Abolitionism after 1830* (Baltimore, 1976); Blanche Glassman Hersh, *The Slavery of Sex: Feminist-Abolitionists in America* (Urbana, Ill., 1978); and Dorothy Sterling, *Ahead of Her Time: Abby Kelley and the Politics of Antislavery* (New York, 1991).

21. Kraditor, *Means and Ends*; the second view derives in part from David H. Donald, "Towards a Reconsideration of the Abolitionists," in *Lincoln Reconsidered* (New York, 1961); Walters, *Antislavery Appeal*.

22. John C. March to Eben Hale, Newbury, July 3, 1837, March Family Papers, Box 1, folder 4, EI.

23. On this approach, see Richard Ellis and Aaron Wildavsky, "A Cultural Analysis of the Role of Abolitionists in the Coming of the Civil War," *Comparative Studies in Society and History* 32 (Jan. 1990): 89–116.

24. Horace Cowles to George W. Benson, Farmington, Jan. 19, 1841, printed in *NASS*, Mar. 18, 1841; the letter was also something of a valedictory statement, for Cowles was shortly to die, and his obituary appeared in the same issue of the *NASS*. George W. Benson to Samuel J. May, Feb. 8, 1841.

25. A report on the founding convention of the Connecticut Anti-Slavery Society,

held in Hartford on February 28, 1838, appeared in *Charter Oak*, Mar. 1838; those present included Benson, Hill, and Hudson, together with Joseph C. Martin of Chaplin, a future member and president of the Northampton community and the father of two other future members. Erasmus Darwin Hudson, Diary, 1840, HN A.m.d.18.51, entry for June 5, 1840 (emphasis in original); Hudson's engagement as agent for the Connecticut Anti-Slavery Society had expired on June 1.

26. Brooklyn Female Anti-Slavery Society, Records, CSL; George W. Benson to Samuel J. May, Feb. 8, 1841; *NASS*, Mar. 18, 1841, reported the Willimantic convention; *NASS*, June 3 and June 10, 1841, the Hartford meeting and the protest. Abby Kelley to George W. Benson, Pawtucket, Sept. 13, 1841, BPL MS A.1.2.12, part 1.107.

27. Susan Byrne to William Lloyd Garrison, Willimantic, June [22?], 1841, BPL MS A.1.2.12:1,47; Hill quoted in Hinds, *American Communities*, 279.

28. Leo Tolstoy, quoted in Lewis Perry, *Radical Abolitionism: Anarchy and the Government of God in Antislavery Thought* (Ithaca, N.Y., 1973), 5. Perry's work remains crucial to an understanding of nonresistance, and I have relied heavily on it for the discussion that follows. On the relationships between peace, nonviolence, and abolitionism, see also Valarie Ziegler, *The Advocates of Peace in Antebellum America* (Bloomington, Ind., 1992); Carleton Mabee, *Black Freedom: The Nonviolent Abolitionists from 1830 through the Civil War* (New York, 1970); and Margaret Hope Bacon, "By Moral Force Alone: The Antislavery Women and Nonresistance," in *The Abolitionist Sisterhood: Women's Political Culture in Antebellum America*, ed. Jean Fagan Yellin and John C. Van Horne (Ithaca, N.Y., 1994), 275–97.

29. Perry, *Radical Abolitionism*, 56–57. See also Louis P. Masur, *Rites of Execution: Capital Punishment and the Transformation of American Culture, 1776–1865* (New York, 1989).

30. Perry, *Radical Abolitionism*, 57.

31. Nonresistants were identified from notices, reports, and subscription lists in *Liberator, Non-Resistant* (Boston), *Practical Christian* (Milford, Mass), and *Reformer* (Worcester); Northampton attitudes are reflected in Sylvester Judd, "Notebook," vol. 2, Judd MS, FL, entry for Dec. 27, 1841; Sylvester Judd to Arethusa Hall, Northampton, Jan. 13, 1842, Judd Papers, Box 2, HCL.

32. Benson's encounters are referred to in *Liberator*, July 13, 1838, and *Non-Resistant*, Jan. 22, 1840. On anti-abolitionist violence generally, see Leonard L. Richards, *"Gentlemen of Property and Standing": Anti-Abolition Mobs in Jacksonian America* (New York, 1970); and Michael Feldberg, *The Turbulent Era: Riot and Disorder in Jacksonian America* (New York, 1980), esp. 44–53.

33. The Harwinton incident was recorded in *Charter Oak*, Sep. 1838, the others in Erasmus Darwin Hudson, Journal 1838–39, HN A.m.d.18.50, entry for Nov. 29, 1838; idem, Diary 1841, HN A.m.d.18.52, entries for Apr. 3 and Apr. 10, 1841.

34. *Union Herald* (Cazenovia, N.Y.), June 17, 1841.

35. David Mack, William Larned, and Enos L. Preston to William Lloyd Garrison, in *Liberator*, Jan. 27, 1843.

36. *Twelfth Annual Report, Presented to the Massachusetts Anti-Slavery Society, by the Board of Managers, Jan. 24, 1844* (Boston, 1844), 55.

37. See John R. McKivigan, "The Antislavery 'Come-Outer' Sects: A Neglected

Dimension of the Abolitionist Movement," *Civil War History* 26 (June 1980): 142–60; idem, *The War against Pro-Slavery Religion: Abolitionism and the Northern Churches, 1830–1865* (Ithaca, N.Y., 1984).

38. Willimantic First Baptist Church, Records, vol. 1, pp. 4, 68, 88, First Baptist Church, Willimantic, Conn. (copies kindly provided me by Mrs. Earl W. McSweeney).

39. Erasmus Darwin Hudson, Case and Sketch Book, 1834–37 and 1840, Shaw-Hudson Letters, Box 7, Folder 1, HN, A.m.d.18.51, entries for Jan. 25, Jan. 26, 1835 (emphasis in original).

40. The Bloomfield group, which included the Bumstead family and Roxcy A. Brown, is described in Erasmus Darwin Hudson, Diary, Feb.–May 1841, HN A.m.d.18.52., entry for Apr. 24, 1841; Judd's involvement is mentioned in Hudson, Journal, Oct. 1840–Feb. 1841, Hudson Family Papers, Box 1, folder 12, UMass, entry for Dec. 14, 1840.

41. Joseph C. Martin to William Lloyd Garrison, Chaplin, Dec. 17, 1843, published in *Liberator,* Jan. 5, 1844, contained his account of the conflict with the minister over the previous three years; manuscript annotations in the CSL's copy of *A Brief Historical Sketch of the Church of Christ in Chaplin, Connecticut, including the Confession of Faith and Covenants adopted by said Church* (Hartford, 1840) show that this letter was written shortly after Martin and several others were excommunicated from the church on Dec. 6, 1843. Martin had been a church officer: Chaplin Ecclesiastical Society, Records, 1809–1906, CSL (microfilm), p. 80, show his appointment as collector in 1840.

42. The report of the Chardon Street Church, Ministry and Sabbath Convention printed in *Liberator*, Nov. 27, 1840, listed among the participants David Mack, Sidney Southworth, William Bassett, Joseph S. Wall, and Herbert Scarborough, all of whom would join the Northampton community between 1842 and 1844.

43. George W. Benson to Samuel J. May, Feb. 8, 1841.

44. George W. Benson, report of the annual meeting of the Windham County Anti-Slavery Society, Mar. 1840, in *Charter Oak*, Apr. 1840. William Adam, draft of a letter of introduction for John A. Collins and Charles L. Remond as delegates of the American Anti-Slavery Society to raise funds in Great Britain, London, Nov. 27, 1840, BPL MS A.1.2.10.57.

45. Margaret Fuller to [William H. Channing?], about Oct. 31, 1840, in *The Letters of Margaret Fuller*, ed. Robert N. Hudspeth (Ithaca, N.Y., 1983–88), 2:180.

46. Carl J. Guarneri, *The Utopian Alternative: Fourierism in Nineteenth-Century America* (Ithaca, N.Y., 1991), 44–51; Rose, *Transcendentalism as a Social Movement*, 93–108.

47. Perry, *Radical Abolitionism*, 136–37; Edward K. Spann, *Hopedale: From Commune to Company Town, 1840–1920* (Columbus, Ohio, 1992).

48. Erasmus Darwin Hudson, Diary, Feb.–May 1841, HN A.m.d.18.52, entries for Mar. 12, 14, 15, 1841. William Lloyd Garrison to George W. Benson, Boston, Jan. 7, 1841, *Letters of William Lloyd Garrison*, 3:9; reference to William M. Chace's interest in a community is made here and on 38n. Buffum's remarks appeared in *NASS*, Oct. 14, 1841.

49. *Non-Resistant*, Oct. 13, 1841.

50. Perry, *Radical Abolitionism*, 131 and chap. 5; Spann, *Hopedale*.

51. Arthur G. Hill, "Antislavery Days in Florence" (typescript), Florence Civic and Business Association, Florence, Mass.

52. Henry S. Gere, *Reminiscences of Old Northampton: Sketches of the Town as it Appeared from 1840 to 1850* (n.p., 1902); Robert Doherty, *Society and Power: Five New England Towns, 1800–1860* (Amherst, Mass., 1977); Christopher Clark, *The Roots of Rural Capitalism: Western Massachusetts, 1780–1860* (Ithaca, N.Y., 1990).

53. Northampton, Tax Assessors, Assessment on the Inhabitants of Taxable Property in Northampton, 1843, Town Papers Collection 5.88, FL; David Lee Child's handbill is in Slavery and Abolition file, HN; the *Liberator*, Jan. 31, 1835, referred to the editor of the *Northampton Courier* as "a very decided and active opposer of Abolition doctrines." Lydia Maria Child catalogued the town's southern connections in a letter to Theodore Dwight Weld, Northampton, Dec. 18, 1838, CCLMC no. 156.

54. Northampton Anti-Slavery Society, Record Book, FL; Lydia Maria Child to Caroline Weston, Northampton, Mar. 7, 1839, CCLMC no. 172, remarked: "I do not know of one Garrison abolitionist here. Moses Breck . . . is so, when left to his own good sense and spontaneous feeling; but he is very easily influenced by the members of the church." The *Ninth Annual Report of the Board of Managers of the Massachusetts Anti-Slavery Society* (Boston, 1841), 59–64, noted that the adjacent town of Hatfield had raised $86 for the "new organized" Massachusetts Abolition Society.

55. Horace B. Chapin, *Women Forbidden to Speak in the Church* (Northampton, [1837]).

56. Eliza Strong to Sidney Strong, Northampton, July 18, 1843, MS Collection, Box 34, FL.

57. Quotations of Lydia Maria Child in this and the previous two paragraphs are from letters written in Northampton, all in CCLMC: to Louisa Loring, June 3, 1838, no. 135; to Ellis Gray Loring and Louisa Loring, July 10, 1838, no. 137; to Caroline Weston, July 27, 1838, no. 141, and Aug. 13, 1838, no. 143; to Abby Kelley, Oct. 1, 1838, no. 149; to Henrietta Sargent, Nov. 18, 1838, no. 151; and to Louisa Loring, Northampton, Feb. 17, 1841, no. 226. George Ripley, *The Claims of the Age on the Work of the Evangelist: A Sermon Preached at the Ordination of Mr. John Sullivan Dwight, as Pastor of the Second Congregational Church in Northampton, May 20, 1840* (Boston, 1840), 20; see Rose, *Transcendentalism as a Social Movement*, 103–4.

58. [Anna Benson Percy?], "When I Was a Girl," in Sheffeld, *History of Florence*, 123. Hill's recollections were published in *Hampshire Gazette*, Apr. 2, 1867. The purchase of the silk company property, dated Oct. 21, 1841, was recorded in Deeds, 92:270.

59. The Adams' first two months in Northampton are documented in Esther Dixwell to George B. Dixwell, Boston, Oct. 30 and Nov. 11, 1841, and in Henrietta Sargent to George B. Dixwell, Boston, Nov. 14 and Dec. 22, 1841, all in Wigglesworth Family Papers, Box 3, MHS. Adam's purchase from Coe is recorded in Deeds, 95:16, dated Feb. 26, 1842. He borrowed a copy of Emmerich de Vattel, *The Law of Nations*, from the lawyer Charles E. Forbes in December 1841 for one month; he and Conant also took legal advice from Forbes. See entries in Forbes, Account Book (marked "Income"), Charles E. Forbes Papers, FL.

60. The property transactions of Apr. 8, 1842, are recorded in Deeds, 95:230, 232.

61. *Hampshire Gazette*, Apr. 2, 1867; Hinds, *American Communities*, 279 (emphasis added).

62. Hinds, *American Communities*, 279.

CHAPTER THREE
"They Will Soon Convince the World"

1. Quotations in this paragraph and the next are from NAEI, Preamble and Articles of Association, Jan. 18, 1843, A. J. Macdonald Collection, p. 72, CtY.

2. Galatians, 3:28.

3. John Humphrey Noyes, *History of American Socialisms* (1870; rpt. ed., New York, 1966), 154. Noyes regarded Brook Farm, Hopedale, and Northampton as "forerunner[s] of Fourierism." Though this was so in the case of Brook Farm, which became Fourierist in 1844, Hopedale and Northampton remained largely independent of that movement and took different directions.

The belief that the Northampton community was Fourierist originated with contemporary critics, who out of ignorance or malice failed to make a distinction that radical abolitionists and other proponents of moral suasion would have insisted upon: for one of several examples, see *Journal of Commerce* (New York), Jun. 30, 1843, rebutted in *Onondaga Standard* (Syracuse, N.Y.), Aug. 16, 1843. Of later writers Olive Rumsey, "The Northampton Association of Education and Industry," *New England Magazine* 12 (1895), was slightly muddled on the issue, but real damage was done by George K. Smart, "Fourierism in Northampton: Two Documents," *New England Quarterly* 12 (June 1939): 370–74, which should not be used without noting the criticisms of Arthur Bestor, "Fourierism in Northampton: A Critical Note," *New England Quarterly* 13 (Mar. 1940): 110–22. The modern authority on American Fourierism, Carl J. Guarneri, agrees with Bestor that Northampton was "independent" of the movement: see Guarneri, *The Utopian Alternative: Fourierism in Nineteenth-Century America* (Ithaca, N.Y., 1991), 83. There was interest in Fourierism there, but Northampton never followed Brook Farm into the movement.

4. The only version of the Preliminary Circular that I have located is a transcription in Charles A. Sheffeld, ed., *The History of Florence, Massachusetts, Including a Complete Account of the Northampton Association of Education and Industry* (Florence, Mass., 1895), 69–73, from an original that Sheffeld described as "printed on two sides of an eight by ten inch sheet." The 1842 constitution is in A. J. Macdonald Collection, p. 71, CtY.; a copy was published in *Liberator*, Sept. 9, 1842, and it was also transcribed into Deeds, 95:233–40.

5. On communities based on common property, see, for example, Steven J. Stein, *The Shaker Experience in America* (New Haven, Conn., 1992), 53, 133; John L. Thomas, "Antislavery and Utopia," in *The Antislavery Vanguard: New Essays on the Abolitionists* (Princeton, 1965), esp. 255–59; and J.F.C. Harrison, *Quest for a New Moral World: Robert Owen and the Owenites in England and America* (New York, 1969). On joint-stock communities, see Anne C. Rose, *Transcendentalism as a Social Movement, 1830–1850* (New Haven, Conn., 1981), chap. 5; Edward K. Spann, *Hopedale: From*

Commune to Company Town, 1840–1920 (Columbus, Ohio, 1992); and Guarneri, *Utopian Alternative*, esp. chap. 5. Conflict between outside investors and members helped cause serious problems at the North American Phalanx in the 1850s; see Guarneri, 327, 413.

6. Sheffeld, *History of Florence*, 69.

7. Rose, *Transcendentalism as a Social Movement*, 105; Guarneri, *Utopian Alternative*, 32, 126–28.

8. So the statement in a recent article, that the "Northampton Association . . . was . . . based on some of the social philosophies of Robert Owen and Charles Fourier. The founders were New England men and women interested in translating their interest in Transcendentalism into social reality," is misleading, because it dwells on the vaguer influences on them and omits the more significant ones; see Wendy E. Chmielewski, "Sojourner Truth: Utopian Vision and Search for Community, 1797–1883," in *Women in Spiritual and Communitarian Societies in the United States*, ed. Wendy E. Chmielewski, Louis J. Kern, and Marlyn Klee-Hartzell (Syracuse, N.Y., 1993), 29.

9. Sheffeld, *History of Florence*, 69; A. J. Macdonald Collection, p. 71, CtY.

10. A. J. Macdonald Collection, p. 71, CtY.

11. There were significant overlaps between the abolitionist and labor movements in towns where both were active in the 1830s. The Lynn (Mass.) Mutual Benefit Society of Journeymen Cordwainers, for instance, organized against cuts in wages and payment in store orders, claiming "the full value of their labor"; Edward P. Magdol, *The Antislavery Rank and File* (Westport, Conn., 1986), p. 49, found that nineteen of twenty-nine officers of the society signed antislavery petitions and ten were members of the Lynn Anti-Slavery Society.

12. A. J. Macdonald Collection, p. 71, CtY.

13. NAEI, vol. 2, pp. 5–11.

14. NAEI, vol. 2, p. 9, entry for May 8, 1842.

15. The numbers of community residents cited here and elsewhere in the book have been established from NAEI, vols. 1, 2, and 4. The membership register, NAEI, vol. 1, is incomplete and has been supplemented with data from minutes in vol. 2 and correspondence in vol. 4. I have counted "residents," rather than "members," because this more accurately reflects the composition of a community in which individuals' formal status varied and was not always clearly defined.

16. On the rush of migrants to join New Harmony, see Anne Taylor, *Visions of Harmony: A Study in Nineteenth-Century Millenarianism* (Oxford, 1987), 103–7. A blank application form for the North American Phalanx is in James T. Fisher Papers, MHS. Prospective members at Hopedale had to answer questions posed in the "Standard of Practical Christianity," a document covering nearly three printed pages: see Record of Proceedings of Fraternal Community No. 1, 1841–51, pp. 12–14, Hopedale Community Books, Pamphlets, Serials, and Manuscripts, 1821–1938 (Microfilming Corporation of America).

17. NAEI, vol. 2, p. 67, entry for July 1, 1843.

18. Occupational data were compiled from NAEI, vols. 1, 2, and 4; U.S. Sixth Census, Population Schedules, 1840 (microfilm); U.S. Seventh Census, Population Schedules, 1850 (microfilm); and published city directories. For the occupational pro-

files of Brook Farm and other Fourierist communities, see Guarneri, *Utopian Alternative*, 415, table 11.

19. Data in this and the following paragraph are from Brooklyn, Conn., Tax Abstract, 1840, Town Clerk's Office, Brooklyn; Chaplin, Conn., Tax Abstracts, 1836, 1839, and 1841; Mansfield, Conn., South Society, Tax Abstracts, 1835–1842; Windham, Conn., Grand List, 1835, all in CSL.

20. Age data were compiled from NAEI, vol. 1; U.S. Seventh Census, Population Schedules, 1850 (microfilm); and published genealogies and vital records. The ages of fifty individuals could not be found. In addition, sixteen children were born into the community.

21. Sojourner Truth's period in The Kingdom is best detailed in Paul E. Johnson and Sean Wilentz, *The Kingdom of Matthias: A Story of Sex and Salvation in Nineteenth-Century America* (New York, 1994). See also: *Narrative of Sojourner Truth* [1850], ed. Margaret Washington (New York, 1993), 69–76; Carleton Mabee, *Sojourner Truth: Slave, Prophet, Legend* (New York, 1993), chap. 3; and Chmielewski, "Sojourner Truth," esp. 26–29. Susanna Bassett is listed as a visitor (that is, a temporary resident without full membership) at Brook Farm in Brook Farm Papers, vol. 1, p. 9, MHS (microfilm).

22. For the "one dollar pledge," see *NASS*, June 17, July 1, 15, 22, 29, Aug. 5, 12, 19, Sept. 9, 1841; at least another ten subscribers sought to join the community, made contributions to it, or had close relatives among the members. On the Walls, see *Reformer* (Worcester, Mass.), 1839–41; and Joseph S. Wall to Abby Kelley, Worcester, Oct. 12, 1840, Abigail Kelley Foster Papers, Box 1, folder 4, AAS. The Haywards' long connection with abolition is recorded in the Anti-Slavery Society of Salem and Vicinity, Record Books, A-SSSV Records, Box 1, folders 1–2, EI; Salem Female Anti-Slavery Society, Records, both in EI; and the obituary of Josiah Hayward in *Salem Recorder* (Salem, Mass.), Apr. 20, 1874. Sophia Foord to Robert Adams, Northampton, May 8, 1843, in the collection of Lisa Baskin, Northampton, Mass.; I am grateful to Ms. Baskin for permission to cite this letter and to Paul Gaffney for informing me of it and providing a copy.

23. William Lloyd Garrison to Laura Stebbins, Franklin, Conn., Oct. 7, 1843, *The Letters of William Lloyd Garrison*, ed. Walter S. Merrill and Louis Ruchames (Cambridge, Mass., 1971–81), 3:214; the twenty-two included Stebbins herself, but not the Bensons, to whom he had written separately. On the Garrison clique, see Lawrence J. Friedman, *Gregarious Saints: Self and Community in American Abolitionism, 1830–1870* (Cambridge, 1982), esp. chap. 2.

24. On Boston abolitionism, see Donald M. Jacobs, ed., *Courage and Conscience: Black and White Abolitionists in Boston* (Bloomington, Ind., 1993); on Lynn, Magdol, *Antislavery Rank and File*, and Howard P. Walthall, "Abolitionism in Lynn, Massachusetts: A Case Study in the Origin and Development of Antislavery Sentiment, 1820–1860" (Honors thesis, Harvard University, 1964).

25. Anti-Slavery Society of Salem and Vicinity, Records, Box 1, folder 3, EI; Salem Female Anti-Slavery Society, Record Book, 1834–46, EI; Elizabeth L.B. Wright to Harriet Foster, Newburyport, May 24, 1839, Salem Female Anti-Slavery Society Records, Box 1, folder 3, EI; Ipswich Anti-Slavery Society Records, 1838–44, EI.

26. Erasmus Darwin Hudson to Martha Turner Hudson, June 17, 1842, Hudson Family Papers, Box 2, folder 48, UMass.

27. On Calvin Stebbins, see Rufus P. Stebbins, *An Historical Address Delivered at the Centennial Celebration of the Incorporation of the Town of Wilbraham, June 15, 1863* (Boston, 1864), 186.

28. On the reorganization of the shoe industry, see Alan Dawley, *Class and Community: The Industrial Revolution in Lynn* (Cambridge, Mass., 1976); Paul G. Faler, *Mechanics and Manufacturers in the Early Industrial Revolution: Lynn, Massachusetts, 1760–1860* (Albany, N.Y., 1981); Mary Blewett, *Men, Women, and Work: Class, Gender, and Protest in the New England Shoe Industry, 1820–1910* (Urbana, Ill., 1988).

29. Bassett's account of events up to 1839 is printed in [Elizabeth Pease, comp.?], *Society of Friends in the United States: Their Views of the Antislavery Question, and Treatment of the People of Colour. Compiled from Original Correspondence* (Darlington, Eng., 1840), 5–18. Later events are outlined in William Bassett, *Proceedings of the Society of Friends in the Case of William Bassett* (Boston, 1840).

30. Bassett, *Proceedings*, 24.

31. Rosetta Hall, a former slave who had been assisted by Frederick Douglass, was invited to join the Hopedale community on June 28, 1845; Guarneri, *Utopian Alternative*, 258, 265–66; John R. McKivigan, *The War Against Pro-Slavery Religion: Abolitionism and the Northern Churches, 1830–1865* (Ithaca, N.Y., 1984), 302–20, notes that whereas there were eleven black members of the board of the American Anti-Slavery Society in the period 1834–40, there were very few after the 1840 split. See Carolyn Williams, "The Female Antislavery Movement: Fighting Against Racial Prejudice and Promoting Women's Rights in Antebellum America," in *The Abolitionist Sisterhood: Women's Political Culture in Antebellum America*, ed. Jean Fagan Yellin and John C. Van Horne (Ithaca, N.Y., 1994), 159–77.

32. David Ruggles to William Lloyd Garrison, in *Liberator*, Feb. 10, 1843; Stephen C. Rush to Garrison, Northampton, July 21, 1844, BPL MS A.1.2.14.43; *Narrative of Sojourner Truth*, in which Truth tells her story through the medium of a white writer, Olive Gilbert. Frederick Douglass, "What I Found at the Northampton Association," in Sheffeld, *History of Florence*; Henry Richards Crummell to editor, *NASS*, published in *Liberator*, Apr. 26, 1846.

33. C. Peter Ripley, "Introduction," in *The Black Abolitionist Papers*, vol. 3, *The United States, 1830–1846* (Chapel Hill, N.C., 1991); Benjamin Quarles, *Black Abolitionists* (New York, 1969); Jane H. Pease and William H. Pease, *They Who Would Be Free: Blacks' Search for Freedom, 1831–1860* (1974; rpt. ed., Urbana, Ill., 1990), 75–76; and the essays in *Courage and Conscience: Black and White Abolitionists in Boston*, ed. Donald M. Jacobs (Bloomington, Ind., 1993).

34. Data on the black population, compiled by Paul Gaffney from U.S. Sixth Census, 1840, Population Schedules, Massachusetts, and U.S. Seventh Census, 1850, Population Schedules, Massachusetts, and kindly supplied to me; the number of black households rose slightly faster than the black population, from seven to twenty.

35. Sophia Foord to Robert Adams, May 8, 1843. George Washington Sullivan is listed in NAEI, vol. 1, p. 78, without reference to his color; that was only mentioned in a report, in the *Hampshire Gazette*, June 4, 1844, that he had fallen forty-five feet

to the ground from the roof of the factory building, but escaped serious injury by remaining erect and landing in a large puddle.

36. Ruggles's date and place of birth are listed in NAEI, vol. 1, p. 73; brief sketches of him are in *Letters of William Lloyd Garrison*, 3:194 n. 8, and Ripley, *Black Abolitionist Papers*, 3:168–80; see also *NASS*, Aug. 20, 1840, Jan. 28, 1841; *Mirror of Liberty* (New York), 1838–40; and Dorothy B. Porter, "David Ruggles, An Apostle for Human Freedom," *Journal of Negro History* 28 (Jan. 1943): 23–50.

37. NAEI, vol. 2, p. 35, entry for Nov. 15, 1842; *NASS*, May 11, 1843; Pease and Pease, *They Who Would be Free*, 181.

38. *Narrative of Sojourner Truth*, 92, makes clear that she considered alternatives to going to Northampton for the winter of 1843–44, including the Fruitlands community at Harvard, Mass.; possibly she had learned that this was on the point of folding. On her background, see Nell Irvin Painter, "Sojourner Truth (1797–1883)," in *Notable Black American Women*, ed. Jessie Carney Smith (Detroit, 1992), 1147–51; idem, "Sojourner Truth in Life and Memory: Writing the Biography of an American Exotic," *Gender & History* 2 (Spring 1990): 3–16; idem, "Representing Truth: Sojourner Truth's Knowing and Becoming Known," *Journal of American History* 81, no. 2 (Sept. 1994): 461–92; Mabee, *Sojourner Truth*, chaps. 1–3.

39. This account is based on Stephen Young, "A Veteran Associationist," *Credit Foncier of Sinaloa* July 6, 1886, 552. NAEI, vol. 2, p. 70, minutes a letter to Smith regretting that his application could be given "no encouragement" at present; the absence of any correspondence with Young is consistent with the latter's own account, that he joined Smith on his journey and presumably arrived at the community unannounced.

40. Rose, *Transcendentalism as a Social Movement*, 241–42. Individuals counted as having kin were those whose spouse, parent, child, sibling, cousin, uncle, aunt, nephew, or niece were also members of Brook Farm. Rose's figures include David and Maria Mack, who signed the Brook Farm articles of association in 1842, but never lived there, having decided to move to the Northampton community instead. If the Macks are removed, the Brook Farm proportions shift to 54 percent with kin and 46 percent without. Rose's "unattached" category includes men and women who were single when they joined Brook Farm, but subsequently married.

41. Kinship data were compiled, using the same criteria as Rose, from NAEI, vol. 1, and from numerous other sources, including published genealogies. Frances Judd and the Birges are listed in NAEI, vol. 1, pp. 6–7. For the Stebbins Family, see Ralph Stebbins Greenlee and Robert Lemuel Greenlee, *The Stebbins Genealogy* (Chicago, 1904): I, 348–49, 568. Mary Ann Smith's relatives at the community are mentioned in passing in Cyrus M. Burleigh, Journal, p. 14, HSP, entry for Aug. 4, 1844. Whipple's relationship to Eliza Hammond was traced in Charles Henry Chandler, *The History of New Ipswich, New Hampshire, 1735–1914* (Fitchburg, Mass., 1914), 563.

42. [Anna Benson Percy?], "When I Was a Girl," in Sheffeld, *History of Florence*, 123.

43. George W. Benson to Samuel J. May, Northampton, Jan. 20, 1844, BPL MS. A.1.2.14.7, offered the Alcotts accommodation at Northampton, but noted that it would not be available until the spring.

44. Judith Wellman, "Women and Radical Reform in Antebellum Upstate New

York: A Profile of Grassroots Female Abolitionists," in *Clio Was a Woman: Studies in the History of American Women*, ed. Mabel E. Deutrich and Virginia C. Purdy (Washington, D.C., 1980); John L. Brooke, *The Heart of the Commonwealth: Society and Political Culture in Worcester County, Massachusetts, 1713–1861* (Cambridge, 1989), 363–66.

45. Population and occupational data in this and the previous paragraph are from *Sixth Census or Enumeration of the Inhabitants of the United States . . . in 1840* (Washington, D.C., 1841). The pattern of recruitment to the Northampton community was broadly similar to that of abolitionism in general during the late 1830s. Wellman, "Women and Radical Reform," 119, table 2, compares 1840 census data for thirty-four townships that sent antislavery petitions to Congress in 1838–39 and for seventy-nine townships that did not. The mean population of the former was 2,790, 70.2 percent of the workforce were in agriculture, and 23.2 percent in manufacturing. The nonpetitioning townships were smaller and more agricultural: they averaged 1,992 people, with 76.7 percent in agriculture and 16.6 percent in manufacturing.

46. For example, James Brewer Stewart, *Holy Warriors: The Abolitionists and American Slavery* (New York, 1976), 67, 78–79, notes abolitionist strength in "rural areas which had successfully come to terms with the new cosmopolitan economy."

47. I have discussed some of the social implications of depression in rural economic life in Christopher Clark, *The Roots of Rural Capitalism: Western Massachusetts, 1780–1860* (Ithaca, N.Y., 1990), 199–203; the quotation is from S. G. Goodrich, *Recollections of a Lifetime, Or Men and Things I have Seen* (New York, 1857), 1:75.

48. Article 35 of the 1842 constitution provided that a member resorting to law would be liable to expulsion; article 11 of the 1843 constitution made it an act of withdrawal. Mack's disgust with law is noted in *Obituary Record of Graduates of Yale College deceased during the Academical Year ending in June 1879* (n.p., n.d.), 337, and Isabella Mack Hinckley, "Recollections of Some Interesting People I Have Known and Met" (typescript, n.d.), 18–20, Belmont Historical Society Collection, Belmont Memorial Library, Belmont, Mass.; *Non-Resistant*, Apr. 20, 1839, noted that "many of our lawyers are worthy men, but . . . the less a person has to do with them (as lawyers) the better."

49. George Ripley to James T. Fisher, West Roxbury, Apr. 16, 1846, James T. Fisher Papers, MHS.

50. On Hammond, see Charles Lane to William Oldham, Sept. 29, 1843, in Clara Endicott Sears, *Bronson Alcott's Fruitlands* (Boston, 1915), 115. Child's remark was in *NASS*, Sept. 22, 1842. Sophia Foord to Robert Adams, May 8, 1843. *Narrative of Sojourner Truth*, 93, apparently quoting a report of a letter dictated by Sojourner Truth to friends in Springfield after her arrival at the community.

51. Erasmus Darwin Hudson, Journal 1842–43, Hudson Family Papers, folder 22, SSC, entry for June 12, 1842; Erasmus Darwin Hudson to Martha Turner Hudson, Victor, N.Y., Sept. 2, 1842, Hudson Family Papers, Box 1, folder 19, UMass.

52. Abby Kelley to Erasmus Darwin Hudson, Frankford, N.Y., Feb. 7, 1843, Hudson Family Papers, Box 1, folder 20, UMass; Hudson to Kelley, Northampton, Mar. 2, 1843, Abigail Kelley Foster Papers, Box 1, folder 6, AAS.

53. *Liberator*, July 28, 1843; *Hampshire Gazette*, Aug. 8, 1843; *Liberator*, Sept. 27,

1844. *NASS*, May 15, 1845 reported that Sojourner Truth spoke at the American Anti-Slavery Society's annual meeting in New York.

54. Stephen C. Rush to William Lloyd Garrison, Northampton, July 21, 1844, BPL MS A.1.2.14.43.; Bacon's account was in *Liberator*, June 30, 1843.

55. Charles Sellers, *The Market Revolution: Jacksonian America, 1815–1846* (New York, 1991), 212–14.

56. Michael D. Blanchard, "The Politics of Abolition in Northampton," *Historical Journal of Massachusetts* 19 (Summer 1991): 175–96; Reinhard O. Johnson, "The Liberty Party in Massachusetts, 1840–1848: Antislavery Third Party Politics in the Bay State," *Civil War History* 28 (1982): 237–65; Richard H. Sewell, *Ballots for Freedom: Antislavery Politics in the United States, 1837–1860* (New York, 1976).

57. Martha Turner Hudson to Erasmus Darwin Hudson, Northampton, Apr. 9, 1844, Hudson Family Papers, Box 1, folder 21, UMass.

58. *A Voice from the Jail* (Newburyport, Mass.), Dec. 11, 1842; Beach published his paper on Sundays.

59. Erasmus Darwin Hudson, Journal "Antislavery Campaign, 1842–43," Hudson Family Papers, folder 22, SSC, entry for July 9, 1842; Hudson to Abby Kelley, Northampton, Mar. 2, 1843.

60. *Liberator*, Mar. 31, 1843.

61. Sylvester Judd, Notebook, vol. 2, Judd MS, FL, entry for Feb. 8, 1843.

62. William Lloyd Garrison to Edmund Quincy, Northampton, July 6, 1843, in *Letters of William Lloyd Garrison*, 3:170; *Northampton Courier*, Mar. 7, 1843, criticized Adam's presence at the convention in Connecticut; James Boyle noted the interconnection of reform issues in *Liberator*, Nov. 24, 1843; Boyle is quoted from *Liberator*, Sept. 11, 1840.

63. William Bassett, *Letter to a Member of the Society of Friends, in Reply to Objections against Joining Anti-Slavery Societies* (Boston, 1837), 29; on Ruggles, see Ripley, *Black Abolitionist Papers*, 221.

64. *Narrative of Sojourner Truth*, 93–97; on Sojourner Truth's speaking in the community, see Dale Cockrell, *Excelsior: Journals of the Hutchinson Family Singers, 1842–1846* (Stuyvesant, N.Y., 1989), 268; George R. Stetson, "When I Was a Boy," in Sheffield, *History of Florence*, 121. See also Nell Irvin Painter, "Difference, Slavery and Memory: Sojourner Truth in Feminist Abolitionism," in Yellin and Van Horne, *Abolitionist Sisterhood*, 139–58.

65. Stetson, "When I Was a Boy," 120; *Hampshire Herald*, July 8, 1845.

66. *Journal of Commerce*, Aug. 30, 1843 (emphasis in original).

67. Quoted in Cockrell, *Excelsior*, 270 (emphasis in original).

68. Quoted in Noah Jackman to [Adin Ballou?], North Attleboro, Mass., May 12, 1844, reprinted in *Essex County Washingtonian* (Lynn, Mass.), June 13, 1844 (emphasis in original).

69. *Hampshire Gazette*, July 2, 1844.

70. Reprinted in *Liberator*, Sept. 29, 1843.

71. Reprinted in *Liberator*, May 24, 1844.

72. *Liberator*, June 14, 1844, also reported that a New England Anti-Slavery Convention had passed a resolution calling for disunion and condemning political abolitionism supported, among others, by the Northampton Community's James Boyle,

John Prouty, Thomas Hill, and E. D. Hudson. On Leavitt, see Hugh Davis, *Joshua Leavitt: Evangelical Abolitionist* (Baton Rouge, La., 1990), chaps. 9–11.

73. On the shift from nonresistance to anticonstitutionalism in the movement as a whole, see Lewis Perry, *Radical Abolitionism: Anarchy and the Government of God in Antislavery Thought* (Ithaca, N.Y., 1973), 159–61.

CHAPTER FOUR
"To Live in the Common Cause"

1. Erasmus Darwin Hudson to Martha Turner Hudson, Auburn, N.Y., Sept. 19, 1842, Hudson Family Papers, Box 1, folder 19, UMass.

2. James Brewer Stewart, *Holy Warriors* (New York, 1976), chap. 4; Charles Sellers, *The Market Revolution: Jacksonian America, 1815–1846* (New York, 1991), chap. 13. Important essays in the recent debate on capitalism and abolitionism by David Brion Davis, Thomas L. Haskell, and John Ashworth have been collected in Thomas Bender, ed., *The Antislavery Debate: Capitalism and Abolitionism as a Problem in Historical Interpretation* (Berkeley, Calif., 1992). On abolitionists and "free labor," see Eric Foner, "Abolition and the Labor Movement in Ante-bellum America," in Foner, *Politics and Ideology in the Age of the Civil War* (New York, 1980), 57–76; Jonathan A. Glickstein, " 'Poverty is not Slavery': American Abolitionists and the Competitive Labor Market," in *Antislavery Reconsidered: New Perspectives on the Abolitionists*, ed. Lewis Perry and Michael Fellman (Baton Rouge, La., 1979), 195–218; and, in a wider context, Eric Foner, *Free Soil, Free Labor, Free Men: The Ideology of the Republican Party before the Civil War* (New York, 1970).

3. James N. Buffum, in *NASS*, Oct. 14, 1841, with reference to employees' obligation to enforce railroad companies' rules denying black passengers equal access to seating on trains.

4. *NASS*, Sept. 16, 1841; Erasmus Darwin Hudson, Journal, 1842–1843, Hudson Family Papers, folder 22, SSC, entry for June 10, 1842. On employers' legal authority, see Christopher L. Tomlins, *Law, Labor and Ideology in the Early American Republic* (Cambridge, Eng., 1993), part 3.

5. Orestes Brownson, "The Laboring Classes," *Boston Quarterly Review* 3 (July 1840): 358–395. Anthony F.C. Wallace, *Rockdale: The Growth of an American Village in the Early Industrial Revolution* (New York, 1978), chap. 8; see also Alan Dawley and Paul Faler, "Working Class Culture and Politics in the Industrial Revolution: Sources of Loyalism and Rebellion," *Journal of Social History* 9 (1976): 466–80, and Teresa Anne Murphy, *Ten Hours' Labor: Religion, Reform and Gender in Early New England* (Ithaca, N.Y., 1992).

6. Olive Rumsey, "The Northampton Association of Education and Industry," *New England Magazine* 12 (1895): 24.

7. Charles Lane and A. Bronson Alcott to A. Brooke, in Clara Endicott Sears, comp., *Bronson Alcott's Fruitlands* (Boston, 1915), 47.

8. Minutes of these discussions and votes are in NAEI, vol. 2, pp. 14, 17, 19–21. Benson's proposal to the May meeting was rejected by twelve votes to five; Hudson and Judd's was approved by thirteen to five.

9. Erasmus Darwin Hudson, Journal, 1842–43, Hudson Family Papers, folder 22, SSC, entries for May 1842.

10. Ibid., entry for July 9, 1842. Hudson and Benson had already disagreed before the July meeting; a few weeks earlier Benson had written to apologize for remarks he had made and to express the hope that the two of them could "harmonize"; see Benson to Hudson, June 26 or 28, 1842, and Erasmus Darwin Hudson to Martha Turner Hudson, Sept. 2, 1842, both in Hudson Family Papers, Box 1, folder 19, UMass.

11. William Adam to John Bailey, Mar. 16, 1843, NAEI, vol. 4, pp. 16–17 (emphasis in original). Conant, Chaffee, and Swift withdrew in October 1842; the reduction of hours from twelve to eleven for employees in the silk factory is mentioned in Frances P. Judd, "Reminiscences," in *The History of Florence, Massachusetts, Including a Complete Account of the Northampton Community of Education and Industry,* ed. Charles A. Sheffeld (Florence, Mass., 1895), 116–17; see Alice Eaton McBee, "From Utopia to Florence: The Story of a Transcendentalist Community in Northampton, Massachusetts, 1830–1852," *Smith College Studies in History* 32 (1947): 39.

12. Arthur Bestor, "Fourierism in Northampton: A Critical Note," *New England Quarterly* 13 (Mar. 1940): 110–22.

13. NAEI, vol. 2, p. 38. Paying wages on the basis of six cents an hour for adults left the community with resources enough to pay the interest due on its loans, but there was no dividend for stockholders: Sylvester Judd, Notebook, vol. 2, Judd MS, FL, entry for Jan. 23, 1843.

14. NAEI, vol. 2, pp. 38–45.

15. NAEI, vol. 2, pp. 47, 57–58. Adults were allowed eighty cents a week for board, and twenty dollars a year for clothes.

16. NAEI, Preamble and Articles of Association adopted Jan. 18, 1843, in A. J. Macdonald Collection, p. 72, CtY; David Mack to Daniel Pound and John J. Wilson, July or Aug., 1843, NAEI, vol. 4, p. 33.

17. The anonymous critic wrote in the *Christian World* (Boston), Sept. 30, 1843; the visitor was H. H. Joslyn, writing in the *Onondaga Standard,* Aug. 16, 1843.

18. The meetings, held between Sept. 9 and 30, 1843, were minuted in NAEI, vol. 2, pp. 74–80. A copy of the revised constitution, mistakenly labeled "1842," but in fact that of late 1843, is in HN.

19. Nathaniel P. Rogers, in *Liberator,* Sept. 8, 1843; Joslyn, in *Onondaga Standard,* Aug. 16, 1843; David Mack to Elisha L. Hammond, Northampton, n.d., reprinted in [James Boyle], *Social Reform: Or an Appeal in Behalf of Association, Based upon the Principles of a Pure Christianity* (Northampton, Mass., 1844), 71–72.

20. William Bassett to Elizabeth Pease, Northampton, July 22, 1844, BPL MS A.1.2.14.44.

21. A. J. Macdonald Collection, p. 281, CtY.

22. Frances P. Judd, "Reminiscences," 115; *Narrative of Sojourner Truth* [1850], ed. Margaret Washington (New York, 1993), 97–98; transcription from Margaret Fuller's memoirs in A. J. Macdonald Collection, p. 8, CtY; Sophia Foord to Robert Adams, Northampton, May 8, 1843, collection of Lisa Baskin, Northampton, Mass..

23. *Essex County Washingtonian,* Aug. 29, 1844; David Ruggles to editor, Albany *North Star,* n.d., in *Liberator,* May 24, 1844; Benjamin S. Jones to the editor of

the *Pennsylvania Freeman*, reprinted in *Liberator*, June 20, 1845; Finch's account was published in *New Moral World* (London), Apr. 13, 1844.

24. *The Learned Blacksmith: The Letters and Journals of Elihu Burritt*, ed. Merle Curti (New York, 1937), 16–17; *Journal of Commerce*, Aug. 30, 1843.

25. Dale Cockrell, *Excelsior: Journals of the Hutchinson Family Singers, 1842–1846* (Stuyvesant, N.Y., 1989), entry for Apr. 27, 1844; Rogers, in *Liberator*, Sept. 8, 1843; *Learned Blacksmith*, 16; *Essex County Washingtonian*, Sept. 12, 1844.

26. Esther Dixwell to Catherine Sargent, Northampton, [July 1842]; Esther Dixwell to George B. Dixwell, Boston, May 21, 1843, both in Wigglesworth Family Papers, Box 3, MHS.

27. Apphia Judd to Arethusa Hall, Northampton, May 1, 1842, Judd Family Papers, Box 2, HCL.

28. Cyrus M. Burleigh, Journal, "The Little Things of Life," p. 230, entry for Jan. 6, 1845, Burleigh Collection Am 8192, HSP; "Northampton Association," *Phalanx*, Sept. 7, 1844, 275, reprinted from the *Boston Laborer*. The article, written under the pseudonym "Agent," included what was presented as the direct speech of an unidentified Northampton Association member; the quotation is taken from this.

29. Descriptions of meetings were published in *Liberator*, June 30 and Sept. 8, 1843, and *Onondaga Standard*, Aug. 16, 1843.

30. Giles B. Stebbins, "A Young Man in the Community," in Sheffeld, *History of Florence*, 126–27. Woodbridge was among the most conservative Congregational ministers in the Connecticut Valley. In the early 1840s the majority of the Hadley church left him with a small rump of followers, and literally moved their meetinghouse to a new site; see Dan Huntington to Frederic Dan Huntington, Hadley, Jan. 1, 1841, Porter-Phelps-Huntington Papers, Amherst College Archives, and Sylvester Judd, Notebook, vol. 2, Judd MS, FL, entries for Dec. 5, 1841, and Jan. 1843.

31. Eldad Stebbins, "Record of Letters Written," Eldad Stebbins Papers, MHS, entry for June 25, 1843.

32. *Hampshire Gazette*, July 25, 1843, quoted in McBee, "From Utopia to Florence," 51.

33. Finch, in *New Moral World*, Apr. 13, 1844; the other visitor at the meeting was B. C. Bacon, whose account was in *Liberator*, June 30, 1843.

34. Sylvester Judd, Notebook, vol. 2, Judd MS, FL, entry for June 1, 1842.

35. The Ashley-Forward marriage was described in *Liberator*, June 14, 1844; the Southworth-Hayden intentions were entered in NAEI, vol. 2, p. 96, entry for July 3, 1844.

36. The Benson funeral was noted in *Liberator*, Sept. 29, 1843, the flowers recalled by George R. Stetson, "When I Was a Boy," in Sheffeld, *History of Florence*, 122; Sylvester Judd to Sylvester Judd Jr., Northampton, Oct. 21, 1845, Judd Family Papers, Box 2, HCL, described his grandson's burial; he referred to "a black woman," without naming Sojourner Truth, but this is unlikely to have been anyone other than she. There is an oblique reference to a disturbance at a funeral in early 1844 in Martha Turner Hudson to Erasmus Darwin Hudson, Northampton, Apr. 7, 1844, Hudson Family Papers, Box 1, folder 21, UMass.

37. "A Glimpse of Christ's Idea of Society," *Dial* 7 (Jan. 1842): 227.

38. On transcendentalists and education, see Anne C. Rose, *Transcendentalism as*

a Social Movement, 1830–1850 (New Haven, Conn., 1981), 61–65 and 138–39, and Carl J. Guarneri, *The Utopian Alternative: Fourierism in Nineteenth-Century America* (Ithaca, N.Y., 1991), 208–13. Samuel L. Hill is quoted from *Hampshire Gazette*, Apr. 2, 1867. See also Lawrence A. Cremin, *American Education: The National Experience, 1783–1876* (New York, 1980), chap. 3.

39. At the Greenfield Boarding School for Young Men, for example, pupils mixed work with study, both reducing the school's costs (hence its fees too) and—according to the principal—saving time, because work provided "recreation from mental exertion." A report in the *Co-operator* (Utica, N.Y.), Apr. 17, 1832.

40. *Journal of Commerce*, Aug. 30, 1843.

41. Esther Dixwell to George B. Dixwell, Northampton, July 7, 1842, Wigglesworth Family Papers, Box 3, MHS.

42. NAEI, vol. 5, pp. 138–39; Porter's arrival and departure are documented in NAEI, vol. 2, p. 68; he is identified as a French teacher in Kate deNormandie Wilson, *Dolly Witter Stetson* (n.p., 1907), 30.

43. [Anna Benson Percy?] "When I Was a Girl," in Sheffield, *History of Florence*, 121; George R. Stetson, "When I Was a Boy," ibid., 123–24. Sophia Foord continued to teach by observation and "object lesson" after she left Northampton. As tutor in the Chace family in Valley Falls, Rhode Island, "she taught botany; she walked with the children over the fields . . . and made her pupils observe the geographical features of the pond and its banks, and carefully taught them to estimate distances by sight." See Lillie Buffum Chace Wyman and Arthur Crawford Wyman, *Elizabeth Buffum Chace, 1806–1899: Her Life and Its Environment* (Boston, 1914), 1:131.

44. David Mack to David P. Harmon, Apr. 29, 1844, NAEI vol. 4, p.[51].

45. The Adams' workday was mentioned in Esther Dixwell to George B. Dixwell, Northampton, [July, 1842], Wigglesworth Family Papers, Box 3, MHS; David Mack to Protection Insurance Co. of Hartford, May 29, 1843, NAEI, vol. 4, p. 32. It is likely that the company refused the request, because a few weeks later the recently arrived former slave Stephen C. Rush was given the task of acting as night watchman.

46. Erasmus Darwin Hudson to Martha Turner Hudson, Sept. 2, 1842; Phebe Adam to Helen E. Garrison, Northampton, Oct. 11–15, 1843, BPL MS A.1.2.13.63.

47. NAEI, vol. 2, pp. 12, 28, 35; NAEI, vol. 5, pp. 68–69, 120, 157, 180, 223–25.

48. Esther Dixwell to George B. Dixwell, [July 1842].

49. The silk-dyer James D. Atkins recalled helping Sojourner Truth, who ran the laundry, "wring out the clothes on Mondays when work in his department was dull." Sheffield, *History of Florence*, 96. No comparable references to women assisting with "men's" tasks have been found.

50. NAEI, vol. 2, p. 74.

51. R. Fowler Hudson was admitted to the community in his own right in April 1844, NAEI, vol. 2, p. 93; Gordon Adam is mentioned in Henrietta Sargent to George B. Dixwell, Boston, Mar. 1, 1843, Wigglesworth Family Papers, Box 3, MHS.

52. Hill, in *Hampshire Gazette*, Apr. 2, 1867; Rogers, in *Liberator*, Sept. 8, 1843.

53. *Liberator*, Nov. 24, 1843. At a convention in Connecticut in 1839, George W. Benson wrote, he spoke for two and three-quarter hours, "and though it was late

when I concluded, and the audience somewhat fatigued," everyone stayed to organize the Tolland County Anti-Slavery Society. *Charter Oak*, Feb. 1839. After a series of meetings dogged by long-windedness the Windham County Anti-Slavery Society voted to limit speeches to fifteen minutes. Windham County Anti-Slavery Society, Record Book, CSL, entry for May 31, 1842.

54. NAEI, vol. 2, p. 15; David Mack to A. F. Taylor, Apr. 23, 1843, NAEI, vol. 4, pp. 29–30.

55. Carol A. Kolmerten, *Women in Utopia: The Ideology of Gender in the American Owenite Communities* (Bloomington, Ind., 1989), 101 and passim. See also Lawrence Foster, *Women, Family, and Utopia: Communal Experiments of the Shakers, the Oneida Community, and the Mormons* (Syracuse, N.Y., 1991), and Wendy E. Chmielewski, Louis J. Kern, and Marlyn Klee-Hartzell, eds., *Women in Spiritual and Communitarian Societies in the United States* (Syracuse, N.Y., 1993).

56. Sylvester Judd to Arethusa Hall, Northampton, Jan. 13, 1842, Judd Papers, Box 2, HCL, is the first known source of the story about the Adams' "eighteen Hindoo servants" in India; John Finch's report of his visit to the community, in *New Moral World*, Apr. 13, 1844, repeats the story; since Finch spent time in the Adam household it is likely he was given the information directly by the family. The exhaustion of the Adam women was noted by Epes Sargent Dixwell to George B. Dixwell, Cambridge, Mar. 1, 1842, Wigglesworth Family Papers, Box 3, MHS. William Adam's reference to the director of the boarding house was in *Liberator*, Feb. 24, 1843.

57. [Isabella Mack Hinckley], *In Memoriam D.M. July 24, 1878. L.M.K.M. December 14, 1882* [Cambridge, Mass., 1883], 12–13; and Isabella Mack Hinckley, "Recollections of Some Interesting People I Have Known and Met" (typescript, n.d.), 18–20, both in Mack family file, Belmont Historical Society Collections, Belmont Memorial Library, Belmont, Mass. Reference both to David's decision to sell and to Maria's pregnancy (with Isabella) is made in Ann Weston to Deborah Weston, Weymouth, Mar. 10, 1842, BPL MS A.9.2.17.40.

58. Hall Judd to William C. Barrows, Northampton, Apr. 28, 1846, NAEI, vol. 4, p.[131].

59. Martha Turner Hudson to Erasmus Darwin Hudson, Northampton, Oct. 1, 1843, Hudson Family Papers, Box 1, folder 20, UMass; *Journal of Commerce*, Aug. 30, 1843; *Salem Register*, article reprinted in *Liberator*, Sept. 29, 1843; William Bassett to Elizabeth Pease, Lynn, Aug. 14, 1845, BPL MS A.1.2.15.49.

60. Kolmerten, *Women in Utopia*, 172–75; *Narrative of Sojourner Truth*, 98; Wilson, *Dolly Witter Stetson*, 40; letters of Elizabeth Curson Hoxie, in HCL bMS Am 1175 (356–445), are quoted in Guarneri, *Utopian Alternative*, 205.

61. Guarneri, *Utopian Alternative*, 205.

62. Quotations are from [Frances Birge Judd], in A .J. Macdonald Collection, pp. 68–70, CtY; see also Frances P. Judd, "Reminiscences," 115–18.

63. Wilson, *Dolly Witter Stetson*, 33, 39. Two of the Stetsons' children died young. Another child, their ninth, was born at Northampton in 1844.

64. The quotations are from two versions of this story: Giles B. Stebbins, "A Young Man in the Community," 128, and idem, *Upward Steps of Seventy Years* (New York, 1890), 62.

65. NAEI, vol. 2, p. 102, entry for Jan. 24, 1845.

66. In April 1842, the admissions board declined an applicant, noting that "in the present state of Mr Smith's domestic Relations the Board are not prepared to admit him as a member." NAEI, vol. 2, p. 8. Later a woman was turned down because she intended to leave her husband and join the community with her children. Epes Sargent Dixwell to George Dixwell, Cambridge, Oct. 15, 1843, Wigglesworth Family Papers, Box 3, MHS, claimed that there was a "downward tendency" of morals at the community and expected a sexual scandal "in due course." John C. Spurlock, *Free Love: Marriage and Middle-Class Radicalism in America, 1825–1860* (New York, 1988), 24–25 and chap. 2, suggests that though Fourierist and other communities officially sustained existing marital and family ties, community life did bring them into question.

67. Erasmus Darwin Hudson, Journal, marked "Anti Slavery Campaign, 1842–3," Hudson Family Papers, folder 22, SSC, entry for May 29, 1842.

68. The vote was on June 29, 1844, NAEI, vol. 2, pp. 94–95; Frances P. Judd, "Reminiscences," 117.

69. William Adam to Joseph C. Martin, Northampton, Apr. 3, 1843, NAEI, vol. 4, p. 21.

70. Frederick Douglass, "What I Found at the Northampton Association," in Sheffeld, *History of Florence*, 130.

71. W. P. Garrison and F. J. Garrison, comp., *William Lloyd Garrison, 1805–1879*, (New York, 1885), 2:286 n. 2; Spencer Klaw, *Without Sin: The Rise and Fall of the Oneida Community* (New York, 1993), 28, 34–37, 47.

72. Martha Turner Hudson to Erasmus Darwin Hudson, Northampton, Apr. 9, 1844, Hudson Family Papers, Box 1, f. 21, UMass, refers to Boyle "driving out" James Willey and Moses K. Meader; both men withdrew in March and April that year, see NAEI, vol. 1, p. 54. See also [James Boyle], *The Funeral Sermon of Dr. James Boyle, with Two Appendixes (Written by Himself) Kingsville, Ontario, June 1884* (Amherstburg, Ont., 1884).

73. Sylvester Judd, Notebook, vol. 5, Judd MS, FL, entry for Mar. 1850.

74. William Bassett to Elizabeth Pease, Lynn, Mass., Aug. 14, 1845, BPL MS A.1.2.15.49.

75. Hutchinson's concern about Sunday games is noted in Cockrell, *Excelsior*, 268. Frances Judd's memoir of 1853 is in A. J. Macdonald Collection, pp. 67–70, CtY. A check of accounts in NAEI, vols. 3, 5, 6, and 7, reveals only a very few entries for liquor, almost certainly for medicinal purposes.

76. Esther Dixwell to George B. Dixwell, Boston, Sept. 8, 1842, Wigglesworth Family Papers, Box 3, MHS.

77. NAEI, vol. 2, p. 12, entry for May 22, 1842.

78. They also doubted that Adam was capable of becoming "a popular lecturer." Esther Dixwell to George B. Dixwell, Boston, Jan. 21, 1844, and Epes Sargent Dixwell to George B. Dixwell, Cambridge, Feb. 1, 1845, both in Wigglesworth Family Papers, Box 4, MHS. Adam's classes were advertised in *Winter Classes for Young Ladies* (n.p., 1844), MHS broadside collection. The Adams were not alone in enjoying dancing; at least two community residents had fiddles, for which they bought new strings at the store: see NAEI, vol. 6, pp. 143, 265.

79. In 1828, Adam had "resigned in high dudgeon" a post connected with Ram Mohun Roy's school in Calcutta after practices he had introduced had been criticized; see Sophia Dobson Collet, *Life and Letters of Raja Rammohun Roy*, ed. Hem Chandra Sarkar ([Calcutta, 1913]), 102–3. The quotations are from Esther Dixwell to George B. Dixwell, Boston, June 11, 1843, Wigglesworth Family Papers, Box 3, MHS, and John Finch's description of his visit to Northampton, in *New Moral World*, Apr. 13, 1844.

80. David Mack to James Mackay, Nov. 13, 1843, NAEI, vol. 4, p.[42], which notes that the letter was confirmed by a community meeting on November 25.

81. Martha Turner Hudson to Erasmus Darwin Hudson, Apr. 7, 1844.

82. William Adam to Henry C. Wright, Northampton, Feb. 27, 1843, NAEI, vol. 4, pp. 9–10; Adam to Ansel L. Snow, Apr. 19, 1843, NAEI, vol. 4, p. 27; NAEI, vol. 2, entry for Aug. 19, 1843, pp. 88–89, entries for Jan. 13 and 15, 1844.

83. Erasmus Darwin Hudson to Martha Turner Hudson, Oct. 7, 1843, Hudson Family Papers, Box 1, folder 20, UMass.

84. G.W.S., "The Community Enterprise," *Liberator*, Oct. 9, 1846 (emphasis in original); Roger Wunderlich, *Low Living and High Thinking at Modern Times, New York* (Syracuse, N.Y., 1992).

85. *Narrative of Sojourner Truth*, 98; on Truth's individualism, see Carleton Mabee, *Sojourner Truth: Slave, Prophet, Legend* (New York, 1993), 143. Esther Dixwell to George Dixwell, Boston, June 11, 1843, Wigglesworth Family Papers, Box 3, MHS. David Mack to Elisha L. Hammond, n.d., in [Boyle], *Social Reform*, 71–72; Stephen C. Rush to William Lloyd Garrison, Northampton, July 21, 1844, BPL MS A.1.2.14.43.

CHAPTER FIVE
The Business of Utopia

1. NAEI, "Preliminary Circular," in Charles A. Sheffeld, *The History of Florence, Massachusetts, Including a Complete Account of the Northampton Association of Education and Industry* (Florence, Mass., 1895), 69–73. NAEI, vol. 5, p. 1, valued the Association's property on Apr. 8, 1842 at $30,986.43, of which $26,413.43 was real estate.

2. NAEI, Preamble and Articles of Association, in A. J. Macdonald Collection, p. 71, CtY.

3. Lists of assets and notes payable are in NAEI, vol. 5, p. 1.

4. A visitor in 1843, for example, reported that the association's property was worth double the $30,000 that had been paid for it. *Onondaga Standard*, Aug. 16, 1843.

5. Anne C. Rose, *Transcendentalism as a Social Movement, 1830–1850* (New Haven, Conn., 1981), 136, n. 67. David Mack's correspondence with Nathaniel Hawthorne led him to the conclusion that Northampton was financially sounder than Brook Farm.

6. *Onondaga Standard*, Aug. 16, 1843.

7. Benjamin S. Jones, in the *Pennsylvania Freeman*, reprinted in *Liberator*, June 20, 1845.

8. Arrangements for the store were noted in NAEI, vol. 2, p. 9, entry for May 1, 1842. On the community's efforts to exchange goods see Henrietta Sargent to George B. Dixwell, Boston, Mar. 1, 1843, Wigglesworth Family Papers, Box 3, MHS, based on information from Gordon Adam; the report on expenditure was noted in NAEI, vol. 2, p. 63, entry for June 7, 1843.

9. NAEI, vol. 5, pp. 20, 82–83 give examples of custom sawing work for locals. On the rapid depletion of woodland in this period, see Christopher Clark, *The Roots of Rural Capitalism: Western Massachusetts, 1780–1860* (Ithaca, N.Y., 1990), 291–93.

10. Metalworking and cutlery are referred to in NAEI, vol. 2, pp. 36, 68; on July 5, 1843, the director reported that the mechanical department had recently produced no goods for outside sale because of calls to carry out repairs.

11. References in NAEI, vol. 2, p. 68 (baking), 36 (boot- and shoemaking), 54 (tanning), and William Adam to David L. Child, Oct. 3, 1843, BPL MS A.4.1.92 (horticulture).

12. [Franklin Allen], *Manual of the American Silk Trade, 1873* (New York, [1874]), 13, and passim. On the silk industry in general, see *New York Weekly Tribune,* July 29, 1843; Alfred T. Lilly, "The Silk Industry of the United States from 1766 to 1874," *American Wool Manufacture* (New York, 1876); L. P. Brockett, *The Silk Industry in America: A History Prepared for the Centennial Exposition* ([New York], 1876); William C. Wycoff, "Report on the Silk Manufacturing Industry of the United States," in U.S. Census Office, *Report on the Manufactures of the United States at the Tenth Census (June 1, 1880)* (Washington, D.C., 1883), 901–35; Shichio Matsui, *History of the Silk Industry in the United States* (New York, 1930); Kazuko Furuta, "Technology Transfer and Local Adaptation: The Case of Silk-Reeling in Modern East Asia" (Ph.D. diss., Princeton University, 1988). On silk raising by the Harmonists in Pennsylvania, see William Kenrick, *American Silk Grower's Guide* (Boston, 1839), 154. On the Kansas Co-operative Farm, or Silkville (1869–92), see Carl J. Guarneri, *The Utopian Alternative: Fourierism in Nineteenth-Century America* (Ithaca, N.Y., 1991), 386–89.

13. Ezra Stiles to William Livingston, New Haven, Mar. 30, 1789, William Livingston Papers II, MHS (microfilm); Daniel Stebbins to Rev. Perkins, Northampton, Oct. 17, 1842, Lathrop-Stebbins Collection, folder B-1, MS Collection, Box 34, FL.

14. Ann Fairfax Withington, "Republican Bees: The Political Economy of the Beehive in Eighteenth-Century America," *Studies in Eighteenth Century Culture* 18 (1988): 39–77. Some late eighteenth-century children's stories compared silkworms unfavorably with bees: see Thomas Day, *The History of Little Jack. Embellished with a Number of Engravings. To which is added, the Little Queen, a Moral Tale. Natural History of the Bee. Natural History of the Silkworm* (Boston, 1795). On the smell of silkworms, see Carlo Cipolla, *Miasmas and Disease: Public Health and Environment in the Pre-Industrial Age* (New Haven, Conn., 1992).

15. Jonathan H. Cobb, *A Manual Containing Information with Respect to the Growth of the Mulberry Tree, with Suitable Directions for the Culture of Silk* (Boston, 1831); quotations are from Samuel Whitmarsh, *Eight Years' Experience and Observation in the Culture of the Mulberry Tree and in the Care of the Silk Worm, with Remarks Adapted to the American System of Producing Raw Silk for Exportation* (Northampton, Mass., 1839), 23, 104, 107, and Lilly, "Silk Industry," 264.

16. The stages of silk production are outlined in Cobb, *A Manual*, 4th edition (Boston, 1839); Whitmarsh, *Eight Years' Experience*, 45–59, 74–85; and *The Silk Culture in the United States*, Extra New-York Tribune Useful Works for the People, no. 6 (New York, 1844), 72–80.

17. Wycoff, "Report on the Silk Manufacturing Industry," 16.

18. Daniel Stebbins to Rev. Perkins, Oct. 17, 1842. The Northampton community's yields were almost certainly lower than Stebbins's estimates. In 1843 William Adam reported that 44 pounds of silk were raised from five acres of mulberry, an average of 8.8 pounds per acre; see *The Silk Question Settled: The Testimony of One Hundred and Fifty Witnesses. Report of the Proceedings of the National Convention of Silk Growers and Silk Manufacturers, Held in New York, Oct. 13th and 14th, 1843* (New York, 1844), 69–70.

19. E. G. Howe to Eleazer Bennet, Mansfield, Dec. 21, 1827, photocopy at Mansfield Historical Society, Mansfield, Conn.; Lilly, "Silk Industry," 271.

20. *Silk Question Settled*, 69–72.

21. The first (1831) edition of Cobb, *Manual*, dwelt most on the white mulberry, but mentioned *morus multicaulis* on 68; the fourth edition, published in 1839 at the peak of the craze for *morus multicaulis*, devoted a long section of text and an appendix to it, though Cobb was not uncritical of the variety. Lilly, "Silk Industry," 270.

22. Daniel Stebbins to Rev. Perkins, Oct. 17, 1842; Whitmarsh, *Eight Years' Experience*, 23, 107. On raising silkworms in China and Japan, see Furuta, "Technology Transfer," pp. 120–21.

23. Cobb, *Manual*, 42, 48; Whitmarsh, *Eight Years' Experience*, 63–66.

24. Lists of premiums (prizes) awarded at the annual agricultural fair in Northampton are in *Hampshire Gazette*, Oct. 18, 1842, Oct. 24, 1843, Oct. 15, 1844, and Oct. 21, 1845. The *Hampshire Gazette*, Sept. 6, 1842, carried a report from a Hartford newspaper about a sample of sewing silk from the community, praised as "the most splendid specimen of American excellence in reeling, spinning and dyeing silk that we have ever seen." The report on profit was made in *Onondaga Standard*, Aug. 16, 1843.

25. On Atkins's training as a dyer, NAEI, vol. 2, pp. 34; on employment, NAEI, vol. 5, p. 120; on Preston, NAEI, vol. 2, p. 65, and NAEI, vol. 4, p. 40.

26. *Silk Question Settled*, 69–70.

27. NAEI, vol. 5, pp. 34, 42, 63, 93, 114, 118, George W. Benson to Erasmus Darwin Hudson, Northampton, June, 1842, and Erasmus Darwin Hudson to Martha Turner Hudson, June 17, 1843, both in Hudson Family Papers, box 1, folder 19, UMass.

28. The change of strategy is mentioned in William Bassett to S. T. Jones, May 20, 1844, and Bassett to James A. Stetson, May 20, 1844, both in NAEI, vol. 4, p.[53].

29. The number of silk workers was cited in *Silk Question Settled*, 70; see also NAEI, vol. 5, p. 180. Hill's recollections of capital requirements were in *Hampshire Gazette*, Apr. 2, 1867.

30. Massachusetts, vol. 46, p. 108, R. G. Dun and Co. Collection, Baker Library, Harvard University Graduate School of Business Administration.

31. NAEI, vol. 2, p. 84, entry for Nov. 8, 1843, noted the appointment of Boyle

and Mack as agents to travel in New England and New York, forming auxiliary societies and raising subscriptions.

32. Advertisements for cocoons and of Paine's silk reel appeared in *Hampshire Gazette*, July 30 and Aug. 8, 1844.

33. References to early use of imported silk are made in NAEI, vol. 2, p. 14, and NAEI, vol. 5, p. 38.

34. On Chinese re-reeled silk, see Wycoff, "Report on the Silk Manufacturing Industry," 18; Trustees and Directors to Abner Sanger, Northampton, Jan. 28, 1845, NAEI, vol. 4, pp.[84–86].

35. William Bassett to Elizabeth Pease, Lynn, Aug. 14, 1845, BPL, MS A.1.2.15.49; an example of complaints about poor raw silk is in Samuel L. Hill to D. H. Davis, Feb. 20, 1846, NAEI, vol. 4, p.[120].

36. Samuel L. Hill to Erasmus Darwin Hudson, July 5, 1845, NAEI, vol. 4, p.[103]; Hall Judd to Hudson, Feb. 16 and Mar. 10, 1846, NAEI, vol. 4, pp.[122, 127]. Correspondence about the bequest of Ruth Stebbins extended from David Mack to Henry Douglas, Mar. 9, 1844, NAEI, vol. 4, p.[46] to Samuel L. Hill to Bates and Gillett, Mar. 21, 1846, NAEI, vol. 4, p.[128].

37. Bagley's request for membership had been declined in David Mack to Sarah Bagley, Northampton, Mar. 19, 1844, NAEI, vol. 4, the contact renewed in Mack to Bagley, Feb. 24, 1845, NAEI, vol. 4, p.[94].

38. Samuel L. Hill to Abner Sanger, Northampton, Dec. 4, 1845, NAEI, vol. 4, pp.[114–15].

39. Correspondence about these activities appears in NAEI, vol. 4, pp.[88–143].

40. Samuel L. Hill to J. F. Harding and Co., Sept. 4, 1845, NAEI, vol. 4, p.[107], declined an order for ratchets, "as the quantity is small . . . and we are harried with work at this time we had rather not furnish them"; on shoemaking: NAEI, vol. 2, p. 101, entry for Jan. 24, 1845.

41. The 1848 estimate was published in *Massachusetts State Record and Year Book of General Information, 1848* (Boston, 1848), 217. On business failures in the Northampton region, see Clark, *Roots of Rural Capitalism*, 217–18; this estimate, based on R. G. Dun and Co. credit reports, does not include businesses that closed because their owners moved, retired, or died.

42. Working hours in Northampton silk mills were reported in *Voice of Industry* (Lowell, Mass.), Dec. 13, 1845.

43. The continuation of silk production throughout the 1840s by, among others, the network of manufacturers linked to Mansfield, Conn., and Northampton, Mass., refutes a myth propagated in the 1850s that the industry had died out when the mulberry bubble burst in 1839, and was revived by English immigrant silk workers over a decade later; see C. L. Frieshmann, *Trade, Manufacture and Commerce in the U.S.A.* (n.p., 1852).

CHAPTER SIX
"Too Despotic Power"

1. Epes Sargent Dixwell to George Dixwell, Cambridge, Mass., Oct. 30, 1842, Wigglesworth Family Papers, Box 3, and Apr. 14, 1844, Wigglesworth Family Papers, Box 4, MHS.

2. Sydney E. Ahlstrom, *A Religious History of the American People* (New Haven, Conn., 1972), 491; Karl J.R. Arndt, *George Rapp's Harmony Society, 1785–1847* (Philadelphia, 1965); Richard L. Bushman, *Joseph Smith and the Origins of Mormonism* (New York, 1984); Edward K. Spann, *Hopedale: From Commune to Company Town, 1840–1920* (Columbus, Ohio, 1992); Paul Elmen, *Wheat Flour Messiah: Eric Jansson of Bishop Hill* (Carbondale, Ill., 1976); Robert D. Thomas, *The Man Who Would Be Perfect: John Humphrey Noyes and the Utopian Impulse* (Philadelphia, 1977); Spencer Klaw, *Without Sin: The Rise and Fall of the Oneida Community* (New York, 1993).

3. Nathaniel Hawthorne to David Mack, West Roxbury, July 18, 1841, BPL Am 1067(4); Elizabeth Peabody, "Plan of the West Roxbury Community," *Dial* 2 (1842): 361–72.

4. *New York Weekly Tribune*, Oct. 15, 1842, Nov. 4, 1843.

5. Works that shift the emphasis away from excessive focus on the personal qualities of leaders have included Rosabeth Moss Kanter, *Commitment and Community: Communes and Utopias in Sociological Perspective* (Cambridge, Mass., 1972); Dolores Hayden, *Seven American Utopias: The Architecture of Communitarian Socialism, 1790–1975* (Cambridge, Mass., 1976); Carol A. Kolmerten, *Women in Utopia: The Ideology of Gender in the American Owenite Communities* (Bloomington, Ind., 1990); Carl J. Guarneri, *The Utopian Alternative: Fourierism in Nineteenth-Century America* (Ithaca, N.Y., 1991); and Stephen J. Stein, *The Shaker Experience in America: A History of the United Society of Believers* (New Haven, Conn., 1992).

6. *New Moral World*, May 31, 1844.

7. The account of this meeting is in Martha Turner Hudson to Erasmus Darwin Hudson, Northampton, Apr. 7, 1844, Hudson Family Papers, Box 1, folder 21, UMass.

8. NAEI, vol. 2, pp. 94–95, entry for June 27–29, 1844.

9. NAEI, vol. 2, p. 66, entry for June 24, 1843.

10. E.g. *Liberator*, Mar. 14, 1845.

11. George W. Benson to Samuel J. May, Boston, Sept. 26, 1844, BPL MS. A.1.2.14.59, and Northampton, Dec. 23, 1844, BPL MS. A.1.2.14.82; the latter is marked "Confidential." Neither minutes in NAEI, vol. 2, nor correspondence in NAEI, vol. 4, throw light on Benson's approach to May, and he may have made it on his own initiative without authorization from the community.

12. David Mack to A. Kingsley, Northampton, Apr. 29, 1845, NAEI, vol. 4, pp. [98–99].

13. NAEI, vol. 2, p. 62, entry for May 27, 1843.

14. Adam to John Bailey, Mar. 6, 1843, NAEI, vol. 4, pp. 11–12; Mack to Lydia Maria Child, Aug. 20, 1843, NAEI, vol. 4, p. 34; Mack to Ashbel Cone, Dec. 9, 1843, NAEI, vol. 4, p.[42].

15. David Mack to Sarah G. Bagley, Northampton, Feb. 24, 1845, NAEI, vol. 4, p.[94]; Mack wrote "we can also furnish 20 or 30 children."

16. NAEI, vol. 2, p. 100, entry for Jan. 23, 1845; p. 126, entry for Sept. 26, 1846.

17. The discussion and vote were minuted in NAEI, vol. 2, p. 25, entry for July 23, 1842.

18. NAEI, vol. 2, p. 71, entries for July 29 and Aug. 2, 1843.

19. William Bassett to Abner Sanger, July 15, 1844, NAEI, vol. 4, pp. [63–64].

20. For the Worcester and Boston conventions, see *Liberator*, Dec. 1, 8, and 22, 1843; Guarneri, *Utopian Alternative*, 57 comments on the Boston meeting's significance for Fourierism.

21. On Brigham, see W. I. Tyler Brigham, *The History of the Brigham Family* (New York, 1907); by a vote of 28–3 the Allens were invited on Jan. 13, 1844, to join the community for a year, "because he is an intelligent and active advocate of reform, deeply interested in the success of Associations," and would subscribe $300 to stock. NAEI, vol. 2, p. 89. On Allen, see Guarneri, *Utopian Alternative*, 517.

22. A note in Burleigh Papers, no. 10, HSP, indicates that Mack was at Hopedale on Aug. 27, 1844, immediately before the community convention held at Northampton at the end of that month.

23. [James Boyle], *Social Reform, Or an Appeal in Behalf of Association, Based upon the Principles of a Pure Christianity* (Northampton, 1844). Having reviewed other community schemes, Boyle noted, "We do not fully adopt any of the various plans proposed—yet in some respects we prefer Fourier's to any other." At a social reform convention held in Boston in May 1844, Boyle outlined his religious differences with other community theorists. *Investigator* (Boston), June 12, 1844.

24. *Harbinger*, Sept. 13, 1845.

25. David Mack to Francis Hinckley, Jan. 20, 1845, NAEI, vol. 4, pp.[87–88].

26. This and the previous paragraphs are based on minutes of the 1845 annual meeting in NAEI, vol. 2, pp. 99–109 (emphasis in original). The term "Intendant," once applied to officials of the French royal government, was used for some officers at the Hopedale community, and Northampton may have borrowed it from there.

27. At the 1845 annual meeting the proposed annual allowances for members were approved unanimously. NAEI, vol. 2, p. 102, entry for Jan. 24, 1845.

28. On machine making generally, see David Montgomery, "Workers' Control of Machine Production in the Nineteenth Century," *Labor History* 17 (Fall 1976): 485–509; for a contemporary example of informal accounting methods in a Northampton blacksmith's shop see Christopher Clark, *The Roots of Rural Capitalism: Western Massachusetts, 1780–1860* (Ithaca, N.Y., 1990), 219–20.

29. Elizabeth Curson to Mary R. Curson, Brook Farm, Feb. 15, 1846, HCL bMS Am 1175 (438), commented "you would be gratified to see poor old aunty cudgel her brains with the groupe accounts."

30. NAEI, vol. 2, p. 102, entry for Jan. 24, 1845; *Hampshire Herald*, May 27, 1845.

31. Mack's objection to being secretary and its withdrawal are noted in NAEI, vol. 2, pp. 107, 109; his and Benson's resignations are on p. 112.

32. Martha Turner Hudson to Erasmus Darwin Hudson, Apr. 7, 1844.

33. The decision to invest in manufacturing was made on Jan. 24, 1845. NAEI,

vol. 2, p. 104. On stockholders' claims for repayment and the dangers of collapse, see Samuel L. Hill to David Mack, June 30, 1846, NAEI, vol. 4, pp.[137–38]. Referring to earlier difficulties, Hill wrote, "Any attempt then to close the affairs of the Asso. suddenly would have proved sadly disastrous to all concerned."

34. NAEI, vol. 2, p. 118, notes receipt of David Mack's letter of notification of his intention to withdraw stock. Hill to Mack, June 30, 1846, NAEI, vol. 4, pp.[137–38], written with barely suppressed anger, sought to convince Mack of the wisdom and justice of waiting to press his claim. NAEI, vol. 2, p. 126, minuted a discussion on Sept. 26, 1846, in which members contemplated ending the community and an informal meeting on Nov. 7 at which the final decision was taken.

CHAPTER SEVEN
From Community to Factory Village

1. This and the following paragraph draw on Erasmus Darwin Hudson to Martha Turner Hudson, Medfield, Nov. 9, 1845, Hudson Family Papers, Box 1, folder 22, UMass. Owen's visit to Hopedale was described in *Liberator*, Dec. 12, 1845, and his current community scheme in Norman Ware, *The Industrial Worker, 1840–1860: The Reaction of American Industrial Society to the Advance of the Industrial Revolution* (1924; rpt. ed., Chicago, 1964), 216–17. I am grateful to Edward Royle for information about Owen and the Queenwood community.

2. Otohiko Okugawa, "Annotated List of Communal and Utopian Societies, 1787–1919," in *Dictionary of American Communal and Utopian History*, ed. Robert S. Fogarty (Westport, Conn., 1980), 173–233; Stephen Young, "A Veteran Associationist," *Credit Foncier of Sinaloa*, July 6, 1886, 552.

3. Carl J. Guarneri, *The Utopian Alternative: Fourierism in Nineteenth-Century America* (Ithaca, N.Y., 1991), 155–58; Samuel L. Hill, undated memoir quoted in William A. Hinds, *American Communities and Cooperative Colonies*, 3d ed. (Chicago, 1908), 280.

4. Clara Endicott Sears, *Bronson Alcott's Fruitlands* (Boston, 1915); Guarneri, *Utopian Alternative*; Anne C. Rose, *Transcendentalism as a Social Movement, 1830–1850* (New Haven, Conn., 1981); Edward K. Spann, *Hopedale: From Commune to Company Town, 1840–1920* (Columbus, Ohio, 1992).

5. A letter from Masquerier to this effect was published in the Boston *Investigator*, Aug. 18, 1841; on Judd and Hill, see Martha Hudson to Erasmus Darwin Hudson, Apr. 7, 1844, transcript in Hudson Family Papers, Box 1, folder 21, UMass.

6. Store accounts are in NAEI, vol. 3, pp. 110–294; the marriage was of Luther Brigham's daughter Sarah to Sylvester J. Bosworth in 1846; see W. I. Tyler Brigham, *The History of the Brigham Family* (New York, 1907), 636.

7. The quotation is from a report in Springfield *Gazette*, May 11, 1846, of Barron's attack and suicide, reprinted in *Liberator*, May 15, 1846, which stated that he had "killed his wife on Sunday morning, by beating her brains out with a hammer, as she lay in her bed." *Hampshire Gazette*, June 2, 1846, however, printed a letter correcting this; Mrs Barron had survived, was recovering "with homeopathic remedies," and was now able to walk. Barron was known to the community, how-

ever: he traded at the store and had carried letters for Samuel L. Hill on community business.

8. See Deeds, 116:168, 196–97, for a record of Hall Judd's purchase of a house lot from Eaton on Nov. 13, 1846, less than one week after the formal dissolution of the Northampton community; page 168 also includes a plan of "Eaton's Village Lots, near Bensonville," drawn on Nov. 12, 1846. Dealings between Hill and Sojourner Truth are recorded in 133:106, 124; between Hill and Wells, 151:169; and between Hill and Hammond, 196:24.

9. *Harbinger*, Sept. 13 1845; John Humphrey Noyes, *History of American Socialisms* (1870; rpt. ed., New York, 1966), 154.

10. Brook Farm Papers, vol. 1, p. 9, MHS (microfilm).

11. Cyrus Bradbury is listed in Hopedale Community, Ledger 1850–1853, pp. 124 and 134, Hopedale Community Collection (microfilm, reel 1, no. 12); May is listed on p. 124 of the same volume; Gove is mentioned in Record Book of the Hopedale Community, vol. 2, p. 39 (microfilm, reel 1), and in Hopedale Sewing Circle and Tract Society, Minutes 1848–1862, no pag. (microfilm, reel 1, no. 7); their marriage is noted in William Henry Gove, *The Gove Book: History and Genealogy of the American Family of Gove and Notes of European Goves* (Salem, Mass., 1922), 209. Bradbury was one of the signers of *Declaratory Resolutions of the Hopedale Community with Reference to the Existing Civil War, Reaffirming their Original Principles, Positions, and Testimonies, Unanimously Adopted, September 15, 1861* (n.p., n.d.).

12. Eldad Stebbins, Account Book, 1808–1845, pp. 227, 230–31, and "Record of Letters Written," 1830–1845, entries for Apr. 1, May 7, Dec. 16, 1844, July 5–8, 1845, both in Eldad Stebbins Papers, MHS; the comment about Gordon Adam was by Anna Sargent Parker to George B. Dixwell, Roxbury, Apr. 26, 1846, Wigglesworth Family Papers, Box 4, MHS; Allen and Southworth are listed in Boston Religious Union of Associationists, Records, MHS (microfilm). A contribution by Benson to Associationist funds was noted in James Freeman Clarke to James T. Fisher, Boston, July 27, 1849, James T. Fisher Papers, MHS (microfilm); David Mack to James T. Fisher, Belmont, Apr. 9, 1855, Fisher Papers, conveyed his regrets at being unable to attend a gathering to meet the leading French Fourierist Victor Considerant; Carleton Mabee, *Sojourner Truth: Slave, Prophet, Legend* (New York, 1993), 58–59, 99–101, 244–45.

13. Mabee, *Sojourner Truth*, 57–59; Harriet B. Gardner, "Elisha Livermore Hammond," in *A History of Florence, Massachusetts, Including a Complete Account of the Northampton Association of Education and Industry*, ed. Charles A. Sheffeld (Florence, Mass., 1895), 221–24; Wilbur H. Siebert, "The Underground Railroad in Massachusetts," American Antiquarian Society *Proceedings*, 2 ser., 45 (1935): 95–96; disunion petitions in Slavery in the United States Collection, Box 1, folders 2–4, AAS.

14. On Meade, see Henry M. Meek, comp., *The Naumkeag Directory for Salem, Beverly, Danvers, Marblehead, Peabody* (Salem, Mass., 1882), 357, and *Old Anti-Slavery Days: Proceedings of the the Commemorative Meeting, Held by the Danvers Historical Society at the Town Hall, Danvers, April 26, 1893* (Danvers, Mass., 1893), xv, photograph on xxv; on the Haywards, see Salem Freedman's Aid Society, Subscription Book, EI; *Salem Directory 1866* (Salem, n.d.), p. 87; and obituary in *Salem Register* (Salem, Mass.), Apr. 20, 1874.

15. Correspondence about the Hudsons' controversy with the Torringford church is in Hudson Family Papers, Box 6, folder 3, UMass. Accounts of the Linda case appeared in *Hampshire Herald*, Aug. 12, 19, Sept. 30, Dec. 1, 1845, and *Liberator*, Sept. 19, Oct. 3, 1845, Nov. 20, 1846. Hudson's correspondence with Phillips is in HCL bMS Am 1953(720), folders 2–3; the quotation is from an undated letter in folder 3.

16. *Harbinger*, Sept. 27, 1845, 255–56, reported on the New England Working-Men's Association convention at Fall River on Sept. 11. John R. Commons, et al., ed., *A Documentary History of American Industrial Society*, vol. 3, *Labor Movement, 1840–1860, part 2* (1910; rpt. ed., New York, 1958), 26, lists James Boyle as a representative to the Industrial Congress from Northampton, Mass. (though Boyle had left the town months before); I am grateful to Carl J. Guarneri for this reference.

17. William Adam to Maria Weston Chapman, Northampton, May 23, 1844, reprinted in *NASS*, June 13, 1844. Adam's naturalization petition is in Hampshire County Court of Common Pleas, Records, vol. 30, p. 81 (1844), FL (microfilm).

18. O. P. Hatheway and J. H. Taylor, *Chicago City Directory and Annual Advertizer for 1849–50* (Chicago, 1849), 12.

19. S. C. Sanial, "The Rev. William Adam," *Bengal Past and Present* 8 (1914): 254, noted a Bengali's visit to Phebe Adam in 1887, when she would have been ninety years old.

20. [William Adam], *An Inquiry into the Theories of History, with Special Reference to the Principles of the Positive Philosophy* (London, 1862); in addition to that at the British Library there are copies at the Harvard Divinity School and the Andover-Harvard Theological Seminary libraries; the attribution of this work to Adam, and other comments on his later life are in Sanial, "The Rev. William Adam," 255–56.

21. On Bassett's later career, see an advertisement in the *Essex County Washingtonian*, Dec. 19, 1844; *The Sizzler* (Lynn, Mass.), Aug. 19–Sept. 26, 1848; Alonzo Lewis, *The Directory of the City of Lynn*, (Lynn, Mass., 1851), 58; [Sampson, Davenport, and Co.], *Lynn Directory, 1867* (Lynn, Mass., 1867), 212–20; James R. Newhall, *History of Lynn, Essex County, Massachusetts: vol. II, 1864–1893* (Lynn, Mass., 1897), 111–12; documents relating to his estate are in Essex County Probate Records, vol. 252, p. 717, and vol. 256, p. 685, Essex County Courthouse, Salem, Mass.

22. Article by Wall in *Health Journal* (Boston), reprinted in the Boston *Investigator*, Sept. 29, 1841.

23. Garrison mentioned Sylvester Graham in *Liberator*, Jul. 28, 1843. Purchases of Graham flour or meal are recorded throughout NAEI, vols. 3, 5, 6, and 7.

24. The discussion of hydropathy in this and subsequent paragraphs owe much to recent specialist works, in particular Susan E. Cayleff, *Wash and Be Healed: The Water-Cure Movement and Women's Health* (Philadelphia, 1987), and Jane B. Donegan, *The Hydropathic Highway to Health* (Westport, Conn., 1986). Hydropathy was not the same as "taking the waters" at mineral spas, and Cayleff, p. 5, also stresses that it should not be confused with "hydrotherapy" or other modern methods of treatment with water; she notes particularly the emphasis on the moral reformation of the patient that was so important to the practitioners and commentators we shall be discussing here.

25. This republican attitude was not universal, however, even outside established

medical traditions. Some elites in particular were suspicious of Priessnitz's methods. When Sylvester Graham expressed guarded approval of hydropathic remedies in certain cases, he was obliged to defend himself against the charge of J. P. Williston in the *Hampshire Herald*, Aug. 12, 1845, that he had confidence in the system of "a poor and unlettered peasant."

26. Cayleff, *Wash and Be Healed*, 5 and 12, discusses several facets of hydropathy, including its reliance on self-help and self-control, and its connection with other medical techniques, including homeopathy and Graham's dietary reforms.

27. Advocates of hydropathy at Hopedale included Harvey Fish, who wrote about it in the *Practical Christian*. There was a water-cure establishment on the grounds of the Hopedale community for a period in the late 1840s; see Hopedale Community Records, vol. 2, p. 137 (microfilm reel 1). At Brook Farm, John Orvis and George W. Curtis both evinced interest: when Curtis visited Graefenberg, Priessnitz's home and the center of hydropathy, in 1847 he described it as "so like Brook Farm in a better state of health than it enjoyed near the unwholesome morality of Boston." Curtis to Christopher P. Cranch, Nov. 12, 1847, Cranch Papers, MHS.

28. David Lee Child's article announcing Priessnitz's work appeared in *NASS*, Nov. 24, 1842. By a vote of May 27, 1843, the community authorized David Mack to construct a bathing house. NAEI, vol. 2, p. 62.

29. Apphia Judd to Arethusa Hall, Northampton, Dec. [28?], 1844, Judd Papers, Box 2, HCL; Erasmus Darwin Hudson to Martha Turner Hudson, Oct. 7, 1843.

30. References to abolitionists' subscriptions for Ruggles are in *Liberator*, Aug. 2 and 9, 1844; his treatment of other members is referred to in Samuel L. Hill to Abner Sanger, Dec. 4, 1845, NAEI vol. 4, p.[115]. Samuel L. Hill to Charles E. Forbes, Northampton, Apr. 28, 1846, Charles E. Forbes Papers, folder 11, FL, contains a request that legal papers to be drawn up for Ruggles's purchase of his "water-cure infirmary"; *Hampshire Gazette*, Aug. 4 and Oct. 27, 1846, reported the town subscription for Ruggles and the expansion of his building.

31. Robert Wesselhoeft and William Grau, *A Second Report of the Brattleboro Hydropathic Establishment* (Brattleboro, Vt., 1849), describes the water cure and its treatments.

32. Ruggles's theories, discussed in this and the next two paragraphs, are set out in David Ruggles to David Mack, Northampton, Mar. 30, 1846, printed in *Green Mountain Spring* (Brattleboro, Vt.), May 1846, 71–72, and in Ruggles to editor, Northampton, Oct. 25, 1846, in *Water-Cure Journal and Teacher of Heath* (New York), Nov. 15, 1846.

33. David Mack to William Lloyd Garrison, Brattleboro, Vt., July 22, 1845, printed in *Liberator*, Aug. 1, 1845.

34. David Mack, "Editorial," *Green Mountain Spring*, Apr. 1846, 49–50.

35. David Ruggles to William Lloyd Garrison, Dec. 6, 1847, BPL MS A.1.2.17.77, made an offer of free treatment; Helen E. Garrison to Ann Phillips, Northampton, Aug. 9, 1848, HCL, bMS Am 1953 (1427), describes the Garrisons' visit; Francis Jackson to James and Eliza Eddy, Boston, Nov. 17, 1848, Bowditch Family Papers, Box 13, folder 7, EI, reported that "Garrison has returned from Northampton, looking much better, and has been washed bright and clean with cold water."

36. Charles Lane to Joseph Palmer, New York, Sept. 10, 1846, quoted in Sears, *Bronson Alcott's Fruitlands*, 138–39, referred to an invitation to Mack to join a proposed community to be called the Leominster and Harvard Association. David Mack to Horace Mann, Brattleboro, Oct. 11, 1846, Horace Mann Papers, MHS (microfilm), outlined his plans for a boarding school. The Macks did establish a school, at Orchard Hill, Belmont, Mass., in 1847.

37. Massachusetts, vol. 46, p. 104, R. G. Dun and Co. Collection, Baker Library, Harvard University Graduate School of Business Administration.

38. Siebert, "Underground Railroad in Massachusetts," 96, refers to black workers at the Bensonville mill; [Wendell Phillips Garrison], *The Benson Family of Newport, Rhode Island* (New York, 1872), 53, mentions wages and Sunday repairs; *Proceedings of the Anti-Sabbath Convention, held in the Melodeon, March 23d and 24th* (Boston, 1848), and William Lloyd Garrison to Nathaniel Barney, Northampton, Sept. 8, 1848, in *The Letters of William Lloyd Garrison*, ed. Walter M. Merrill and Louis Ruchames (Cambridge, Mass., 1971–81), 3:585–86, document Benson's role at the convention, and its consequences.

39. The debt suits against Benson are in Hampshire County, Court of Common Pleas Records, vol. 32, pp. 508, 588–90, 638–40, 704–7, 724–25, 734–35, 739–40, 747–48, 767–68, 793–94; the credit reports are in Massachusetts, vol. 46, p. 104, R. G. Dun and Co. Collection (emphasis in original).

40. Hill, memoir in *Hampshire Gazette*, Apr. 2, 1867.

41. Some light on Hill's silk-manufacturing activities is shed by NAEI, vol. 8, which includes some accounts for the period 1849–53. U.S. Seventh Census, Non-Population Schedules, 1850: Manufactures, National Archives, Washington, D.C. (microfilm), shows that Hill's silk mill employed nine men and thirty women, with a capital of $15,000.

42. Agnes Hannay, "A Chronicle of Industry on the Mill River," *Smith College Studies in History* 21 (1935–36): 77–79. According to U.S. Eighth Census, Non-Population Schedules, 1860: Manufactures, National Archives, Washington, D.C. (microfilm), the Nonotuck Silk Company operated two mills, with $65,000 of capital, forty-six male workers, and ninety female workers between them.

43. Partnerships and directorships were traced in the following manuscript records: Massachusetts, vol. 46, R. G. Dun and Co. Collection; A. P. Critchlow and Co., Journal 1857–62, Littlefield, Parsons and Co., Journal B 1862–66, and Florence Manufacturing Co., Ledger 1866–73, all in ProBrush Company Collection, Carton 13, HN; the incorporators of the savings bank are listed in Massachusetts Senate Document, no. 24 (1873); see also Hannay, "Chronicle of Industry," 77–79, and Sheffeld, *History of Florence*, pp. 237–45.

44. Samuel L. Hinckley to Henry Rose Hinckley, Boston, Jan. 2, 1861, Henry Rose Hinckley Papers, folder 3, no. 79A, HN, commented that "Negro slavery is not in my opinion the greatest evil in this evil world," and his wife added: "I go for the South in many respects, only rejoicing that I am not a southerner, but I think they have a great deal to complain of in the North & the name of *Abolitionist* is hateful" (emphasis in original).

45. Giles B. Stebbins, "A Young Man in the Community," in Sheffeld, *History of Florence*, 128.

46. See credit reports in Massachusetts, vol. 46, pp. 113, 114, 116, 119, 233, 236, and Massachusetts, vol. 47, pp. 360, 399, 417, 435, R. G. Dun and Co. Collection; Samuel L. Hill, Will, Hampshire County Register of Probate, file 208, no.35, Hall of Records, Northampton.

47. The strike at Wells's shop was mentioned in Daniel Wyatt Hudson to Erasmus Darwin and Martha Hudson, Florence, Mass., July 28, 1854, Hudson Family Papers, folder 3, SSC; accounts of the boiler explosion appeared in *Hampshire Gazette*, July 12 and 19, 1859.

48. On working hours, see *Report of the Special Commission on the Hours of Labor, and the Condition and Prospects of the Industrial Classes*, Mass. House Document, no. 98 (1866), appendix, p. 57; on child labor, see *Report of the Hon. Henry K. Oliver, Deputy State Constable, Specially Appointed to Enforce the Laws Regulating the Employment of Children in Manufacturing and Mechanical Establishments*, Mass. Senate Document, no. 21 (1868), p. 10, and letter from J. P. Williston on p. 60. Caroline H. Dall, Report to the Woman's Convention, Boston, Apr. 26, 1866, C. H. Dall Papers, Box 22, folder 13, MHS, praised Samuel L. Hill's silk mill for the "classes, libraries and privileges" women workers enjoyed, though she made no comment on working hours and noted that wages were no higher than average.

49. Stebbins, "A Young Man in the Community," 128.

50. On the Martins, see obituary of Joseph C. Martin Jr., *Hampshire Gazette*, Mar. 15, 1899. Helen E. Garrison to Ann Phillips, Northampton, Aug. 9, 1848, HCL bMS Am 1953 (1427); Ross's 1851 tax list is in Northampton Town Papers Collection 5.74, FL.

51. Arthur G. Hill, "Antislavery Days in Florence" (typescript, n.d.), Florence Civic and Business Association, Florence, Mass.

52. Indirect evidence of black insecurity comes from comparison of U.S. Census schedules for 1850 with the Massachusetts Census of 1855; this suggests a reversal during the first half of the decade of a significant increase in the black population of Northampton that had occurred during the 1840s. Direct evidence of the fear instilled by the Fugitive Slave Act is provided in J. P. Williston to Rev. I. S. Spencer, Northampton, Feb. 20, 1851, Williston Collection, MSS 42, subgroup I, series B, subseries 9, folder 2, NEHGS.

53. Sylvester Judd, Notebook, vol. 5, Judd MS, FL, entry for Aug. 13, 1848; Elisha G. Cobb, the former pastor of the Florence Congregational Church, described his early years there (in the 1860s), "confronted by a constant fusillade against the Bible, the Sabbath, the character of professed Christians," and with lectures on geology and evolution that "outran science in order to run out religion. The Creator was abolished, miracles declared to be impossible and Christian faith a superstition." *Daily Hampshire Gazette*, Oct. 27, 1915.

54. Free Congregational Society, Statement of Purpose [1863], copy at Florence Civic and Business Association, Florence, Mass.; membership lists are in Records of the Free Congregational Society of Florence, Unitarian Society of Northampton and Florence, Records, Box 14, folder 2, Unitarian Church, Northampton; see also Free Congregational Society, Records, 1873–1975, HN, A.A.18.115; Hill's remark was printed in *Hampshire Gazette*, Apr. 2, 1867. Praise for the Florence society was given

in *Proceedings at the Third Annual Meeting of the Free Religious Association, held in Boston, May 26 and 27, 1870* (Boston, 1870), 49, by a speaker who compared the movement's triumph over the Christian church as comparable with the North's triumph over the Confederacy (p. 51). Strong interest in reform Hinduism, the Vedanta, and particularly the Brahmo Samaj also linked the movement to the tradition derived from Ram Mohun Roy that had been so important in William Adam's career before he came to the United States (pp. 113–21). See Stow Persons, *Free Religion: An American Faith* (New Haven, Conn., 1947), and David Robinson, *The Unitarians and the Universalists* (Westport, Conn., 1985).

55. *Hampshire Gazette*, Aug. 21, 1866 reported Hill's previous year's income. Rumors about Hill's wealth and information about his holdings were noted by credit reporters; see Massachusetts, vol 47., pp. 360, 399, R. G. Dun and Co. Collection, Baker Library, Harvard University Graduate School of Business Administration. Evidence of Hill's and others' philanthropic activities is contained in [Arthur G. Hill, et al.] *Memorial. Alfred Theodore Lilly* (Florence, Mass., 1890), p. 36. An excellent study of factory towns and their philanthropies is John S. Garner, *The Model Company Town: Urban Design through Private Enterprise in Nineteenth-Century New England* (Amherst, Mass., 1984), which examines Hopedale, Peace Dale, R.I., South Manchester, Conn., and St. Johnsbury, Vt.

56. This account is based on Spann, *Hopedale*, 174–75, from which contemporary quotations are taken. Adin Ballou, *History of the Hopedale Community*, ed. William S. Heywood (Lowell, Mass., 1897), 291–301, gives his own account of "an attempt to realize the Kingdom of God on earth . . . [that] founder[ed] at last on the shallows of worldly ambition and desire."

57. The terms for admission to the Florence Kindergarten (later renamed the Hill Institute) were set out in Samuel L. Hill, Will, Register of Probate, file 208, no. 35.

58. On Peabody, see Ruth M. Baylor, *Elizabeth Palmer Peabody: Kindergarten Pioneer* (Philadelphia, 1965); Bruce A. Ronda, ed., *Letters of Elizabeth Palmer Peabody: American Renaissance Woman* (Middletown, Conn., 1984); and Peabody's periodical, the *Kindergarten Messenger*. [Hill, et al.], *Memorial. Alfred Theodore Lilly*, 26, dates the kindergarten's origins at 1872. Sheffeld, *History of Florence*, 156–57, attributes Hill's interest to his own realization of the importance of educating the very young, and that he then invited Peabody to Florence to lecture on Froebel. If Sheffeld is correct that the lecture was given in Cosmian Hall, this would have been between 1874 and 1876.

59. E[lizabeth] P[owell] B[ond], "The Florence Kindergarten," *Kindergarten Messenger*, n.s., 1 (July–Aug. 1877): 110–13. Other quotations are from Bertha von Marenholtz, "Education by Labor, According to Froebel's Principle," *Kindergarten Messenger* 2 (Aug. 1874): 1–12; on page 6, von Marenholtz referred to Froebel as heir to the principles of education and labor developed by "Pestalozzi, Fellenberg, Fourier, Lancaster, Owen, &c," whose influence on communitarian educational schemes in the 1840s was so important.

60. *Kindergarten Messenger*, n.s., 1 (May–June 1877): 85.

61. Sheffeld, *History of Florence*, 156.

62. *Hampshire Gazette*, June 9, 1874. On the flood and its background, see Williamsburg Reservoir Company, Records, FL, and W. B. Gay, *Gazetteer of Hampshire County, Massachusetts, 1654–1887* (Syracuse, N.Y., [1886?]), 237.

63. [Hill], *Memorial*, 88. On strikes and labor relations in Florence, see Hannay, "Chronicle of Industry," 99–104; Hannay comments on the anti-union principles of Florence's manufacturers and the absence of a stable union in their mills until 1921.

CHAPTER EIGHT
The Communitarian Moment

1. [Arthur G. Hill, et. al.], *Memorial. Alfred T. Lilly* (Florence, Mass., 1890), 95.

2. Charles Nordhoff, *The Communistic Societies of the United States, from Personal Visit and Observation* (1875; rpt. ed., New York, 1965), 11, 13–14; for Arthur G. Hill's criticisms of unions, see his letters in *Daily Hampshire Gazette* (Northampton), Aug. 25, 26, 1914, during a streetcar workers' strike; Frederick Engels, *Socialism: Utopian and Scientific*, trans. Edward Aveling (1892; rpt. ed., New York, 1975).

3. Wendell Phillips Garrison and Francis Jackson Garrison, eds., *William Lloyd Garrison* (New York, 1885), 2:25-26.

4. Joseph B. Whitehouse, "Florence and the War," in *The History of Florence, Massachusetts, Including a Complete Account of the Northampton Association of Education and Industry*, ed. Charles A. Sheffeld (Florence, Mass., 1895), 197–201; John Adams Vinton, *The Richardson Memorial: Comprising a Full History and Genealogy of the Three Brothers, Ezekiel, Samuel, and Thomas Richardson* (Portland, Maine, 1876), 492–93.

INDEX

Note: NAEI = Northampton Association of Education and Industry. Residents' names appear in **bold type**

Abolitionism, 7–8, 10, 18, 95–97, 190–96, 220; anniversaries, 88; and capitalism, 8–9, 14, 99–100, 203; and communities, 7, 41–42, 153–54; divisions in, 29, 34–38, 86; evangelical, 11, 35, 44, 51–52, 72, 89–91; historiography of, 7, 10, 35–36; at NAEI, xi, 66–71, 80–82, 87–89; political, 11, 40, 96, 204; radical, 12, 28, 34–35, 72–73, 87, 191; social roots of, 82–85; tactics, 10–11, 35–36; and women's rights, 35–36. *See also entries for individual anti-slavery societies*
Account keeping, 127, 172–73, 176–78
Adam, Gordon, 115–16, 120–21, 190
Adam, Helen, 119
Adam, Phebe Grant, 26, 28, 53, 116, 123, 194
Adam, William, 15, 24, 30–31; background, 26–29, 98; on communities, 45, 61; later career, 193–94; at NAEI, 17, 53, 110–11, 118, 123, 165–70; as teacher, 131; on wage system, 103–4; withdraws from NAEI, 130–32
Adams, Robert, 67, 193
Adventist movement, 13
Alcott, Abigail May, 82
Allen, John, 174, 189–90

American and Foreign Anti-Slavery Society, 35, 90, 96
American Anti-Slavery Society, 19, 26, 40, 45, 96
Anti-abolitionist violence, 34, 39–41, 94
Anti-sabbath conventions, 45, 204
Anti-Slavery Society of Salem and Vicinity, 68
Asceticism, 23–24, 111–12, 125, 187
Ashley, George, 114
Atkins, James D., 62, 152, 188, 207; photograph, 209

Bacon, B. C., 89, 112
Bagley, Sarah, 158, 171
Baking, 140
Ballou, Adin, 3, 47, 48, 164–65, 215
Bassett, Susanna, 66
Bassett, William, 68, 94; background, 69–71; on capitalism, 108, 195; later career, 194–95; at NAEI, 124, 129, 155–57, 163–64, 172–73
Bath, Maine, 86
Beach, Thomas P., 91–92, 128
Bellamy, Edward, 219
Benson family, 79–80, 188
Benson, George, 18

Benson, George W.: background, 18–20, 30–31, 36–38; and communities, 22, 45–47; cotton manufacturer, 159, 184, 187, 204; and Fourierism, 173–76, 190; later career, 204–5; at NAEI, 15, 17, 53, 82, 113–114, 137, 155, 165–69; photograph, 19; on wage system, 98, 102–5

Bensonville. *See* Broughton's Meadow; Florence

Bestor, Arthur E., 4, 105

Birge family, 78, 81

Bishop Hill community, 164

Black abolitionists, 34, 72–74, 78, 88–89

Black members at NAEI, 71–75

Bloomfield, Conn., 30, 44, 80, 84, 86

Bond, Elizabeth Powell, 217

Boston, 27, 68, 72, 84, 154

Bottum, Samuel A., 67

Boyle, James: and abolitionism, 67, 87, 92–93; background, 129; and Fourierism, 173–75; and land reform, 193; at NAEI, 113, 117, 121, 168, 176–77, 197; withdraws from NAEI, 179

Boyle, Laura, 67, 87, 190

Bradbury, Cyrus, 190

Breck, Moses, 51

Brigham, Luther, 174

Brisbane, Albert, 46, 59, 185

Brook Farm, xi, 3, 28, 30, 58–59, 97, 173–74; debt of, 137; decline, 86, 185–86; leadership at, 25, 165; members of, 66, 76–78, 189; school, 114–15, 170; and social reform, 11, 47, 57, 100; women's experience at, 109, 124, 178

Brooklyn, Conn., 18–20, 64–65, 80, 83–84

Brooklyn Female Anti-Slavery Society, 20, 37

Brooks, Samuel, 15, 17, 23

Broughton's Meadow, 15, 72, 187–88; map, 16

Brownson, Orestes, 100

Buffum, James N., 47

Burleigh, Cyrus M., 111

Burleigh, Gertrude K., 9

Burritt, Elihu, 110–11

Byrne, Susan, 38, 67

Capitalism, 6, 8–10, 70, 99, 102, 162, 203–11; and cooperation, 13–14, 210;

criticized, 99, 102–8, 132, 222; and social harmony, 215

Chaffee, Lucina (Conant), 22

Chaffee, Orwell S., 22, 31, 79, 162

Chaplin, Conn., 44, 64–65, 67, 80, 84, 86

Child, David Lee, 50, 51–52, 143, 197

Child labor, 108, 117, 119–120, 152, 170–72

Child, Lydia Maria, 13, 51–52, 86, 197

Children at NAEI, 115–17, 169, 171

Christianity. *See* Churches; Come-outerism; Evangelical revivals; Religion at NAEI; *entries for individual denominations*

Churches, 9, 24, 36, 39–40, 42–45, 92, 212–13

Civil rights, 72–73, 94–95

Civil War, 14, 190, 222

Clapp, Henry, Jr., 111

Class conflict, 104, 218–19

Cobb, Jonathan H., 147, 148

Coe, William, 20, 38, 40, 53

Collins, John A., 58

Colver, Nathaniel, 37, 89

Come-outerism, 10–12, 14, 42–45

"Communitarian moment," 1–2, 10, 14, 36, 97–98, 189, 191, 202–3, 220–23

Communitarianism, xi–xii, 108–9; and capitalism, 8–9, 32, 33, 56; decline of, xi, 183–86; historiography of, xii, 6; ideals of, 47–49, 86–89, 185; and social reform, 2, 7–9, 12, 32, 46–47, 161, 189

Communities: admission of members to, 62; failure of, 5, 80–81, 163, 184–86; gender in, 122–24; life in, 108–9, 112, 126; in Massachusetts, 3, 11; memories of, 221–23; migration among, 23, 66, 189–90; plans for, 54–61; property in, 101. *See also* Account keeping; Leadership at communities; *entries for individual communities*

Community conventions, 173–75

Competitiveness, 12, 14, 32, 38, 57, 85, 99–100, 208

"Conant group," 3, 81, 104, 139, 149, 152, 154

Conant, Joseph: and abolitionism, 22; and founding of NAEI, 2, 53, 57, 136; president of NAEI, 17, 23; and silk industry, 2, 15, 31–32, 98, 102, 146, 162

Conant, Pamelia, 79

Connecticut Anti-Slavery Society, 25–26, 37–38
Cowles, Horace, 36
Crandall, Prudence, 18, 19, 41
Credit, 136
Credit reports, 155, 204–5
Critchlow, Alfred P., 207–8
Crummell, Henry Richards, 71
Cultural conflict, 89–95, 129–32
Curson, Elizabeth, 124–25, 178

Danvers, Mass., 67–68
Democracy, 9, 167. *See also* Equality; Moral suasion; Politics at NAEI
Distribution of earnings, 58, 106
Disunionism, 96–97, 191–92
Dixwell family, 27, 111, 163
Domestic work, 119, 122
Dorsey, Basil, 187
Douglass, Frederick, 71, 88, 94, 129
Draper brothers, 186, 215
Dwight, John S., 52

Eaton, Edwin, 181, 188, 207
Economic depression, 22, 29–33, 84–85, 161
Education, 25–28; at NAEI, 3, 67, 108, 114–17, 131–32, 168–72
Equality, 28, 32, 56–57, 93, 104–8, 112, 120–121, 133–134, 172–73, 203, 211
Evangelical revivals, 9, 34, 44

Factory system, 9, 100, 104, 108
Factory villages, 183–84
Family life, 60, 65, 123–124, 127–28
Farming, 28, 30–31; at NAEI, 109, 119, 140, 160, 176, 178
Farm labor, 119, 137
Farwell, Emily, 67, 116, 170
Finch, John, 109, 113, 167
Florence, Mass., 206–19; "Florence group" of manufacturers, 207–11
Fogarty, Robert S., 1, 6
Foord, Sophia, 67, 73, 81, 87, 116, 166, 169–70, 217, 246
Forward, Eliza, 114
Fourierism, 3, 11, 46, 48, 190; at NAEI, 4, 6, 57, 173–76
Fourierist communities, 48, 58–59, 97, 100, 127, 165, 185

Free Congregational Society, 213, 215–16, 218, 221
Free labor. *See* Wage labor
Free Soil movement, 91, 195, 222
Fruitlands community, 3, 11, 102, 185
Fugitive slaves, 72–73
Fuller, Margaret, 46, 109
Funerals, 114

Garrison, Helen (Benson), 18–19, 67, 211
Garrison, William Lloyd: and abolitionism, 10–11, 36–39, 67–68, 88–89, 92–93; and communities, 47, 67, 121–22, 221; and George W. Benson, 18–19, 204; and moral suasion, 11, 202; and social inequality, 99
Gender, 29, 34–38, 44–45, 57, 93, 104, 120–28, 142–43; and race, 94–95
Gilbert, Olive, 124, 187
Gove, Caroline, 184, 190
Gove, Mary S., 113
Graham, Sylvester, 24, 113, 196
Greeley, Horace, 165
Guarneri, Carl J., 71, 185

Hammond, Elisha L., 67, 86, 123, 174, 176, 188, 191
Hammond, Eliza Preston, 67, 79, 123, 191
Harmony Society, 141, 164
Haven family, 213
Haven, Louisa Ann, 171
Haven, William, 64, 67, 188
Hawthorne, Nathaniel, 25, 165
Hayden, Harriet, 67, 82, 86, 114
Hayden, Joel, 91, 96, 159, 204
Hayden, Lucy C., 67, 82, 86
Hayward family, 67–68, 168
Hayward, Josiah, 192
Health reform, 46, 196
Hill, Arthur G., 212, 219–21
Hill, Roxana Maria Gaylord: photograph, 79
Hill, Samuel L.: and abolitionism, 15, 38, 49; background, 20–21, 30–31, 98; business interests of, 162, 180–82, 205–10; and debts of NAEI, 158, 181, 205; and founding of NAEI, 17, 53–54; at NAEI, 114–17, 121, 139, 159, 166–67; as philanthropist, 213, 216; photographs,

Hill, Samuel L. (*cont.*)
21, 209; and property development, 188–89; on religion, 43, 212–13, 216; treasurer of NAEI, 179–81
Hill, Thomas, 117
Hinckley, Samuel L., 205–8; photograph, 209
Hopedale community, 3, 71, 132, 173, 183–84, 190, 215; decline of, 186, 215; leadership at, 164–65; religion at, 48, 62, 129; and social reform, 11, 47–49, 57–58, 97, 100
Housing at NAEI, 75, 77, 106, 109–11, 126–27, 137, 166, 168–69
Hudson, Erasmus Darwin: and abolitionism, 25–26, 37–38, 41, 67, 87–88, 192–93; background, 24–26; on capitalism and wage system, 99–100, 103–7; on communities, 47, 127–28, 133; and founding of NAEI, 15, 17, 54; later career, 196; and religion, 43–44, 69, 92; withdraws from NAEI, 120, 132–33
Hudson, Martha Turner, 104, 106, 120, 124, 131–32
Hunt, Seth, 90
Hutchinson family singers, xi, 88, 95, 111, 130
Hydropathy, 123, 196–203

India, 26–28, 143
Individualism, 132–34
Industrial capitalism. *See* Capitalism
Ipswich, Mass., 68–69

Jamaica, 33
Johnson, Oliver, 11, 69
Joint–stock principle, 98–100
Joslyn, H. H., 107, 112
Judd, Frances P. (Birge): and abolitionism: 191; later career, 211, 213; marriage of, 24, 113–14; at NAEI, 78, 109, 121, 125–26, 130, 168; on women's rights, 104, 128, 192
Judd, Hall: and abolitionism, 37, 191; asceticism of, 23–24; and founding of NAEI, 15, 17, 26, 30, 54; illness and death, 197–98; marriage of, 24, 113–14; on "neighborhood community," 186–88; on religion, 44, 129; as secretary of NAEI, 179–80; as storekeeper, 138; on wage system, 99–100, 103

Kelley, Abby, 13, 37–38, 40, 87–88, 92
Kerr, James, 171
Kindergarten movement, 216–18, 221
Kingdom, The, 66, 74
Kinship, 22, 24, 77–81
Kolmerten, Carol A., 122–27

Labor movement, 11, 60, 132, 219–21
Labor theory of value, 101–2
Land reform, 11, 14, 193
Lane, Charles, 102
Language teaching, 115
Larned, William, 172
Latimer conventions, 88
Lawyers, 24, 85
Leadership at communities, 6, 48–49, 98, 107, 122, 164–82
Liberty party, 35–36, 42, 90–91, 159
Lilly, Alfred T., 207
Loomis, Gorton G., 176
Lumbering and sawmilling, 119, 139, 159–60
Lynn, Mass., 68, 70, 195

Mack, David: background, 24–25, 45, 85; communitarian ideals, 133–34, 167, 200; as director of education, 116–17, 131, 168–71; and founding of NAEI, 15, 17; and Fourierism, 173–74, 190; on hydropathy, 198–202; later career, 202; at NAEI, 53, 122–23, 130–32; as secretary of NAEI, 118, 132, 172, 176–79; on wage system, 99–100, 103–7, 132; withdraws from NAEI, 158, 179
Mack, Maria, 25, 113, 121, 217; at NAEI, 123
Mansfield, Conn., 20, 22, 31–32, 64, 80, 83–84, 141, 145
Manual labor schools, 115
Market economy, 9, 84–85, 138, 160; criticized, 100
Marriage, 24, 60, 127; at NAEI, 113–14, 123–24, 126, 187
Martin family, 213
Martin, Joseph C., 44, 65, 166, 180, 211
Masquerier, Lewis, 186
Massachusetts Anti-Slavery Society, 13, 28, 42, 191
May, Charles, 82, 184, 190
May, Samuel J., 18, 82, 166, 169

McBee, Alice Eaton, 4
Meade, Abner S., 67, 192
Metalworking, 119, 139–40, 159–60, 178
Millennialism, 12–13
Mill River, 2, 15, 109, 118, 206; flood disaster of 1874, 218
Modern Times community, 133
Moral economy, 11, 99–101, 178, 203
Moral suasion: and hydropathy, 199–203; at NAEI, 59–61, 133–34, 165, 176–79, 223; and reform movements, xii, 10–11, 13, 34, 43, 89
Mormonism, 113, 164
Mulberry trees, 31–32, 143, 147

Napier, Thomas, 52
Neighborhood, 20–21, 77, 80–81, 85
"Neighborhood community," 180, 186–87
New Bedford, Mass., 72
New Covenant Believers, 92–93
New England Non-Resistance Society, 11, 39, 40, 70
New England Working-Men's Association, 193
New Harmony community, 62, 101, 165, 183
New Lanark, 183–84
Newburyport, Mass., 68–69
New York City, 73, 84, 154, 156
Nickerson, Roxcy Brown, 111, 190
Nonotuck Silk Company, 207, 210, 218–19
Nonresistance, 10, 24, 38–43, 45, 49, 96, 175, 190; at NAEI, 40–41, 55, 59–60, 66–68, 88, 92, 97, 113–15
Nonsectarianism, 6–7, 49, 69, 71, 91, 113, 128–29
Nordhoff, Charles, 221
North American Phalanx, 62, 76, 186
Northampton Anti-Slavery Society, 50
Northampton Association of Education and Industry: achievements, 220; admission of members, 17, 62–63, 66, 75–78, 106; annual meeting 1843, 105–6; annual meeting 1845, 176–79; boarders at, 77, 127; capital stock of, 3, 23, 98–101, 105, 108, 132, 136–37, 181; circular of 1843, 106; conflicts at, 129–32; constitution of 1842, 59–61, 101, 106, 136; constitution of 1843, 56, 107; critics of, 92–95, 107, 115; debts of, 3, 108, 135–38, 155–

58, 180–81, 188; described, 109–13; disbands, 1, 181, 186; earnings and expenditure, 120, 136, 139, 152, 157; food at, 111; founding of, 1, 15–17, 20–22, 25–26, 29, 51–55, 136; historiography of, xii, 3–4; "Industrial Community," 58, 101–2, 104, 107; meetings at, 91, 112–13, 121–22, 128, 167–68, 186; members' ages, 65; members' occupations, 64; members' origins, 7, 64–69, 80–85; memories of, 221–22; organization at, 16–17, 61, 101, 107, 158–60, 165; output, 136–40; plans for community building, 169, 174; Preliminary Circular, 53, 57–60, 101, 136; property of, 2–3, 15, 101, 108, 137, 158–59; pupils at, 63, 116–17, 168–70; records of, 4–5; silk factory, 108, 110, 118, 169; size of membership, 2, 61, 77, 80–82, 120, 159, 163, 171; stockholders, 2, 17, 58, 101–2, 107, 158; store, 138, 187; subscription drive, 155; supplies, 138–39; voting rights, 63, 101–2, 107; work at, 117–20
Northampton, Mass., 2, 30–32, 84, 192; black population of, 72, 204, 212; described, 49–52; hydropathy at, 197, 198, 212
Northampton Silk Company, 2, 15, 20, 22, 31–33, 135–37
Noyes, John Humphrey, 3–4, 12, 57, 164

Oneida community, 4, 141, 164
Owen, Robert, 3, 11, 62, 101, 113, 183

Paine, Oliver D., 153, 156, 160
Parker, Susan, 67, 176, 190–91
Parker, William, 67, 190–91
Peabody, Elizabeth Palmer, 165, 217
Peace societies, 18, 39
Perfectionism, 12–13
Philanthropy, 211–14
Phillips, Wendell, 28, 99, 192
Politics at NAEI, 98, 102–7, 167–68, 171–73
Porter, Fortune R., 113, 116
Prairie Home Community, 108–9
Preston, Enos L., 31, 152
Priessnitz, Vincent, 196–97

Quakers, 18, 20, 39, 66, 69–71, 91
Quincy, Edmund, 47–48

Racial equality, 7, 57, 60, 71, 93–95
Racism, 50, 94–95
Radicalism, 4, 6, 9–10, 12–14, 38–40, 58, 60, 92–93; retreat from, 189–96, 202–3
Rapp, George, 141, 164
Raritan Bay Union, 124
Religion at NAEI, 6, 42–43, 48–49, 57, 69, 91–93, 112–14, 128–30
Richardson, Nancy, 126
Ripley, George, 30, 45–47, 52, 86, 165
Rogers, Nathaniel P., 6, 107, 111, 115, 121
Roosevelt, Clinton, 175
Rosbrooks, Louisa, 176
Rose, Anne C., 78
Ross, Austin, 65, 188, 211–12
Ross, Fidelia, 211–12
Roy, Ram Mohun, 26–27
Ruggles, David, 71, 82, 88, 94–95, 109, 191–92; background, 73–74; and hydropathy, 188, 197–202
Rumsey, Olive, 4, 219
Rural society, 6, 9–10, 82–85, 125
Rush, Stephen C., 71, 73, 82, 87–89, 134

Sabbath, 113. *See also* Anti-sabbath conventions
Salem Female Anti-Slavery Society, 68
Sanger, Abner, 155
Scarborough, Theodore, 15, 17, 20, 40, 65, 119–20, 140
Schooling. *See* Education
Sewing, 140, 176, 178
Sexuality, 60, 127
Shakers, 2, 13, 23, 61, 87, 165
Sheffeld, Charles A., 4, 218–19
Shoemaking, 140, 160
Silk, 140–42; raw, 153, 156–57; sales of, 153–54; for sewing, 144
Silk manufacture, 3, 22–23, 31–33, 135–62; dyeing, 119, 152, 154; prizes for, 149; reeling, 144, 148–49, 156; stages of production, 144–45; workers, 104, 118–19, 139, 152, 154
Silk raising, 3, 22, 31, 32, 117, 119, 142–52
Silkworms, 141–143, 148; illustrated, 150–51

Skaneateles community, 58
Slavery, 7, 10, 12, 34, 39, 86, 99–100
Smith, A. L., 76
Smith, Mary Ann, 78–79, 81–82
Social Darwinism, 215
Social harmony, 4, 32, 100, 215–23
Socialism, 8, 54. *See also* Equality; Subsistence allowances at NAEI
Society of Friends. *See* Quakers
Southworth, Sidney, 114, 190
Spann, Edward K., 215
Stacy, George W., 133
Stebbins, Calvin, 69, 78
Stebbins, Daniel, 141, 145
Stebbins, Eldad, 113, 190
Stebbins, Giles B., 89, 113, 117, 126, 190, 210–11
Stebbins, Sarah E., 78
Stetson, Dolly Witter, 116, 125–26
Stetson family, 172
Stetson, George, 116
Stetson, James A., 31, 65, 80, 116; agent for NAEI, 126, 153–54
Stiles, Ezra, 141
Stoddard, William H., 90
Strikes, 210, 219
Subsistence allowances at NAEI, 101, 105–8, 120, 134, 159, 172, 177
Sullivan, George W., 73, 239–40
Sulloway, Jason, 176
Sulloway, Mary, 176
Swift, Earl Dwight, 15, 17, 22, 79, 98, 137, 139
Swift, Olive (Conant), 22

Talbot, Charles Nicholl, 30, 33, 137, 154–55
Tappan family, 51, 90
Tappan, Lewis, 35, 94, 155
Temperance, 11, 25, 46, 90, 130
Ten-hour day. *See* Working hours
Thurber, George, 123
Topolobampo colony, 185
Transcendentalism, 3, 4, 30, 59, 115
Truth, Sojourner, 66, 71, 81, 87, 114, 121, 168; and abolitionism, 89; background, 74; illustrated, 75; later career, 187–88, 190–91, 204; at NAEI, 109, 124, 133; as speaker, 89, 94

Underground railroad, 22, 73, 191
Unitarianism, 9, 26–27
Utopian communities. *See*
  Communitarianism; Communities; *entries
  for individual communities*

Van Wagenen, Isabella. *See* Truth,
  Sojourner

Wage labor, 14, 63, 70, 99–102, 108, 118–
  19, 203, 208–11
Wage rates, 103, 105, 172
Wages system, 100–107, 130. *See also*
  Capitalism, Equality
Wall, Eliza Boyce, 66–67, 70, 81, 103, 121
Wall, Joseph S., 66, 70, 196
Walters, Ronald G., 35–36
Water-cure. *See* Hydropathy
Wealth, 64–65, 195, 211–13
Weber, Max, 164–65
Wells, Hiram, 15, 17, 20–21, 98, 139, 179,
  207–11

Wells, Julia A., 122
Wesselhoeft, Robert, 197–99, 202
Whig party, 9, 90
Whipple, B. F., 79
Whitmarsh, Samuel, 32–33, 135, 147
Whitmarsh, Thomas, 33
Willimantic, Conn., 20, 30, 37–38, 64, 80
Williston, John P., 72, 90–91, 96, 159, 192,
  204, 207, 211
Windham County Anti-Slavery Society,
  19
Withington, Ann Fairfax, 142
Women at NAEI, 93, 120–28, 178
Women's rights, 7, 10, 27–28, 35–36, 44–
  45, 51, 60, 67, 93, 104
Women's work, 117, 119, 122–23, 163–64
Woodbridge, John, 113
Working hours, 104, 106, 161, 211
World's Anti-Slavery Convention, 28
Wright, Henry G., 113

Young, Stephen, 76, 185